SALES

THE PROCESS FOR SUCCESS

JB Zegalia

Llumina
Press

SALES

THE PROCESS FOR SUCCESS

thesalesbook.net

Requests for permission to make copies of any part of this work should be mailed to Permissions Department, Llumina Press, 7915 W. McNab Rd., Tamarac, FL 33321

ISBN: 978-1-60594-515-6

Printed in the United States of America by Llumina Press

Library of Congress Control Number: 2010905048

TABLE OF CONTENTS

INTRODUCTION   i

THE BASICS
1 WHY A CUSTOMER BUYS   1
2 LET ME ASK YOU A QUESTION   21

THE SALES PROCESS
3 GREETING AND RAPPORT   41
4 MAKE A SELECTION   53
5 PRESENT THEIR SELECTION   75
6 APPRAISE THEIR TRADE   89
7 BUILD VALUE   97
8 PREPARE FOR THE NEGOTIATION   103
9 PRESENT THE FIGURES   115
10 CLOSING THE SALE   127
11 MY FAVORITE CLOSES   145
12 OVERCOME OBJECTIONS   159
13 STILL CLOSING   183

UNDERSTANDING OUR CUSTOMERS
14 SENSE OF UNDERSTANDING   189
15 RECOGNIZING THE SIGNS   203
16 BUYING PERSONALITIES   213

UNDERSTANDING OURSELVES

17 TRAITS OF A TOP SALESPERSON   231
18 QUESTIONS ANSWERED   247

SUPPORTING KNOWLEDGE

19 THE TELEPHONE   255
20 LISTENING   281
21 PROSPECTING   289
22 THE INTERNET   297
23 KEEPING YOUR FOCUS   307

INTRODUCTION

A career in sales is more than just a job; it is like being the director of your own company. It gives you the unlimited potential to succeed and the ability to do it at any stage in your work history. It is a career in which you are not limited to a set goal or range of income. It is also a career in which your ability to learn and your quest for knowledge are the keys to your production.

There are basic steps in selling, each of which will build off the preceding one toward the completion of the sale. Sales is a business of progression. It involves a combination of skill and knowledge, all while adhering to a set plan. It is a series of steps that will have to be understood, believed, and followed with resolve to achieve any true level of success. From building rapport to overcoming objections, there is no unimportant step in the sales process. You must complete each step successfully and advance to the next to best position yourself to influence a purchase. In this book, each chapter will outline the goal of each step and give you real world advice on what to do and how to do it. This book will take you through the steps of the sale and will show you how to smoothly transition your customers through the decision process.

Sales is also a business where success in any individual experience will often require many factors to develop perfectly and yet where an objection or hesitation can occur quickly and at any time. There is a fine line between making a sale and not making a sale. Although there will always be the customer who just walks in and buys, most of your customers will have to become open to your efforts and influence before they will ever consider buying anything. People want to buy, however they also want to feel both comfortable and confident in making a purchase. There is a reason that certain salespeople will consistently outperform others. Some will choose to learn their trade, and some will not. The most encouraging fact about our business is that it is a business where anyone with the desire to learn can achieve the level of success that he or she chooses. All top salespeople have chosen to study their trade. Knowledge and skill are factors that can be learned and forever improved upon. By having the desire and investing the time and effort to improve yourself, you soon will.

Please understand that sales is sales. Whether you are selling jewelry, office space, service agreements, automobiles, business proposals, printers, or investments, your objectives are the same. Whether you are offering a product or simply trying to convince your friends to see your point of view, your goal is to understand your audience and influence a direction. Sales is the ability to understand a person's motivating factors and use them to lead to a decision. Sales is successfully providing the influence it takes to lead, alter, correct, or realign another person's point of view and eventual path.

The ability to persuade is important. It is important in our profession and it is important in our regular, everyday life. Although this book is set up for our profession, it will often mirror our lives. Take a minute to read the steps of the sales process. As you do, try to relate each one with your specific offering and with the different interactions that occur in our lives. The knowledge and ability needed to succeed in sales are the exact same knowledge and ability needed to succeed in life. Selling is more than just ringing up an item. It is how our whole life is determined. It is how we are able to navigate in the direction we choose without the resistance that will slow us down or misdirect our path. Every day will involve us in leading the way. Most everything in life, although reachable, will not come with merely a request. Sometimes asking or telling will not be an option, and our only alternative will be to persuade; and for this we will need the skills to do it. We will need the ability to influence our own direction. Some of us will be happy to follow. However, some will want to lead;

they will want to choose their own direction. Well, for this, they will need a plan or path. They will need a process.

Whether long or short, quick or carefully created, understand that all successful persuasions will follow a process. All successful people will have a set plan or path to guide their influence. The best process is one that is effective and imperceptible, meaning one in which the process is so fluid that it seems like there is no process at all. This book will provide you with the process. It will provide you with your best path to start, continue, and finish influencing a decision. It will advise in each step. In addition to the process, we will look at the supporting knowledge needed to better enact our plan.

In all cases, please understand that the best way to influence anyone is to have a process in place. Learn the process to perfection and rapidly adapt it to your specific interaction. The key to perfecting your plan is repetition; catering it only to the offering or goal that each influence will require. Successful people will always take every opportunity to learn the process and always seek to control their own destiny. This understanding is more than just how to sell. It is how successful people provide the atmosphere that will create their future.

When reading this book, read it to understand. Start with a clear and open mind. Allow yourself to examine what you may not know and confirm what you already do. Your goal should be to get the most out of it so you can transfer your learning to future experiences. Our business is not one in which every customer or situation will mirror the last. Each experience you face will require different levels of knowledge. If you were only looking to make one sale, you would not need much of an investment. However, if you are serious about becoming a skilled and successful salesperson, you will need to take the initiative and make the investment to reach your goals.

While reading this book, some may be advised to take a different approach to best receive the knowledge it has to offer. When you are involved in selling, you will often have to monitor your customer's level of interest or receptivity. It may be the same for you here. If you are easily distracted or not good at extended periods of learning, start with the chapters or topics that interest you the most. This way, you will be more likely to become involved and remain engaged. Simply search the table of contents, flip through to the chapter of most interest and explore where your interest might expand. The more interest you have in a topic, the more receptive you will be to learning. Once started, seek to transfer your interest to the supporting chapters and then continue to widen your scope.

If, while reading, you come across something that you might not see the clarity in or the need for, think about it before you arbitrarily dismiss it. The biggest part of learning is the ability and willingness to examine a topic from all levels. This is also an important part of sales. How you are best able to determine and understand your customers' needs is by first clearing your own partiality and listening in an open and receptive manner. You have to be able to seek and recognize the point of view of others before you can be sure of the most beneficial solution. Open yourself to discover all the knowledge you can from this book. Examine each point with an open mind and then incorporate any possible new understanding with your present experience to add to your current abilities. While writing this book, I wanted to list every possible step and an explanation of each in every chapter. I didn't want you to miss something by not fully reading every part of the book. However, I tried to spread the information and advice out in an appropriate sequence. So be sure to ultimately read the entire book, so as not to miss the supporting advice for each step.

Although in many instances the entire scope of each step will not be necessary, please know the understanding will. One-price offerings may negate or alter the need for certain sections, such as the negotiation chapters, and certain management processes or philosophies may vary the extent of added knowledge or practices needed to perform your specific part of the sales process. However, there will always be something that will require influence and there will always be supplementary advice, persuasion, and understanding needed to help initiate a purchase. For example, if your customer does not have a previous solution that they will be trading, you may question the need for the "revaluing the trade" chapter. However, many customers will often have something they will be replacing, and the knowledge learned can always be used for additional support, such as why they should update sooner rather than later. The magnitude or scope of every sale or decision may be different; however, successfully performing each method of influence will often require understanding of the complete process. Developing your knowledge of different approaches will always better enhance your ability to succeed. Even though the process cannot be specific to each situation, it can always easily be adjusted to fit each circumstance.

ALL ABOUT THE KNOWLEDGE

The most important quality for any successful salesperson to have is the desire to learn. When a salesperson is properly trained, a sale is an easy task to achieve. In fact, the only limitation a salesperson may ever face in his or her career will come from no longer feeling the need to polish their skills. A resourceful salesperson will always seek to acquire the knowledge needed to better handle each situation or obstacle. A successful salesperson understands that there is no finish line in learning, that there is always the ability to learn more with exposure to constructive knowledge. This book was written for just such a salesperson. It was designed to describe each step of the sale and offer a comprehensive guide to follow. Please understand that with desire and an accurate guide to follow, anybody can become a top salesperson in a very short time. With this book, you will learn how to set up your business, build rapport, and gain credibility. You will learn to be inquisitive and persuasive, to build relationships, handle objections, and make the sale. Soon you will be one of your company's top sellers. Let's get started.

WHY A CUSTOMER BUYS

A person will buy when he or she feels a solution has been found for his or her individual wants or needs. People will make a decision when they are satisfied that they have somehow found a solution that will make their lives better. Why someone buys is because they want to experience the result that their acceptance will bring. Deciding on a product or service is like any other decision one may make. Your customers want the luxury, safety, status, or enjoyment they feel their selection will provide.

A person's decision to purchase is often the result of the influence in which they have allowed themselves to be persuaded. The exact point of this decision is reached when they have found a solution that they believe will satisfy their objectives and when they feel the solution's value is equal to the investment required. It is when they feel that the value of owning your product is worth the price to be paid.

VALUE

As salespeople, we must understand that the key word here is "value." This is because the definition of value is one of perception and is always open to influence. In sales, it is this perception of value that will be the driving factor in your customers' decision-making process. Understanding this enables you to realize that the key objective that you have as the salesperson is to build the value needed to influence a purchase. Before we can ever request a forward decision from someone, we must first understand their motivations. Knowing that your customers are open to influence is the first step toward persuading them to make a purchase. This gives you the knowledge that your ability and persistence will be rewarded. It allows you to realize that it is you, the salesperson, who is in the best position to influence their selection and persuade a decision. To be successful, you have to be able to determine your customers' wants and needs, identify the items that best satisfy them, and be credible in the advice you offer. You have to create the value needed to influence a purchase.

Almost all purchasing decisions have been influenced in some way. A person's decision to buy may have been influenced by his or her own research, a charismatic salesperson, or even the marketing campaign of the manufacturer or provider. In some way, all purchasing customers were somehow convinced they would benefit from their impending ownership. Please know that if you position yourself as a friendly, knowledgeable, and credible person, your customers will almost always seek their guidance from you as to their ideal selection. You will be seen as a representative of the services you offer, and your customers will see you as their guide.

WHAT MOTIVATES A PURCHASE

In order to influence our customers to purchase, we must first recognize our customers' motivating factors and learn to build upon each one. It is these factors that will help initiate a purchase if we are able to identify, support, and confirm how each will help to satisfy their goals.

EMOTION

Most of our customers will start out driven by specific wants and needs and will often have predetermined parameters set up for themselves. They will try to make a logical decision based strictly on the facts of the offering and the cost involved in purchasing it. They will condition themselves not to make an emotional decision. However, there will always be additional motivating factors involved in what, where, and how someone decides to purchase. Very few will be able to make it through the entire process following their pre-set guidelines. Many will be influenced by the purchasing experience you provide and their consequent emotions. The thought of owning and experiencing a new or newer solution can be exciting, even for the most conservative people. Your customers' emotions, when combined with other reflexive feelings, will often sway their decisions as much as the offering or price in question. This being the case, our efforts should be centered on our customers' emotional wants and needs, as these are most often what determines their final actions.

Make no mistake: People will alter what they buy, where they buy, and from whom they buy, all as a result of their emotions at the time. This is why it is so important for us to follow the steps that allow us to be in a position of influence. This is why it is so important to provide a positive atmosphere and a comfortable experience. We must prepare ourselves to be influential while an acceptable solution is found. We must take the time to build rapport, ask credible questions, and listen to our customers' wants and needs. We must follow and complete each persuasion-building step of the process.

PERSUASION

Everybody is agreeable to some degree of influence. Some people will drive across the state to save a few dollars, and some will gladly pay more to do business closer. However, either of these people could probably have been persuaded to do the opposite. There are valid points in doing each. There is no right or wrong answer in buying. What, when, why, and from whom someone will buy are all open to influence. It is all a matter of perception, which is controlled by the emotions of the customer at the time of each decision. Almost all people will have these emotions and almost all will be receptive to your influence.

If your customers like you, trust you, and feel comfortable in working with you, they will be open to your influence. You can alter and help form their decisions. Your customers will allow you to persuade them if your influence is credible and well-received. Think about how many times you have gone out to purchase a particular product and come back with something you liked better after listening to the advice of others.

People themselves know that they are not always fully in control of their own actions or emotions when making a decision. This is one of the reasons that many people will often state that they are "just looking" upon entering your business or say, "I don't have a lot of time" upon receiving your call. They know they are receptive to outside influences and do not want to identify themselves as serious buyers before they have a chance to form an opinion on their own. Many will want to get a feel for you, your company, and your solution before they will further commit their time. However, never assume that your customers will not be receptive to your open, honest, and credible advice if you are able to present a welcoming experience. Your job is to use your knowledge and understanding to help customers make decisions that are right for them. Once you have assessed their needs and determined the solutions most suited to them, you owe it to them to be persuasive and persistent in your motivating efforts.

ATTENTION TO THE DETAILS

All top salespeople understand that there are often many different solutions that will satisfy a given person's needs. This being the case, it makes sense that most buying decisions are made for less tangible reasons. These reasons can vary, and may seem insignificant to new or inexperienced salespeople.

To be completely successful, you must understand that each person you work with will, in some way, be more or less influenced by every action or reaction that occurs. Customers may like your smile, your location, your financing options, or the fact that your company always has fresh coffee. Or they may dislike all of these things about you or your company. These factors and more will combine with the experience you provide and will be scored, consciously or subconsciously, as pluses or minuses in your customers' decision-making process. For this reason, you must always observe your customers' actions and emotions for the subtle hints that will guide you in giving them the comfort that will promote your buying atmosphere. Always seek to encourage your customers' positive emotions and buffer or soften their negative emotions.

UNDERSTANDING WANTS AND NEEDS

The primary determining factors in our customers' conscious decision to purchase are their wants and needs. These are the factors that must be taken into account before your customers will settle upon an agreeable solution. Earlier, we looked into the importance of setting ourselves up to be persuasive in our interaction. Now let's take a look at understanding our customers' patterns of thought to help determine how they are both influenced and motivated. Let's look at understanding our customers' wants and needs. It is important to understand our specific customers' wants and needs so that we will know how to increase their individual desires and build their perception of value.

A customer's need is recognized as a logical desire, where as a want is more emotionally driven. A person's needs are usually predetermined or set, and their wants are usually created and subject to influence. Again, many offerings will often satisfy a specific person's needs. A need, or a perceived need, may be the reason people initiate a search, but it is often their wants and your selling experience that most influence them to take action. Most purchases are emotionally driven. Please believe that a person will pay more and decide more quickly if he or she is excited about their solution.

NEEDS

A need is the result of an event that necessitates an action. It may be that a previous solution has been damaged, is broken down, outdated, inoperable, or in some way unavailable. It may also be that their current solution no longer suits their present or future needs. Knowing your customer's needs will enable you to help find the solution to their problem and allow you to further persuade and confirm their selection.

LATENT NEEDS

Latent needs are needs not yet realized by your customer. For example, your customer may have a product that will require attention soon. Although they may not have recognized it yet, they have an impending need, and the age or limited servicing opportunities available may not justify keeping it. It may be in your customer's best financial interest to make a move now, while their current solution still has a respectable trade value.

A top salesperson will search for impending needs and develop them into buying motives. Almost all solutions will eventually need maintenance, servicing, or the occasional upgrade. This customer's motive would be to lessen financial risk and increase peace of mind. A new, reliable, and possibly warranted solution will always create more enjoyment and less worry. To uncover your customer's possible future needs, ask the questions that will allow them to see the possibilities. For example, you may ask, "What problems do you anticipate with your current provider?" Their own answer might suggest an impending need and be the start of their newly realized motivation. At what point should someone no longer risk their time, safety, or money on an aging solution? All too often people will put off a decision, only to find out later that they should have made a move earlier. Asking the proper questions may elicit an answer that your customers will recognize as a reason to make a move now.

WANTS

A person's want is the feeling that is created in anticipation of attaining an objective. It is his or her desired intention. It is the feeling that will ultimately help motivate one to achieve what he or she wishes to have. Understand that your customers' wants will often be the driving factor behind most of their purchases.

Knowing your customers' wants will enable you to emotionally encourage their direction. It will give you the knowledge needed to creatively influence a purchase. Your customers' level of desire will always be either increased or decreased by the influences or actions that occur during your sales interaction. It is because of this that you must become skilled in recognizing and building upon your customers' wants as you seek to create a positive and comfortable experience.

INITIATIVE TO BUY

In order to best prepare ourselves to be in a position of influence, we must sometimes look to adapt our initial approach to what will best be received by each of our individual customers. Even though our customers will often be swayed by the emotions that occur while involved in the experience that we are able to provide, it is important to recognize their early motivational factors to know how best to interact with each in the early stages of our meeting. We want to know how to begin to persuade as we seek each of our newly greeted customer's objectives.

The most important factor for us to understand is our customer's level of want versus need. Know that different people will be more motivated by different levels of each.

Those motivated by need have conditioned themselves to act with logic or reason. Those motivated by want are usually more carefree and guided by their emotions. Some people will initially respond more or less to logic or need, as opposed to want or emotion. Some people may even respond exclusively to one or the other in these early stages.

People who are conditioned to think in a structured environment, such as engineers or architects, may respond initially only to logic. This is because their patterns of thought are likely to be influenced by their work and will be similarly structured. With these customers, you would be advised to present the information that you feel will guide them to rationalize a decision. Humor, excitement, and sizzle will not be helpful in the early stages of your meeting. However, with a proper preliminary approach and timely transition, and by effectively following the steps of the process, you will be better able to develop your customer's underlying emotional wants into additional motivational factors.

With other customers, like those who are less structured in their needs or more open to new ideas, a more emotional approach may be better suited. Different people require different approaches and adjustments, depending on how they choose to set their decision-making process and the resolve they have to adhere to their process.

To help establish your early ability to connect with each of these customers, try to determine the dominant motivation they have in visiting and cater your initial presentation just for them. If they are initially need oriented, start by addressing their needs. If they are initially want-oriented, address their wants. Then, as your sales relationship progresses, decide how much attention to spend on each to help further your connection. Anticipate how best to adapt to your customers and look to increase the factors that will influence their individual motivations as your interactions progress. Their level of resolve of each, possibly varying throughout the process, is where you should direct your efforts.

Please understand that a customer's eventual decision will only evolve in the direction of your influence if you are able to successfully open their receptiveness and maintain it throughout your interaction. In the beginning, you will often have to get close to your customers' patterns of thought before they will begin to open up and become receptive in following. Establishing an initial connection with each of your customers will often be the necessary foundation for your success in the continuing formation of your influence.

WHAT A CUSTOMER WANTS IN AN OFFERING

What a customer wants in a new solution will often vary from person to person. Each person will have his or her own set of preferred benefits that he or she will seek to attain. It is here that you will have to know your products and their benefits. You will also need to understand how your customers will view each benefit as it relates to their wants and needs.

Here is a list of some of the wants and needs that people may have in regard to a new solution. Read this list so you can identify with each. Notice that some of these will motivate you personally to purchase and some will not. The purpose of this list is for you to become aware of other people's motivational factors. As you read each one, try to envision how they may appeal to your differing customers and think how to build upon the desire of each.

- Safety
- Luxury
- Status
- Exclusivity
- Style
- Comfort
- Power
- Warranty

- Agility
- Reliability
- Economy
- Time-tested
- Capacity
- Performance
- Proven
- Maintainable

One of the keys to being a top salesperson is being able to recognize your customers' main buying interest, what they desire most. Whether they perceive it as a want or a need, most customers will have some central motive while making their selection. It is probably one of the factors listed above. Your goal is to recognize this interest and build upon it. Separate their desired benefit and make that your key selling point. Use their main motivating factor to focus your persuasive efforts. Seek your customer's motives in the early stages using your discovery questions. Although they might not give you the exact "sales" word, they will often tell you in a manner that you can interpret. They will probably not use the word "status," but you will likely be able to recognize this as their motive by the clues they give or by noticing what choices capture their attention. When your customer inquires about a specific offering, relate back to the reasoning that others shared when showing an interest in that offering. Seek to understand how they were influenced.

Some additional insight may be obtained by recognizing how your products or services are being marketed. Certain offerings are marketed to satisfy certain desires. Become aware of the marketing campaigns of your various offerings. For example, the manufacturers' ads in brochures, in magazines, or on the radio will often present the image that they want their solutions to produce. This "branding" will often have a strong effect and will likely be a telltale sign of their motivation. Your customers' perceptions of the message this branding has created will often transcend to reality for them. Seek to build on this within your influence. Your trucks may be tough, your jewelry may be affordable, your resorts may be luxurious, and your servicing programs may be flexible. Become aware of the key words and slogans that your manufacturers use, as these will help you to better understand your customers' motivations. It should be easy to think of a popular product and visualize its marketing campaign. Take note of its motivating factors.

Recognize your customer's interest, confirm their interest, and then build upon it. If your product's safety is important to your customer, focus on why or how your product is safe. Do not concentrate on features in which they do not have an interest.

WHAT A CUSTOMER WANTS FROM A SALESPERSON

People want a salesperson who is attuned to their needs, is capable of speaking to them on their level, and is respectful and accommodating of their preferred style of comfort. They want a salesperson who projects an open and warm manner, is respectful of others' personalities, and who knows how best to adapt to their own. They want someone who won't prejudge or assume. They want someone who will listen to their needs and tailor a presentation just for them, a salesperson who genuinely seeks their best interests by asking the proper questions and answers theirs with credible guidance.

Make no mistake: The more positive their experience is with you, the more likely they will buy from you. Here is a list of qualities that customers deem important in their salesperson.

- Honest
- Likeable
- Informative
- Credible

- Knowledgeable
- Unique
- Trustworthy
- Sense of humor
- Pleasing personality

I think that at some level, people know that they will somehow tie their ownership experience in with their purchasing experience on big-ticket items. Thus, your customers may consciously or subconsciously defer from making a purchasing decision based upon the experience you provide. If they are having a bad experience, they may avoid purchasing, even if they have found an acceptable choice. Conversely, if they are incurring a good experience, they may be more receptive to purchasing their choice in order to create the pleasant memories that will be prompted every time they interact with their choice. In any case, do not doubt the power of a positive experience.

BUYING SIGNALS

Buying signals are the signs your customers will display when they are moving toward making a decision. When your customers exhibit the signs of wanting to move forward, it is usually preceded by an event or occurrence that has initiated an increased desire. This action or series of events is often a direct indication of why your customer seeks to buy. It is important to recognize these buying signals so you will know to what degree certain motivations exist when helping to confirm their selection and increase their desire. Here are some of the signs that your customers are ready to move forward, placed in the order they may appear.

- Smiling and leaning forward with intent
- Wanting to clarify certain information
- Asking about financing or payment options

- Asking about the time needed to complete the paper-work
- Portraying how they will enjoy your product
- Asking questions about your service hours
- Looking at other members of their party to confirm their interest

It is also important to take notice of your customers' signs of interest so that you will better know when they are likely willing to move forward. Timing is important. If you ask for the sale too early, your customers may deem you too forward and back off. Similarly, if you wait too long, their buying desires may diminish.

Your customers' willingness will occur at various stages and with varying degrees of intent. Monitor their emotions and then react to them. Look to act when their receptivity and desire are at their highest. Encourage their positive feelings and defuse their negative ones. Learn to recognize your customers' signs of interest, build upon their desires, and ask for the sale as their interest builds.

HOW CUSTOMERS BUY

How people decide is likely to be by the process in which they were shaped. Please understand the importance of this. Our process is our guide. It is the reason that we will likely arrive at our intended destination. In order to best aid in the experience that we are able to provide, we must have a format that will help smooth our customers' transition from customers to owners, from unsure to enthusiastic.

As stated in the introduction, our process is the best template for any path. Although adaptable in its use, its consistency in form will provide our best approach to constructing a decision. To help further the understanding of our process's steps, their usefulness, and broad encompassment, let's take a look at an example of a simple everyday occurrence; say, selecting a movie. Let's separate each step, and see how easily each can be incorporated into our process to help provide the structure in achieving our goal. Please note the flow of the steps. When seeking to select a movie of choice; we will greet our intended guest, provide the options of preference, present our selection for consideration, use past experience as a reason to choose, build value in our choice, ensure that our guest will make a decision before we agree to any alternatives, present our closing argument, ask for their agreement, overcome their objections, and ultimately enjoy the show. Each bit of influence, no matter how simple or common, is always adaptable and best achieved by the process. It is how someone is best influenced to "buy." Although the process of the sale will not perfectly align with each decision you seek, its basic structure will always provide your best path of influence.

Most decisions are formed by external factors. If you think about it, even when we seem to come up with something on our own it is still likely that we are influenced. Whether by society, culture, schooling, or our jobs, our whole world is shaped by outside influences. As soon as our parents brought us home, whether through reward or penalty, our conditioning will likely have begun. We do something because it is expected. We wake up at similar times, put on similar clothes, take similar forms of transportation, and complete similar tasks. For as many different people we have in our country, think how many are so, so similar. Wife, husband, 2.5 kids, etc. The structure of our society is based on conformity. We watch the majority and adjust to fit. We follow the process.

Please understand the relevance of this. Learn the process, understand the process, and believe in the process. People's desires, motivations, enthusiasm, and actions are all subject to influence. As long as you are able to present your customer with a comfortable experience and comfortable atmosphere, your process will provide the path he or she will gladly follow.

WHY CUSTOMERS DON'T BUY

A customer will buy because they have found a solution to their wants or needs. However, their final agreement must also be accompanied by a resolution of any concerns or uncertainties. To help further understand why our customers buy, we must also learn some of the many reasons they will choose not to buy. When we can recognize and understand this "reasoning," we can then actively look to offer the new information needed to change the direction of their decision.

Customers do not buy for two specific reasons: They either are not capable of purchasing or do not choose to. It is those that do not choose to that we will look at here. Customers that choose not to buy from us are not able to justify a move forward. For some reason, they have created some blocking force that is keeping them from buying. Understand that these concerns and hesitations are the common objections that we will incur and will have to overcome before we can move toward a decision.

Although we will be dedicating a lot more time to overcoming our customers' various objections later on, let's take a quick look at some of the more common objections here and some simple advice for each to get started in our understanding. Please browse through the following objections to get a quick outline of the obstacles we will often face. However, remain conscious not to slow the flow of your reading. In the early part of any experience, it may be best to simply scan the straight more factual areas to ensure that you will continue and not risk proceeding and miss out on any future interesting and insightful knowledge. Please be sure to monitor your interest and adjust your actions, and always allow yourself the ability to slow down and appreciate the areas that are more thought provoking or interesting to you.

Fear of not getting a good deal: Please understand that a good deal is not a defined measure; it is merely one's perception of an offering's value. So create some value. Build the value in the benefits of their selected solution, in yourself, and in your company. This is where establishing your credibility and creating a comfortable experience will significantly increase your ability to encourage the customer's direction.

Not sure what they want: Clarify their wants and then seek to satisfy them. When your customer is unsure of their next move, ask the questions that will help uncover their wants, needs, and motivations. Help them to determine what they are looking for with your inquiries, and then listen to understand their response.

Fear of the wrong choice: Without acceptance of their choice, your customer will unlikely move to a decision. Question again to re-discover their objectives and then clarify them. Your goal here is to confirm that their selection does in fact satisfy their wants and needs. Support their selection and confirm that it is the solution they helped select. Let your customer know how much your previous customers are enjoying their new solutions.

No hurry: Many buyers will not be in a hurry and even more will say they're not. This is where discovering your customer's underlying wants and latent needs is the recommended path. Seek to open their awareness and gain their excitement. Additionally, if short-term incentives exist, use them to help justify a move logically.

No perceived need: Often, a customer will weigh their desire against their need. Some will want to justify their decisions logically. In this situation, look to question current and future needs. Lead your customers to discover some of their potential future needs with a few of your inquiries. Also seek to develop their wants.

Fear of what others will think: Build confidence in your solution's recognition and public appeal. Let your customer know of the accolades that your product or service has acquired. Be sure to also establish the importance of what they themselves think, because ultimately this should be what matters most.

No value: As we said earlier, value is everything in sales. First, demonstrate the features of your solution and show how its benefits will satisfy your customer's objectives. Then, continue building value in yourself and in your company. Because our customers' perceptions of value are so important, we will be dedicating a whole chapter to it.

No trust: When your customer appears to lack trust in you, it may be advisable to slow down a little and reapply your listening skills. Determine their goals and be credible in the advice you offer. Show empathy for their concerns and present a caring nature. Support your facts. Keep good eye contact and positive body language. Be careful not to tell them more than they will accept or believe.

Uncomfortable: When your customer is uncomfortable, your obvious goal should be to make them more comfortable. Adapt and adjust your approach to your customer's style. Establish a connection with your customer before you seek to lead. Find your common ground and build your rapport. Adapt to their manner of interaction. Welcome them with a tour of your facility.

Has a better deal: Make sure the offering in question is of similar features. Also seek to verify any of the other variables in the deal, such as the value of the trade or any additional terms or qualifiers. Also, similar or not, always be sure to include the benefits of purchasing from you and your company. Seek to have your customer include these in their ownership experience.

People's concerns and objections will often follow a general guide in the purchasing of a new solution. However, there will always be the variances and uniqueness of each. Some of your customers' reasons for not purchasing may be hard to recognize. To help foresee and understand these potential reasons, you will have to actively monitor your customers' actions and emotions for the level of interest and commitment they have. If you feel their receptivity has drifted off or concerns have appeared, try to back up and replay the instance when your feeling started to occur. Picture every move and try to discover what went off-track. Know that their hesitation may be a result of the facts of the deal or a result of their experience. Always be sure to recognize each possibility. Determine their hesitation and then seek to resolve it. Know that in doing so you will often have to be investigative, creative, and persistent for each individual you will meet.

Sales is a continual process of evaluating and adapting to any action or reaction. You will often have to be investigative, creative, and persistent in overcoming your customers' objections. It is not as simple as whether they like your solution or not. At any time, a hesitancy may occur. However, please also know your customers will still move forward if you can recognize and satisfy their concerns. Understand that your customers will often evaluate the whole experience for a purchase of any substantial size. It is usually the total experience that will precipitate a move in one direction or another. As a salesperson, you have to understand this and be willing and prepared. Determine the cause of the hesitation and resolve it. If you have found your customer's ideal solution, you should be informative, persuasive, and persistent in confirming their choice and overcoming their objections. Continue to confirm and satisfy the benefits they are in search of and overcome their concerns.

FINAL NOTE

The biggest factor in a person's decision to buy is based on the quality of the experience the salesperson is able to provide. If a customer likes their salesperson, trusts their advice, and is comfortable with their level of service, the customer will make every attempt to buy from them. The customer will select and purchase their most likely choice. Please understand this. The customer will buy the salesperson before they will buy what is being offered. Most customers will make a decision based more upon their experience than the facts or price of the offering in question. All successful salespeople know this; all failing salespeople do not want to believe this. This is why one person in your company will consistently sell above the standard and others will consistently fall below. The exciting part to recognize here, however, is that with the proper skills, the proper process, and the proper learning ability, anyone can perform at the higher level.

2

LET ME ASK YOU A QUESTION

66 **L**et me ask you a question?" This is the most powerful question in sales. It is also my favorite. It will stop your customers, get their attention, and allow you to steer them in the direction you want with the questions you ask. It gives you the opportunity to lead your customers with their own answers. It is what will encourage them to offer their attention and acceptance for you to further inquire. This is in fact what actually makes this a question. It is your request for their approval to ask. Know that the curiosity created by your following pause will unlikely be ignored.

Being successful in sales requires you to act and react constantly in the best way to sell. You have to be more than knowledgeable and helpful. You have to determine the best way to proceed and chart your course. You have to take control and lead. Very few people will come in and walk you through the steps of the sale, very few. You must investigate, learn, and establish a direction. You must become creative, anticipatory, and uninhibited in your quest to understand your customers and their needs. You must become successful in questioning.

Having a proper questioning technique is the key to being a top salesperson. Asking the appropriate questions is the basis of sales at every step of the process. You question to build rapport, gain credibility, determine the benefits your customers seek, root out their objections, and confirm a selection. Your success in sales is directly related to your ability to use the answers to your questions to confirm each step and advance to the next. By asking the proper questions, you take control of the pace and direction of the sale, all while receiving the information you need to understand your customers' goals. A question is also the easiest way to initiate a conversation; it invites interaction and shows that you care about your customers' needs.

In sales, we use many types of questions. The use and timing of each will be dependent upon where we are in the sales process and what we want our customers' responses to be. For example, with some questions we want to learn their answers, while with others we want our customers to realize their answers. In the first example, we would use a discovery or exploratory question; in the second, we would use a leading or confirming question.

In this chapter, we will take a look at each of these questions and more, all of which are meant to help you sell more effectively. Let's start by looking at these two important question types: discovery and leading. These are the core questions in sales and often the basis from which other questions are derived. From there we will seek to understand the questioning process, examine how to ask our questions, and explore the other questions we will use.

DISCOVERY QUESTIONS

A discovery question is used to gain information. It is how we are best able to determine the objectives our customers have and understand how to create a positive interaction with each. It gives us the information we need to determine how to move forward, all while allowing us to maintain control of the conversation.

With discovery questions, we build our level of credibility while learning of our customers' needs. This line of questioning in itself allows us to show that we are capable of determining the needs our customers have and thus capable of helping them with their selection. This is essential in being able to help influence a purchase throughout the steps of the sale. Understand that your advice will have no credence if your customers feel that you do not have the proper information needed to give them the guidance they desire. They will not allow you to influence them if you do not have the knowledge and understanding of what it is they seek.

Become comfortable and realize that your customers will expect you to ask the questions that are needed to discover their objectives. In addition to better understanding the goals they seek, discovery questions can also be helpful in understanding the buying style of your customers in the early stages and investigating the hesitancies they may have in the later stages. When in doubt, ask. Your discovery questions are essential in helping you navigate through every step of the process, from start to finish. Do not inhibit your success and allow yourself to navigate in the dark. When a question or misunderstanding arises, seek the information needed to proceed, explore your curiosities, and discover your answers.

LEADING QUESTIONS

A leading question is one we would use to help direct our customers to a certain path. The use of this question is where we would seek to have our customers form an opinion or move to a decision based upon their own answers. It is to guide them, or at least to have them reconsider a current thought or point of view.

The key to effectively accomplishing your goal here is to first calculate what you want your customers' answers to be and then carefully construct the questions to guide them to the responses you desire. After you understand your customers' goals and determine their next best step, you want to be able to influence them. When creating your questions, allow them to realize the responses you desire from within their own thoughts. If you are successful in accomplishing this, the result will be simple. There is no doubt that they will be more receptive to their own "discovery" than any statement you may offer. Basically, if you say it, they will listen; if they say it, they will believe. The concept of this is extremely powerful, and is how most successful closers become successful.

The leading question is used throughout our sales process. An example of a leading question in the selection stage may be, "This is the color and option package you were looking for, isn't it?" An example for when preparing to negotiate may be, "Ms. Customer, let me ask you a question. If we were able to agree upon the terms of this deal, you would be in a position to move forward today, wouldn't you?" Note that you are leading them to confirm the commitment needed in order to proceed.

These two examples are direct leading questions. Your customers' responses will directly lead them to the answers you want them to realize. With these questions, please know that much of your desired influence is achieved by your leading facial expression. For example, when you want a positive response, seek to encourage one with your look of approval.

Other "planned realizations" or attempts to alter a more determined view may take some creativity. To further understand how best to adjust some of your more determined customers, let's take a look at one of our most available means of media: the TV. For today's lesson, try to picture a show involving a performing lawyer. That shouldn't be hard. Picture the lawyer interviewing a witness on the stand. Note his positioning and his method. He knows where he wants to go, and he knows how he will get there. How he gets there, of course, is through a series of questions that will ultimately bring to light the lawyer's objective. On any given show, have you ever heard the opposing attorney say, "Objection, Your Honor; he is leading the witness"? Well, of course he is. While we might not want to share the demeanor present in this scene, it is an effective way to watch how the result of leading can be achieved.

During the course of our sales interactions, there will also be times when we will have to prepare for our future. We will sometimes have to influence our customers' future outlook to better accommodate their future possibilities. Meaning, when we are able to foresee that our available offerings are not lining up directly with our customers' current wants, we must often look to widen their outlook. We must look to broaden their horizons. It is here that we must look to ask a question or series of questions in advance of their future decisions to help steer them to realize or envision a new way of thinking.

Let's look at an example. Please know that the learning from this and most all of our listed examples can be easily transferred to your particular field. Always seek to make your comparison.

With your discovery questions, you determine that your customer is looking for a light-colored sports utility with a larger engine for towing and no other options. While checking your inventory you see that you have one that is close, but that also has a third-row seat, an entertainment center and rear air conditioning, a fairly expensive set of options. Before you even mention this particular vehicle as an option, you want to design or lead your customer's acceptance. You want to set the scene. "Sir, is it possible that your wife and kids may at some point need to use this vehicle?" Now pause.

His own reply to this question might alter his outlook and make him more receptive to the vehicle. In this scenario, the customer's future objection of extra expense will be easier to overcome because he has already made the case to consider these options with his own internal response. Know that certain options or features may very well be ones that your customers want; however, if not presented properly, they might not see the benefit in having them and thus resist even considering them.

Learn the benefits of the options that your products or services have and structure your questions accordingly. If your customers can form an opinion with your guidance before they are faced with certain variables, they will typically be more receptive when considering them. If you can lead them with your questions, they will be more flexible in their decisions. All options have some benefit. In some cases, having your customers answer their own questions may be the only way to conclusively gain their agreement. Understand that a customer will often doubt the veracity of a salesperson's words because they will be cautious of the salesperson's motives. Customers will always be curious as to whose best interests a salesperson has in mind. Setting the scene will often be required and this always is best accomplished with this style of question.

Average salespeople will continually seek to answer their customer's concerns with a statement. Successful salespeople know the best way to ensure the customer's agreement is to invite them to come up with the answers on their own. The leading question is the most effective way to answer your customers' concerns, both before and after they are realized. Having the ability to persuade and influence customers using carefully thought-out questions while anticipating their thoughts is the key to leading them to the answers you want. It is essential to have your customers understand and believe what is questioned, so they can add that information to their reasoning and move on to the next.

WHY A QUESTION

The question is unquestionably the most important tool in sales. It is how we get the information we need to help establish our customers' needs and how we are able to further research how to fulfill them. It is how we are able to both take control of the sales process and effectively lead our customers to the sale.

I often visit sales-related businesses, and it surprises me how few salespeople will try to understand or evaluate their customers' needs before showing their products. This is the most common mistake of all beginning salespeople. Please do not follow this example. It is why most beginning salespeople fail to succeed and why most average salespeople fail to excel.

A top salesperson understands that customers want to be understood. They expect you to ask the questions that will tell you how best to help them. They want a salesperson who will give them the proper advice for their needs, not one who will assume what they want or need. They want a salesperson who is not afraid to ask, who understands how to ask, and who is capable of giving credible advice and guidance. We need to understand what is important to our customers, not assume we know. Do not give your customers the opportunity to resist your efforts by confronting them with your own directive; invite them to help discover their opportunities.

QUESTION, QUESTION, QUESTION

Make no mistake: Sales is the creative ability of asking the proper questions. With a question, you create your best opportunity to proceed. If you could come away with one skill from reading this book, understanding why we question would probably be your best choice. It is that important.

Let's now take a more in-depth look at the reasons we question in the order they may transpire, staying within our sales process. Please read each reason slowly while visualizing a scenario. Try to come up with additional questions for each reason as it may relate to your specific business. The easiest way to get better at asking questions and understanding their importance is to become inquisitive and question. Here we go, this is why we question:

- You question to find the information needed to gain common ground and build rapport.
- You question to allow your customers to open up and show their interactive style.
- You question to show your customers you care and want to understand.

- You question to discover the benefits your customers are looking for.
- You question to build the credibility needed to influence your customer.
- You question to narrow the scope of your customer's selection to one choice.
- You question to get your customers to think and reevaluate a current opinion.
- You question to build their desire.
- You question to build value in their selected choice.
- You question to confirm their selection during the presentation.
- You question to involve them in visualizing ownership.
- You question to reevaluate their current product or service.
- You question to build value in their choice of you and your company.
- You question to see if your customers are ready to buy.
- You question to build value in the financial terms that you have offered.
- You question to seek out your customers' objections to moving forward.
- You question to re-clarify the reasons for their choice and ask for the sale.

I hope you are thinking we use questions a lot, because we do. The sale is likely dependent upon it. With a question, you maintain the flow and direction of the sale, engage your customers during each step of the process, and continue to the next. Seeking to initiate and improving your question skills is that important. This cannot be overstated. If you are to be successful in sales, you have to start asking questions.

While in the process of your sale, learn your direction. Think of yourself as a sales detective. Do not let fear or hesitancy limit your ability to learn or succeed. Selling is like solving a problem, and the easiest way to solve a problem is to seek out and analyze the facts. The question accomplishes many purposes, all while showing your customers that you are concerned with them as individuals. It also allows you to present your information in a way that is hard to disagree with, unlike with a statement. It is your job to help your customers discover their best solution and lead them to their best solution. When in doubt, ask.

HOW TO QUESTION

The best way to start is with the small, easy questions. This is to gain acceptance as you go. Your customers want you to understand their needs, and look forward to your questions, however, they also want to feel comfortable with you.

When starting your discovery process, take the time to build some rapport with your customers and allow them to open up with light, open-ended questions. Engage them in regular conversation. Start with the small questions, then work your way up to your information related questions. Your goal in the early stages is not to draw attention to the fact that you are questioning them. Know that if you listen and show an interest in their "light" initial responses, you will be more likely to have willing and open responses in the future. This approach is the easiest way to get them to be forthcoming, giving you the information you need to work with. If you can establish a level of comfort, you will also be better able to lead them with your questions later. It will give you more control in steering your customers in the direction that you feel is best suited for them based upon the information they have given.

When interacting with your customers, take time to listen to their responses and understand their thoughts. Clarify their answers to help further create their receptivity. Do not just listen as an acknowledgement. This is too transparent to the average customer and will not be well received. Also remember to not just rattle off all your questions at once. Your customers may become defensive if they feel they are being interrogated.

CATER YOUR APPROACH

The best way to have your customers open up is to involve them with your genuine concern and adaptive approach. Analyze their willingness and adjust your style to ease their concerns. Mix in a couple of open-ended, rapport-building questions, depending upon the responses you receive. If your customers' answers are closed and narrow in the beginning, use a wider, more open approach.

As you start asking more questions, you will quickly learn which are the most effective and what will work best with the people you meet. To get started, use some of the examples of why we question listed here as a reference and build upon them. As you progress, you will soon learn when and where additional questions will help and how you may incorporate your adjustments. Use this list to create your questions ahead of time.

SPECIAL CARE

In some cases you will need to take extra care in your customer approach. This is advice for the "don't pressure me" customer, as here we will have to walk with a little more care. One way to soften an objection to a question is to introduce a way out. An example might go something like this: "Would you consider sharing your goals for today, or would you prefer not to?"

Another example of when this may be effective is while making a call. Here you might ask, "Hello, Mr. Customer, this is J.B. Did I catch you at a bad time?" Notice that by giving an option not to interact, these customers will feel less pressured and will be more likely to respond. Note in the second example that because you did not offer the reason for your call before seeking acceptance, their curiosity may also help to influence them to consent. They will want to know why you called.

In these cases, gaining consent and adding curiosity is often critical in helping you succeed. This style of questioning is not meant to change your goal; it is merely a creative way to achieve it. It can also be used for the person who feels he has to be in control. "Sir, is it okay if I show you one more feature you might like, or are you not interested?" Note that this question will give him the power and create curiosity, both of which will encourage him to move forward and consider the feature you wish to offer. Know your audience.

CREATE YOUR BALANCE

The key to successful questioning with any customer is to adjust your approach while following your path. Knowing how to question will always be best determined by the presence of your customer and the stage in which you are involved. Within your conversation, you want there to be a balance; a balance of asking, listening, and speaking, all while keeping the conversation flowing at the proper pace and in the proper direction. Do not let one aspect of your interaction dominate the theme, or the flow of communication will fall off. Always seek to keep harmony between you and your customers and proceed with your questions as appropriate. With the proper listening and the proper responses, you can be assured their answers will continue to be informative and forthcoming, and your path to the sale will be one of little resistance.

QUESTION TYPES AND HINTS

Think of the difference between a question and a statement. Think of the response each will produce. Where a statement needs a receptive audience, a question will in fact encourage one. Unfortunately, our business still has some preconceived notions regarding its representation. It is not hard to conjure an image of a pushy salesperson rattling off all the benefits he thinks will appeal to his customer. This image is half the reason that many customers come in with preset time limitations or other escape plans.

A top salesperson, however, understands that the way to create a receptive audience is to engage them, and the easiest way to do this is with a question. Questions will keep you informed and on track while keeping the focus in your interaction by encouraging you to listen as much as you speak. Let's now look at some additional questions here and discuss their uses.

OPEN-ENDED QUESTION

This is a question you would use to get your customers talking. It has no specific answer and will give them the opportunity to answer any way they want. It is a great question to use in the rapport-building stage to help allow your customers to open up. It will invite your customers to tell you a story. It can also help you learn the style and personalities of your customers. It will allow them to offer their outlooks or experiences and give them the latitude to explain and describe in the manner they choose. Example questions may be, "So, how do you like living out there in the country?" or, "What are you looking for in your new agent?"

CLOSED-ENDED QUESTION

This question will give you a specific answer. It is a direct question, and it will help direct your customers' answers to a defined response. It can often be answered with a yes or a no. It is also used to help get your customer to focus on a smaller set of options.

Both open- and closed-ended questions can be used in the discovery stage or when leading customers to a certain response. Your goal in successful questioning should be to start off with open questions to get the overall idea and then move to a more closed set of questions to focus in on your specific objective. Some examples may be, "Will you be trading in your current solution?" or, "Would you consider this option package?"

CLARIFYING QUESTION

The clarifying question will help you further understand your customers' thoughts, concerns, or objectives. It will show that you care about what your customers have to offer and will allow them to explain or clear up what they are saying. It allows you and your customers to be in complete understanding while finding their solution. It will also uncover if something has changed or if you need to establish a new direction. Simply put, it helps explain what your customers are relaying.

MULTIPLE-CHOICE QUESTION

This is where you would ask a question and provide two possible answers. You use this question to narrow down the available choices for your customers, making it easier for them to answer. Remember multiple-choice questions back in school? Weren't they easier than the essay questions? It takes less thought to choose an answer than to create one; therefore, this question is more likely to get a response.

Additionally, this question can be used to lead your customer to a set of options that you prefer. For example, asking, "Sir, would it be easier for you to come in on Wednesday or Thursday?" or, "Mrs. Customer, would you prefer the sport model with the sunroof or the one without?" will more likely produce a definitive response, one in which either answer was also pre-determined as acceptable by you. With this one question you can steer them in the direction you want, make it easy for them to answer, and get a commitment from them, all at the same time.

INVOLVEMENT QUESTION

This is where you will place your customers in an ownership position. It is to help paint a picture of the experiences they will have while enjoying their new solution. To accomplish this, simply ask a question that will create an image your customers can visualize. An example may be, "So, what's the first movie you think your grandson will watch on your new entertainment center?" Another may be, "Well, what do you think your co-workers will think of this one?" or, "Where is the first vacation you will take in your new van?" or, "How do you think she will feel while wearing this?" or even, "I bet this will look good in the driveway!" Know that even a statement can actually be a question, if upon finishing, you will a response with your look of affirmation.

These are powerful images and strong persuaders. Your customers will respond to these on an emotional level. Visualize the picture that each of these questions will paint for your customers and how they may influence pending decisions. Know that very few people will buy strictly for need. A buying decision is often motivated by wants and desires. Help your customers envision their dreams; paint them a picture.

CONFIRMING QUESTION

A confirming question is the complement to the leading question. It is used to help confirm or reconfirm your customers' responses while setting up a close or smaller confirmation. It is how you get the flow of yeses started to lead into the "big yes" down the road. A common confirming or leading question is the commitment question. This is where you add a confirming set of words to lead your customers to the response you want. This question is pretty important when closing your customers, so let's look at some examples.

During a difficult close, try asking a small series of confirming questions before again asking for the close. The momentum you create will greatly increase the odds of your customer agreeing to the sale. As we look at these commitment questions, notice how they will help confirm your customer's choice.

As your customer weighs his decision, continue your approach as follows: "Sir, let me ask you a question." Pause for his attention. "You did say blue was your color of choice, didn't you?" or "Your neighbors have had a reliable experience with theirs, haven't they?" Note his response. Then continue.

"Your wife said she favored this particular one, correct?"

"Its new, more contained features will just about make it maintenance-free, wouldn't you agree?"

"The investment required falls within the budget you set for yourself, doesn't it?"

"It will provide the further coverage that your additional needs require, won't it?"

"The improved operating features will allow you to work faster, right?"

"Your advisor recommended you attain these additional benefits, didn't he?"

"The included features will allow you to eliminate outside servicing, right?"

"With the current incentives, now is the best time to buy, don't you agree?"

Now, after some of these questions, pause again, and continue with, "This is your new solution, isn't it?"

If your customer's last answer was yes, you would start writing it up, wouldn't you? If his last answer was not yet yes, you would keep trying to help him see the light, right?

Please recognize the impact of creating a positive momentum for your customers. This line of questioning can be used to set up the close or adjusted for each agreement needed to help you move through the steps. The use of the confirming question will greatly increase your ability to lead your customer to the sale, wouldn't you agree? You see what's going in here, right?

RETURN THE QUESTION

The next type of question we will go over is similar to the confirming question but meant to work off your customers' questions. Its main goal is to confirm your customers' wants by using the opportunities that they will give. It is a preliminary setup for closing down the road. Basically, it is answering your customers' questions with questions of your own with the goal of leading them to a desired response.

If your customer were to ask, "Does your vacation package offer a water front view with a pool?" you could return, "Would you like one with a pool?" Or if she were to ask, "Would it be available for the upcoming holiday?" you could return, "Would you like to have it ready for the holiday?"

Note the difference here between answering your customer's questions directly and answering with a question. The difference is what you have after they have responded. If you just answered yes, you would not have anything. However, if you returned their question with a question of your own, a positive response will give you the commitment needed to keep them moving forward.

The use of this question can also help lead you directly to the sale. To gain a more decisive commitment, such as with the examples above, you may look to follow up with, "Ma'am, if I had one with a pool and could have it ready for the holiday, would you want to make a reservation?"

HOW MUCH?

When your customers ask, "How much?" should we return the question with a question of our own? Well, let's take a look. Often, customers will not wish to purchase that exact day. They are merely seeking information that they will keep adding to until they happen across a salesperson who can gain a commitment in the course of exchanging information. Understanding this, we need a way to alter our typical customer's time frame to something more in the present. One certain way to slow your customer down and start gaining their commitment is by returning this question with a question of your own.

Here is a look at response questions for the most popular question you will ever hear in our business: "How much?"

If they ask, "How much is that blue model?" ask them:

"Is that the model you like?"

"Is blue your color of choice?"

"Have you settled on this particular model?"

"Are you interested in a cash price or a monthly payment?"

"Hey, I like the blue one too. What is it about that one that you like?"

This form of questioning is not being vague. It gives you something to work with. It allows you to build your customers' interests before assigning a price. It also allows them to hear their own desires from their own thoughts. Choose one of the questions from above and try it. Notice how you can create almost any response you want depending on how you vary your question. This allows you the ability for an open response in the earlier stages and a more focused response in the later stages.

The response you receive here will often give you the forward direction you need to further their commitment. If you just gave out a price, you would have nothing. Use their desire for price information as a way to gain their attention and build your value.

IF I COULD

Have you ever had the customer who never got enough? They just kept asking to have something else thrown in, eternally postponing the sale. "Will you throw in the tint? Will you include a matching set of earrings? Can you extend the term of the policy for the same price? Can you add the auxiliary cooler?" And so on.

Well, wouldn't the salesperson have saved some time, profit, and maybe even the sale itself by simply asking, "Sir, if I can throw in the mats, will you buy the truck?"

"If I could, would you...?" This question may be considered too forward by some, but I disagree. I feel it is a perfectly fair and very effective question when used properly. I admit you can't always start the sale with too many of these, but most of the time it is a great way to close. I think that the vast majority of salespeople under use it, so I will choose to support it here. It will allow you to gain a commitment with your pending offer. Some additional examples may be, "If we could find a facility you liked, would you have time to take a tour today?" or, "If we could get your monthly investment to that figure, would you be in a position to start enjoying it right away?"

When your customer asks if you can accomplish a request, use it as a lead to gain their commitment. Do not be shy in returning their question to influence their commitment. This is where you have leverage. This is one of your best opportunities to gain the commitment you need to make the sale. If a customer has a specific request, such as including an option, leverage a commitment from them before you respond. Take the opportunity they have given you and consider your agreement as a condition of the sale. Use their question to gain the commitment needed to help complete the sale.

KNOW YOUR CUSTOMER

There is no doubt that returning your customer's questions with questions of your own can be very useful in our business. This type of questioning will better allow our customer to commit and will often help us in completing each step in the process. It is effective at slowing the fast-paced customer and helping indecisive customers take action.

However, it is also important to keep in mind the old saying, "It is not what you say, but how you say it." It is here that you may want to vary how serious or light your presentation is, depending on what step of the process you are in or where your level of rapport is currently at. You may want to soften your approach in some circumstances. Always note the timing and the response of your delivery.

Then again, at other times, like in the final stages of closing, you may want to remain straight and serious while seeking your question-based commitments. Some of our customers, depending on their buying processes, may be quite elusive when committing to the final terms. With some, leveraging a commitment may be the only definitive way to initiate a sale. Different customers will often require different actions. However, in any case, do not be afraid to use a question-based response. You want to gain the mini-commitments needed to make the sale and yet still be aware of their willingness to participate. Think of questioning as an act of measured balance. Maintain your forward direction by varying your encouragement with a catered amount of apprehension relief.

FINAL NOTE

If you have ever had a customer say, "Well, thank you for all your help and information," it is likely that he or she was the one asking the questions and also the one who controlled the sale. It is also likely that a sale did not occur.

Sales is not a career in which a reserved or inhibited person will succeed. Your customers will not likely present you with all the information needed to make a sale. You will have to investigate your customers' needs and lead them with their own answers. To be successful, you have to become successful in questioning. You have to become anticipatory, creative, and unconstrained. Ask the proper questions at the proper times and lead your customer through the steps of the sale. Know your customer, know your plan, and always believe that the person asking the questions chooses the path and the direction of the sale. Sales really is the artful ability of asking questions. Overcome your hesitations, become familiar with when and where to inquire, adjust and adapt your manner of approach to fit your customer and the stage of the process you are in, and start asking questions. Be a good salesperson. Uncover your customers' needs and allow them to start enjoying their new opportunity today.

3

GREETING AND RAPPORT

The greeting and rapport stage is one of the most important steps in our sales process. It sets the stage on which all other steps are set. Your goal here is to welcome your customers and create an atmosphere in which they will be comfortable. Customers want and will respond to a good experience.

In the instant before you introduce yourself to a customer, clear your mind and set your focus. Do not let yourself be distracted by anything else that is on your mind. Sales is more than a job; it is a mindset. You cannot effectively sell while you are preoccupied or thinking about your last deal. When a customer walks up, you want to set your focus and let the show begin.

THE GREETING

Have you ever walked into a store where you felt the salesperson just wouldn't leave you alone? You probably have. Was it because the salesperson just seemed to force him or herself on you without your acceptance?

The greeting is your customers' first impression of you. At this early stage, it is essential that you are able to provide them with an immediate feeling of comfort. Learn to welcome your customers with your eyes and your expression. Develop a sincere smile and an open manner. Give them the feeling that they will be comfortable throughout their interaction. In sales, your greeting will always be more successful if you are able to invite your customers to initiate the greeting instead of forcing one upon them. Seek to engage your customers. Do not make your customers feel as though they have to talk to you. Present them with a greeting that they will want to respond to in a positive way.

OBSERVE AND ADAPT

In the first stage of your introduction, it is usually a good idea to allow your customers some space, giving them the time to gradually become comfortable in their new surroundings. It is here that you will want to observe and seek to recognize your customers' initial level of willingness to interact. Engage your customers slowly and try to determine their initial level of outgoingness. When you see an uneasy or defensive customer, take it slow, giving them the time to settle and feel more at ease. If your customer appears to be more confident and outgoing, simply adjust your approach to match theirs. Always greet your customers with similar actions.

When greeting a new customer, always keep in mind that all but the most outgoing will have some degree of anxiety or uneasiness. Know that you must look to diffuse this before you can start to build your rapport. Always use an approach that you feel will relax your customer, allowing them to think about the goals they desire and not be distracted by their early anxieties. Watch their movements and expressions. Listen to their tone of voice. A shy person may look down, face away, and speak softly. An outgoing person will look you in the eye, face forward, and speak with confidence. Varying degrees of outgoingness will always be found in every person you meet. Some people will be reserved, some outgoing, some fearful, and some anxious. To best excel in this stage, you want to be able to analyze your customers quickly and proceed accordingly. Seek to adjust your greeting to match your customers' initial levels of outgoingness and personality. Practice and use several different approaches, adjusting them to match the personality of each.

COMFORT AND STYLE

A person's style is a projection of how they live. It is the environment in which they have chosen to exist. It is their job, their friends, their neighborhood, and where they choose to have dinner. It is where they vacation and where they choose to shop. If you want to be more effective in sales, you have to be able to adapt to the style in which your customers prefer to do business. People like to interact in a manner of their liking, so your greeting should always be adjusted to fit your customers' preferred style.

Picture the difference in atmosphere between a local barbeque and an uptown restaurant, or a ballet and a ballgame. Think of the environments and interactions involving the people attending. Is it safe to say that certain people will feel more comfortable in one place than the other?

To be successful, you must constantly adapt to the styles and personalities of the people you will meet. Observe each person for the type of greeting you should use and start with one you feel will best suit his or her style. Provide an atmosphere that will be comfortable to them. Analyze their actions and mannerisms to get a feel for your preferred approach before you begin. People will always respond better to someone who is able to interact with them on their level. Become aware of your customer's personal and emotional presence and then establish your best approach.

ENAGAGE YOUR CUSTOMERS

Start with an opening that will invite a conversation, not one that will produce a defensive response. Try an opening specific to each individual. Think of the openings they will want to respond to; engage them. For example, when you first see them, take notice of what may stand out, comment positively, and ask a question about it. Your initial opening may be, "A Cowboys fan, I see," while noticing a hat or jacket, or, "So, how often do you get to go biking?" while noticing a customer's bike rack. These openings will start a conversation and will lead into a rapport-building stage. Please know that in almost any situation, there will be the available clues to an engaging approach.

A question that will start a conversation and avoid a defensive response will always promote a good start. The type of question to ask here is an open-ended question. This will allow your customers to expand on their answers any way they want. This will invite a conversation and help create the flow of your communication. If no clues to their interests exist, a simple welcome such as, "Hi, welcome to ABC company. What brought you in today?" will work. I like these types of introductions because they do not involve a yes or no answer. They are question-based and will invite your customers into an exchange. Your customers will be more likely to respond in a positive manner if you are able to create a comfortable interaction before you bring up the business at hand. They will find ease in responding to your approach. The key here is to adjust your questions and approaches to your customers and each situation. Come up with some openings you will feel comfortable using. Try to have several on hand for the varying people you will greet. There are many other similar openings that will engage your customers. Once you have successfully observed and matched their initial presence, you will then be able to further adjust and adapt as your interaction proceeds.

EYE CONTACT

For all greetings, make sure you maintain good eye contact with your customers. Try to produce a welcoming look of trust and understanding while looking into their eyes. Avoid the temptation to look down or away when speaking. Know that it will be your eye contact that will have the biggest impact here. What you say with your eyes will be believed; what you say while looking away will be questioned. Your goal is to create an impression of confidence and honesty, and a warm smile and good eye contact is always your best approach.

To further increase your effectiveness in your greetings, try to visualize how others see you. Become aware of how your approach is received by others. When you can see yourself in an objective manner, you will be better able to understand how others will see and feel about you. This is necessary to understand how to create a more successful first impression.

USE YOUR CUSTOMERS' NAMES

I heard somewhere that the sweetest sound to someone's ears is his or her own name. I couldn't agree more. Learn your customers' names early and use them during the course of your conversation. If a customer has a difficult name, practice the correct pronunciation with him or her. This will show that you care and will also help avoid embarrassment. However, be careful not to bring attention to the fact that you are trying to connect by overusing it. Always use their names casually and in a normal tone. Refer to your customers by name when you are in a light topic or a non-business conversation. If your customers feel that you are using a technique, they will be less likely to trust you. Fortunately, the more you practice this, the more sincere you will become.

MIRRORING YOUR CUSTOMERS

Have you ever gone somewhere, like to a different part of the country, and come back with an accent? If you did, you were mirroring. You were subconsciously fitting in by adjusting your manner and style. Mirroring is a safe and effective way to build rapport. After you have successfully engaged your customers, you want to continue building a comfortable environment. Slowly transform your speech, mannerisms, and actions to mirror theirs. If they walk slowly, walk slowly. If they are outgoing and humorous, be outgoing and humorous. If they are quick and business-like, answer directly and act professionally.

Your customers will always feel more at ease if they are with someone who is like them. As long as you are careful not to exaggerate your efforts, this is a valuable means of helping you establish rapport.

Take the time to learn some of the terms and phrases of the more common professions and activities in the area where you sell. Learn the "language" of your customers. Become knowledgeable in topics such as school, sports, local news, and even recent events to help establish a basis for common-ground topics and preferred styles of communication. When talking to an engineer, be informative; when talking to a businessman, be professional; when talking to a carpenter dressed in a T-shirt, put your foot on a truck bumper and say, "How 'bout this one?" Just kidding, but you get the idea. Always put yourself in the best position possible by providing a level of comfort for each new customer. Please understand that it is often in the early stages of their visit that they will determine how long they will stay. Encourage their willingness; learn to speak their language.

SHAKING HANDS

I think that there is a right time and place to shake a customer's hand. Two such occasions may be when you are welcoming your customer back and a rapport has already been established, and possibly also when you and your customers have agreed upon a deal. Note that in both of these situations, you have had ample time to understand their styles. For your first meeting, however, I feel you should not always be the first to extend your hand. Understand that many customers may be uncomfortable being approached in this manner. At this early stage, your customer may feel that you are invading his or her space. Every customer you greet will have his or her own comfort zone and entering it too soon may increase their level of anxiety.

I understand that this is a topic that may produce differing opinions, and I was even a little hesitant to include it; however, I do feel this is a perspective you may want to consider. Think back to past introductions or watch others in the future. Most of the time, you will notice a lack of ease surrounding the handshake during the first introduction. Well, you can eliminate this uneasiness if you do not force customers to shake your hand. I feel that this is the safest approach when meeting a new customer.

While researching this belief, I found that most customers agreed with this line of thinking and most salespeople did not. I think this is because the salespeople were thinking about their early training, while the customers were thinking objectively about their point of view. Understand that skillful salespeople will always seek to be invited in, not invite themselves in. Always seek to measure your customer's willingness to interact with you before you offer to shake. If they are outgoing and positive, it may be okay. However, if they are shy and reserved, I think it is a mistake. When you approach your customers, know you will still have an opportunity to respond if you misjudged their initial willingness. You should be able to see your customer's hand rise, even while you are looking into their eyes. In any case, I think it is always better to welcome your customers with a warm smile and open manner, not an awkward handshake.

ALL ABOUT THE RAPPORT

A proper greeting is an essential part of your transition into the rapport-building stage. It sets the foundation for your customers' acceptance of you. It allows you to create the interest and attention that will better promote a sale. Once your customers start to see you as a likeable person, they will be more likely to offer you their time and attention; thus giving you the time needed to evaluate their needs and determine their best solution. It affords you the opportunity to further understand and adapt to your customers, all while keeping them willing to proceed. Establishing a rapport will distract them from their early anxiety and will allow you to be on their same level. This is critical down the road. A person is always more easily persuaded by a peer than an outsider.

The first step in building rapport is finding the common ground needed to initiate and carry on a conversation. The goal here is to have your prospective customer open up and share an experience or common interest with you.

The whole time the greeting is taking place, you should be busy observing your opportunities. You should be scanning and developing clues on how to create the common ground needed to help build rapport. The clues that help form the basis of your common ground are always present if you are observant. These clues may be in the accessories on the vehicle your customers drive up in, like a college window sticker or a parking pass for work, or in the objects sitting on their shelves. All of these and more contain clues to possible topics of conversation.

Your town may have diverse customers, but your product and your customer base will usually be similar in some fashion. The idea here is to take them emotionally to a place where they will feel comfortable. There should always be plenty of area-specific topics of conversation. As we spoke of earlier when mirroring, familiarize yourself with the interests that customers you typically meet may have. You might be in a sports town, a sailing town, or a company town. Learn the local flavor and develop some topics of conversation. Every area and person will have an interest that can be uncovered with your efforts. It might be camping, baseball, traveling, or even their kids. Take these examples and think how they can be used to invite a conversation. If you can share a small point or neutral opinion on a topic of interest, your customers will be more likely to open up and share stories about their interests with you. When they do, you will have established rapport.

If you have no clues, lightly ask some questions as you start to interact to get them started. Vary your directness with their responses. "So, what do you do for a living?" "How far was your ride in today?" "What do you do when you're not working?" Engage them with your open-ended questions. Inquire about their hopes, dreams, and favorite places for vacation. Use their own answers as a tool to alleviate their early anxieties and allow a less inhibited path to the discovery of their needs. In this stage, you must be able to portray a friendly, open attitude and pay attention to what they are saying and feeling. Involve your customers. Know that a skillful salesperson will always do more listening than talking. Develop your conversation as an invitation for customers to offer the information you need. Once you start developing rapport, find a careful balance of common-interest and involvement questions to both stimulate a conversation and determine the wants and needs your customers may have. Position yourself as someone who your customers will like and your place of work as somewhere they will want to do business.

Every step of the sale will go more smoothly if you can establish a connection with your customers. People will prefer to spend time with you and ultimately buy from you if they are able to connect with you, as opposed to another salesman they haven't met from another company. Know your path and destination before you start each step and become aware of the importance of each. Visualize the process. Build one step at a time. Greet, develop rapport, question, demonstrate, develop desire, build value, handle objections, persuade, and close. Develop an interest in other people. Do not skip this step or underestimate its importance. Understanding your customers and identifying with their emotions and preferences is how you are best able to meet and work with each. Build your foundation before continuing to the next stage. Rapport is essential in increasing your customers' level of receptivity and acquiring your ability to be persuasive. This, in turn, is essential for you to be able to create the best opportunity for your customer to follow the steps of your sales process. Once you find a common interest or connection, you will be better able to form a bond with your customers. Develop a clear sense of your direction and you will be able to reach your goal: the sale.

CREATE A SENSE OF HUMOR

There is no quicker route to having people like you than making them laugh. Even the most guarded customer will open up with a little humor. It is the mild distraction that will often allow your customers to be more receptive to your persuasion. A good sense of humor is a great way to take the anxiety out of the sales process and will take the edge off most any situation.

My favorite types of humor for the public sales business are clever humor and ridiculous humor. They are both safe and light-hearted. An example would be to say something obviously ridiculous and then look at your customers with a straight face. As they look back with curiosity, as if to say, "Are you serious?" let out a little grin to let them know you are not. They will smile, and you will have shared your first laugh.

Use your imagination and creativity to develop a sense of humor and then become comfortable using it. Choose a presentation style that fits with your personality and the atmosphere you have created. Think of the experiences in which you and your previous customers were able to share a laugh and recreate the experience for your new ones. Remember, you will likely have a different audience every day, so you can use your most successful material every day. Your goal is to put your customers at ease. Here are a couple of my favorites:

- When a husband and wife are together and I am about to leave their presence for a minute, I will look with concern at one and ask him or her to "keep an eye" on the other, and then smile. Since I have just met them, it is fun to watch their reactions to the curious level of trust I have in one of them.

- With my offering on display, I will say with all the pride and seriousness in the world, "That's the blank right there," while pointing out the most obvious feature. When they look over and grin, I will follow up with, "Well, I just went to sales school, and sometimes I just like to show off." Break the ice; loosen the tension. Have some fun with your customers.
- When having a hard time getting your customers to come in and work out a deal, smile and say, "Look, are you going to come in peacefully or do I need to get some help?" Then smile. This, of course, is for when you are in proper character and when the interaction leading up to your request has already been one of light humor.
- If, while negotiating the terms, the negotiation becomes a little tense, lean forward and yell to your manager, "Sir! Sir!" When your manager responds and your customers are curious about your sudden exclamation, lean forward and ask, "Sir, do I have permission to treat my customers as hostile?" Then smile. It may be the break that you and they need.
- If someone asks you a serious question, respond with a bizarre question of your own with a straight face. If they ask the mileage, ask them if they drive more up or downhill. The key is to look serious and analytical. Just when they think you are serious, smile. Let them have fun. If you can make them laugh, you can sell them. This type of humor can also be a gauge for their own level of humor. It will tell you whether you have an emotional or a logical customer. Upon learning new information from their reactions, adjust your approach as necessary.
- Okay, this is my favorite. This will get just about anybody to smile. While working a deal, ask your partner, manager, or even one of their friends a question while speaking normally and in obvious hearing distance of your customer. Start out with, "Look, I don't want them to hear me, but…" and then ask your question. Trust me;

because it is so apparent that your customer can in fact hear you, almost all of your customers will think this is funny. This will also let you say something aloud, directed at them, that you really don't have to take responsibility for, because you're making believe they can't hear you. Get it?

With humor, please know it is often just as effective to mildly break away from the anxiety at hand as it is to have your customers falling over with laughter. If you are able to match a style of humor and lighten or avoid certain situations, you can often aid in your newly created atmosphere. Naturally, too much humor or the wrong style is not advised, however, if your customers are able to see certain situations less seriously, they may become pleasantly distracted and more easily persuaded. The next time you feel you have the right set of customers, a little humor may be the best remedy.

Okay, now try some you like. Oh, and if you are not laughing now, maybe you should work on your delivery, because it's all in the delivery.

FINAL NOTE

The best way to interact is always with a shared enthusiasm. Understand that the best way to lead your customer is to first connect with them. Every successful process will need a solid foundation. You will not be able to tell someone what he or she should buy or have them move to a new decision without first having them willing to listen. Your customers' direction will only follow the path of your recommendation if you are able to successfully open and attain their willingness to proceed. The purpose of our greeting is to create a receptive customer, one who will find comfort in following the process we set out. Observe, adapt, and welcome your customer. As with any process, the best way to begin is by first preparing.

4

MAKE A SELECTION

T he next step in the sales process is to help our customers choose the product or service that will be right for them. Our goal here is to help them select one specific solution, not a type or style of solution. We will not be able to sell a range of products or services; we will only be able to make a sale if one specific choice is found. When a customer walks in your door or accepts your meeting, many will have some idea of what they are looking for; it is our job to narrow their focus to one particular choice.

There will be three unique scenarios that we will be presented with when helping our customers make a selection. In this chapter, we will be taking a look at each scenario and exploring some advice on narrowing their focus in each. First, however, let's take a look at some overall advice on preparing ourselves to better understand and help our customers in their selections.

SET YOURSELF FOR SUCCESS

It is here, in this early stage of the process, that your presence will have its greatest impact. Be confident in yourself and your products. Show concern for your customers' needs and respect for their style. Portray yourself as a person who wants to help find the right choice for them, not someone who just wants to make a sale. Involve and engage your customers with your interest and your questions. Help them determine the solution that would be best for them by the input you request and then help them realize it with the support of your influence.

There are too many similar offerings and competing salespeople to assume that people have to buy from you. They do not and will not, unless you can enlighten them as to the benefits of doing so. Here, more than ever, is where you need to have established rapport and credibility. In other words, your opinion has to count. You have to be informed, likeable, and trustworthy. Understand that your customers want to learn and be educated on what would be the right choice for them. They want guidance. They are looking for a competent, informed professional to help them in their purchase. Know your offerings and understand how their features will match up to the benefits your customers are seeking.

DETERMINE THEIR MOTIVATION

When a salesperson first introduces himself or herself to a customer, he or she should have the end in mind. This end, of course, is the completion of a sale. While envisioning the sale, the salesperson should chart the best path to achieve the sale by understanding the customer's motivation, and effectively satisfy it by adjusting his or her course as more information is gathered.

The selection stage starts with a group of exploratory questions that will help determine what your customers are looking to acquire. It is with these questions that you will seek to understand their motivations. Ask yourself, "What event has occurred to bring us together?" Know the need or want that has precipitated your meeting and then find the solution that will best satisfy them. Is your customer's current solution in need of frequent repairs? Has a new contract created the need for a larger facility? Has a recent promotion created the desire for a nicer suit? Are they looking for safety, status, luxury, or comfort, or do they just want the peace of mind that a new policy may provide?

To help select your customers' best choice, it is important to establish what is important to them. It is their motivation that you must seek and satisfy. Recognize your customers' buying motives before you choose which products to show. Search out the needs or benefits they are looking for and narrow their selections to the choices that will best motivate them to purchase. Do not just randomly demonstrate all the offerings in your line; this will show that you do not care about their wants or needs and that you only care about selling them anything. For example, it would be counterproductive to talk about your model's performance when your customers are looking for an economical solution. However, without taking the time or effort to inquire into your customers' motivations before you start with your demonstrations, this is something that you would never know.

Understand that certain features will motivate people differently. To some, having four-wheel drive may mean traction on the snow days and a better resale value. To others, however, four-wheel drive may mean less fuel economy and a higher initial cost. Some people travel in snow country; some do not. Top salespeople will not demonstrate a particular offering or sell the benefits of their offerings before they know what benefits are important to their individual customers. All top salespeople will look to determine their customers' goals before they start with their selection process.

Additional insight into your customers' motivations may be found in their previous solution. What did they like about their last or current product or service and what might they be interested in improving? If a customer liked their previous choice and it just needs replacing, you might want to help select something with similar features. If they want to improve upon their previous choice, determine what features they are looking to add or change. Once you have determined what they are looking for, you will be better equipped to persuade them by confirming the credible points of their selection.

INVOLVE THEIR EMOTIONS

The selection stage is basically a group of presentations. It is where you present different combinations of offerings to your customers, all of which you feel will satisfy their needs, in order to gauge which you feel they will want the most. The key to successfully completing this stage is to search out the solution that will not only meet their needs but will also excite your customer; the one solution that will create the desire for them to want to own it today. Understand that the presentation stage will always be better received, and sometimes only received, if you can select a choice that they will want to buy. Although your customers may have logical reasons for their purchases, they are much more likely to make a selection and move toward the sale for emotional reasons. There is a big difference between want and need.

Invite your customers to share their goals. Get them emotionally involved. Determine the choices, options, or features that will drive their decisions, and build upon them. If it is luxury that your customer is looking for, reinforce that in your presentation. Let them know that the model you are showing is first class. If comfort is what they seek, show and demonstrate your offering's correlating features. Involve them and all of their senses. Determine their desired benefits and then show how a selection will fulfill those desires. Display the offerings that you feel will most line up with their wants and needs and then help select the one that lines up best.

THE THREE PATHS OF SELECTION

When first meeting a new customer, there will typically be three different situations that will present themselves. In the first, your customer will not have a set plan or service in mind. In the second, they will know what they want and you will have one available. In the third, they will know what they want, but you will not have their choice available.

In each scenario, your ability to present an acceptable choice is directly related to how well you are able to analyze your customer's wants and needs and match them up with your most suitable choice. Whether you are selling cars, bracelets, dresses, homes, networking solutions, or investments is of no consequence. There will always be the need to focus on just one before you can continue toward the sale. For example, your customer may know that he wants an investment plan; he just may not know the exact plan he will prefer. Once you complete your initial discovery and determine in which of these scenarios your customer will fall, it is time to follow your path. Let's now take a look at each scenario and some advice for each.

1. IF THEY DO NOT HAVE A SPECIFIC SELECTION IN MIND: INVITE THEM TO YOUR INVENTORY

When the customer you are working with does not know the exact model they are looking for, invite them to explore your selection. Give them the opportunity to land on something they may like as you review their needs and build your rapport. Many customers are visually oriented, and their likes may be best determined upon seeing the available choices. Because they are visiting without knowing exactly what they want, they are likely to make a selection based on how it appeals to them in person. These are the people who want more than just to look on the Internet or read the consumer books. They want to see and touch the available choices.

QUESTION THEIR NEEDS

Since these customers do not know exactly what they want, you will often need to help them with the narrowing process. Start by determining the basic offering that they have in mind as you proceed toward your display. This process is both started and finished with a series of investigative questions. Remember that in sales, you take control of the path of the sale by the questions you ask. It is here that we will use our questions to discover the features and benefits our customers seek.

The questioning process for this stage may go like this: "Do you think you may be interested in a ring or a bracelet? Okay, would you prefer white gold or yellow gold? Okay, a solid design or with a clasp? With or without a jewel? Would you prefer a diamond or an emerald? And so on. Note how the focus of your questions can be adapted to any product or service.

Start with a wide scope and slowly narrow your focus to a smaller set of choices. This is also how you gain credibility. Your customers will feel that you are better able to guide them if you have the proper information. Listen to their needs and understand what they are trying to accomplish. Seek the information needed to help you guide them from their ideas and visions to a specific selection. From here, continue your narrowing process by including the choices with the features they like and eliminating those that are determined unacceptable.

In this early stage, you may want to vary the number of discovery questions you ask. Depending on your customer's level of comfort, you may be able to ask a series of these all at once, or you may be best advised to mix them in with some additional rapport-building questions. You want to be sure that your customer's receptiveness and comfort level are high to ensure that their answers remain forthcoming. The directness of your questioning should always be tempered to correspond to the rapport you have established and the responsiveness your customers exhibit.

NARROW WITH CAUTION

When initiating your early questioning process, it is important to inquire with a broad scope approach so you do not limit too much of your selection for consideration. This way, there can still be an open group of possibilities while you determine which options or features your customer considers necessary or optional. An example of this would be to ask if they were looking for a light color or dark color, or a selection loaded with options or lightly equipped. This approach will help narrow their selection and will still leave you with a range of offerings that may be acceptable as your customer starts to envision their likely preferences. For example, we may not want to eliminate medium-blue just yet because that may be the only color we have in which their other desired features line up. Know that once a customer eliminates a certain feature, it will be harder to get his or her approval later on, even if they do like it when they see it in person. Try to learn as many of your customers' preferences as you can before focusing on a specific choice. What you are trying to avoid here is finding the perfect selection as related to most of their criteria only to have already eliminated it earlier in the process. If the house your customers will most likely consider, due to its design and location, also has a pool, it would be detrimental to pre-eliminate all homes with pools.

In this stage, it is also good practice to test different combinations of your offerings' attributes visually to help anticipate and avoid future objections. If you see that the most likely choice in your selection will not line up with all of their initial preferences, you may want to pre-influence them on the benefits of additional or optional features your selections may offer. It is always best to allow your customers the opportunity to keep some of their initial preferences acceptable but not mandatory while seeking to determine and then realize their smaller, more defined preferences. As long as your customers are not compromising their specific needs, offering them the opportunity to consider additional features and choices may be in their favor. In addition to increasing the possibility of finding an acceptable choice, your customers may genuinely appreciate the benefits of these additional features.

PRESENT AND THEN HIGHLIGHT THEIR DECISIONS

Your goal in the selection stage is not to make the customer's selection; it is to establish and confirm their goals and create the best opportunity to have them determine their selection. As the salesperson, you must investigate and understand the reasoning for their preferences and then help them realize the best available solution. You must look to keep obstacles from occurring and be prepared to overcome them if they do. Know your offerings and their availability. Be effective in influencing an acceptable decision by offering the proper advice.

PREPARE FOR THE EXPECTED

When making a selection, there will always be unforeseen objections and obstacles that may occur. At any point, something can go off track or we can find ourselves backing up, starting over, or unable to move forward. There will always be hesitations and uncertainties to contend with before a selection can take place. However, if you stay within the guidelines of each step and continue to move forward in an inquiring and understanding manner, you will often realize your next best move. Again, your questions, both discovery and leading, are the key. To help in our preparation, let's look at some of the more common objections or challenges we face in this scenario and some advice in handling them.

THE DECIDING FACTOR

One common obstacle that may occur when making a selection is the decision process for closely related choices. If your customers are unable to make a decision between two or more selected choices because they appreciate the varying benefits of each, meaning they like both blue and burgundy, or they like both the Swiss and the designer series watch, you will often have to help them focus on just one before you can move to the next step.

The key to resolving this is to investigate the preferences they may have in each while you slowly start to focus in on their most likely choice. Look to understand and anticipate your customers' level of resolve for each from the questions you ask, while methodically determining the attribute or option that they will most likely select. As you get closer in your determination of their likely direction, start to raise your level of influence towards the one that appears to be their most apparent choice, to better confirm their selection and further their resolve.

Know that as you are both searching for and determining their choice, you will always best succeed at influencing your customers' decision by lightly presenting the benefits of each without over presenting any one in particular, saving the final closing persuasion for the deciding moment when in fact their most preferred choice becomes more evident. Meaning, present both sides of their preferences equally in the early stages of their decision, then gradually lean your measure of influence to the preference that they start to respond to the most, concluding with your final persuasion for their highlighted choice.

Since this situation is quite common while making a selection, let's take a minute to look at some example questions to help balance the pros and cons of a typical final selection. For this example, we will use something as random as making a color choice in purchasing an automobile. Here again, as in most cases, the influence you provide is always best received when it is created from your customers' own thoughts. If you are effectively able to ask the questions that will uncover their most prominent present and future thoughts and feelings on the differences, your customers will often realize their own best choice. Here we go.

If your customers are trying to decide between a car's color choice, let's say white and dark blue, we may want to start like this:

"Let me ask you a question."

Pause for their attention.

"What color was your last vehicle? Would you prefer a change? What color is your wife's vehicle? Would you like to have the same color or a different color? How about the color of the vehicles of your friends or coworkers; is that something you want to consider? How long do you keep your vehicle, and is it kept in a garage? Do you think one may be less likely to show the effects of the weather? Do you think one will create more attention when all cleaned up and out on the town?" Again, seek to make the comparison to your specific industry.

As they think about their answers, know they will soon start to come up with their most preferred choice. As you analyze their responses and reactions, you can adjust future questions to follow and confirm their direction. Try to balance your influence between the desired features, pointing out the possible benefits of each, as you listen for their direction. With creativity and persistence, allow them to uncover what they care about most. This line of questioning will work well with other decisions as well. Other examples may include leather versus cloth, gold versus silver, a commercial-quality solution versus a portable one, a percentage-based fee versus a flat fee, or an all-inclusive vacation versus a one-way ticket. Know that each solution has its own benefits, and each consumer has his or her own desires. To help identify with this reasoning and help prepare for your future, take a minute here to develop some questions regarding these examples that may help to enlighten your customers.

THE PERFECT CHOICE DOES NOT EXIST

There may also come a time when you realize that your customer's "perfect choice" does not exist. It is here that you and your customer must become aware of this and start to consider the closest fit.

If this is the case, simply offer to let them choose their most suitable choice based upon their current preferences and then present the features that do satisfy their search. Think of it as: "Of all the offerings you are contemplating, which one would likely be the most suitable?" or: "Of all the choices here, which do you like the best?" You could actually ask this exact question.

In this situation, let your customers know that their selection may not have to be perfect, because their likes or dislikes may change in the near future. They may actually grow out of their present desires and grow into their next best choice. If, while selecting, you note that this challenge exists, and the options or features in question are not mandatory to accommodate their needs, be sure to allow your customers the opportunity to be certain of their current decision. Note that many times customers will actually leave a place of business upon not finding their perfect choice, only to go somewhere else and purchase a completely different solution. Always be sure to present your customers with the opportunity to reconsider their current preferences before they leave. Ask your customers if their style or tastes have changed over the years. Most have, and probably will in the future as well. You may not have the exact perfect offering available; however, you will often have one that they may feel to be very close.

In any case, understand that a small cosmetic variance or an affordable added feature will not necessarily stop them from wanting to move forward, especially with a couple of well-thought-out questions to help create a more expanded point of view.

ALLOW YOUR PROCESS TO SUCCEED

Please know that not all customers are complicated in this stage. Actually, in most cases, this process is as simple as selecting the choice with the most preferred features and separating it from the others. This customer-specific step is nothing more than a series of eliminations. If your customer is not complicated, do not complicate your process. If you and your customer are able to select one to their liking that successfully satisfies their wants and needs, move forward and prepare your presentation. Let their selection unfold by the determination of being the most likely choice.

Once these customers, the initially undecided, find and make their selections, it is now time to separate their selection from all the others and make it your focus. This is the offering on which you want to concentrate, the offering that you will now present.

2. IF YOU HAVE WHAT THEY CAME IN FOR: BRING THEIR CHOICE TO THEM

When a customer asks for a specific offering and you have one available, you will want to bring the one you think will best suit their needs up to them. Do not risk your customers changing their minds or confuse them by letting them wander through your inventory. If a customer is already decided, do not increase their option pool; keep them focused. If they have done their own research and feel their choice is specific, leave it that way. Some people are more decisive than others. Point, pull, present, or carry their choice to them. Let them look at your customer photo album as they await your return.

BE PREPARED

This is where being prepared before the customer comes in will come into play. It is essential to know your inventory. Every day, before you settle in, check your stock and availability, constantly updating your knowledge. Try to obtain an updated inventory as often as you can. If a prospect wants a single-story rambler with a garage and a wooded backyard, you want to be able to check if you have one available. Know your available choices so you do not have to take your decided customers, either physically or mentally, through your inventory and risk making them undecided.

VERIFY THEIR CHOICE

Before you exhibit their choice, be sure you understand exactly what they are looking to accomplish in order to determine the best offering. Depending on the confidence they have in their selection, you may want to investigate and even confirm their preferences with some additional investigative questions. Displaying an incorrect choice may unintentionally question their decision.

In other cases, even though your customers may initially appear undecided, you may uncover that they are in fact decided with a couple of your questions. Some people will present what they want without inquiry or further research and some will better convey their choice with the help of your questions. Before you decide that someone is undecided and continue toward your display, be sure they are by asking some questions.

IF ONE IS VERY CLOSE, BRING IT UP

One possible variance for your actions with the decided customer is when you have offerings that are very close, but not exact. It is here that you would still be most likely suited to display one specific choice; however, you will want to be able to anticipate what varying features will be least likely to negate your choice. For example, your customers may be more or less likely to alter their preference when it comes to certain features than they would for other features.

For this circumstance, know that people are often quite complex when altering their pre-set plans. Always be sure to investigate their current and possible future preferences before you display what you feel is their most suitable choice. It is human nature, when making a selective decision, for people to be afraid of missing something they may want or paying extra for something they do not need.

When determining their most preferred selection, do your research in a light manner. Be careful not to push them away or limit their interest by forcing them to make a decision before presenting your display. It is here that you simply want to get a feel for the direction they will likely lean to best position a selection. If they are receptive, you may also start to have them become aware of additional features.

When in the situation of having very close offerings, I have found it is easier to display one that may have an extra option or is of higher quality or more comprehensive, because you can usually emotionally attach someone to an "add" if you can help him or her realize its benefit. I also believe that as long as they can afford it, customers are more likely to be pleased with their ownership experiences if they choose to include an option that they were contemplating rather than not.

THEIR NEXT BEST CHOICE

It is essential to understand that one customer's preference for a particular feature may differ from another's. The value placed on each preference and the ability to develop new desires will differ with each customer as well. When evaluating your next best move, do not assume your customers' preferences and do not assume when or if they will adjust their plans or even pay more for an additional or upgraded option or benefit.

Determine the features that your customer most prefers, match them up with your most suitable choice, verify that it satisfies their goals and needs, and then introduce your choice without prejudging their decision. Remember, our goal is not to select their solution; it is to afford them every opportunity to realize their preference and allow them to make their own selection. You could never have every available product, plan, or service in every possible combination of options or features, so be prepared to creatively offer a new outlook if necessary. Learn the features and benefits of your selections, know what they have to offer, and always allow the opportunity for a selection to be made.

KEEP YOUR DECIDED CUSTOMERS DECIDED

When working with a decided customer, newly decided as well, always be sure to help oblige them to stay that way. When you display the offering that you feel will best meet their goals, be extra certain to keep it away from other available choices as you prepare for your presentation. Be sure not to present it next to or near another offering that may draw their attention.

You also in no way want to let your decided customer browse your printed information or materials while they are waiting. They will inevitably see some interior trim pattern or shade of blue they will want to investigate. This may give them an excuse to leave without making a commitment. You always want to make sure your customers are occupied when you retrieve their choice. If they are already decided, and we have their desired choice, we want to take every step possible to keep them that way.

3. IF YOU DO NOT HAVE WHAT THEY CAME FOR: OPEN THEIR OPTIONS

If your customer knows what they want, but it is not available, treat this scenario as you would if your customer came in and did not know what they wanted. It is here that you will want to offer other options. This is not the time to say you do not have anything for them, or to say, "I'll see if I can find one." You always want to give your customers the opportunity to broaden their horizons in case they are not completely determined. "Walk" them around to see if they land on something else. As you walk, ask the investigative questions that may uncover new or possibly overlooked objectives.

PRESENT THE ALTERNATIVES

Please know that if a customer spent some time in determining a choice, they will probably be reluctant to just throw away all of their research. They may close their mind to other possibilities. However, you have to realize that they might not be aware of all the other similar offerings that may be available. It is here that you will want to present the alternatives. If they are initially unyielding and reluctant, you may have to encourage a new, more open point of view. Slowly walk through your inventory, "looking" for their choice. Encourage them to look as well. As you look, ask the questions that may help reshape their current thoughts.

Understand, and have them understand, that this may be the best chance for them to realize what they really want. When a person is surrounded by a new set of choices, something will stand out. They will likely notice an additional interest. Remember the time you went to buy a television you saw in a sales catalog, but when you got there, you chose an entertainment center instead? You owe your customers the same opportunity. Do not take away their ability to change their minds. How many times have you gone to buy one thing, only to come home with something you saw and liked better? Tell your customers this story; they will probably be able to relate to it and be more receptive to looking.

BE PERSUASIVE

It is human nature to be afraid of making a bad decision. Customers know this as well. Ask yourself, and ask them, what if they find and buy their choice and then see one they like better but didn't know about? Will they regret their decision? Even if they don't, might they be upset that they chose not to explore all of their options? If you have a settled choice, keep your customers focused. If you do not, offer them opportunities.

BE PERSISTENT

Make no mistake, your best chance to have your customer make a selection in this scenario is to have them explore their other opportunities. Leave "finding them one" alone; only consider it as a last option. Too many things can happen while waiting. Too many times, another salesperson who was willing to present some alternatives will cancel your impending sale. Be committed to giving your customers all the opportunity in the world to consider and reconsider all of the options, features, and benefits that you and your company have to offer.

GAINING A COMMITMENT

Our goal in the selection stage is to select a solution. It is our goal to effectively eliminate all of the other possibilities and select one choice. However, it is also our goal to gain a commitment to move forward. Please understand that with out a commitment, we will have no place to go.

Many beginning salespeople will meet their customers, explain and show all of their choices, and even find a suitable solution, only to be rewarded with a thank-you. To be successful, we must be better than this. We must always put our self in the best position to best succeed. We must seek and gain a commitment to purchase if an acceptable solution could be found.

Our best approach in gaining a commitment is to seek it when our customer's desire is at its highest, and this is most likely to be before their goals are met. Understand it is always easier to gain a commitment when leveraging it against a preferred, yet not realized goal, and it is also easier to move forward when you have a commitment in place upon realizing the goal. Confirm that your customers will in fact move toward a purchase, if an agreeable choice can be found, before you show them your complete selection. If you wait, they may not make a commitment afterward, even if you do find a match. Understand for most people, there is a more active want factor for what is desired than for what has already been achieved. For many people, the drive and motivation is in the search. Know that once something is achieved, it is usually not as desirable because it already exists. The curiosity in the uncertainty and the anticipation in the attainment will often no longer be present with the same level of intensity.

ENACT YOUR PLAN

When seeking to gain your commitment, try to create a question that will help willingly lead them there. Seek to create a question that they will want to or even have to say yes to when responding. After discovering their needs and some initial set-up, your commitment question may go like this:

"So what you're saying is, if we were to have this model with all of your desired features, and it was available in either green, burgundy, or dark blue, you would like it, even if it were just a little over your budget. Is that correct?"

Now simply pause and wait for their answer. Then verify their commitment further by adding: "And if we were lucky enough to have it available and the terms of delivery could be worked out, you would consider owning this today, right?"

This question will not only confirm their commitment, it will also help to confirm their choice. They will not want to commit to a goal they would not want, just in case it was found. If they answer in the positive, you will have something to work with and can lead them to the next step. If they do not answer in the positive, know your research into why will often lead you to the source of their evasiveness.

Do you see how this works? Do you see how this will both set and verify your path? Do you recognize how valuable gaining a commitment is in making a sale? If necessary, you may need to ask this question more than once or follow up with additional inquiries. Remember, the key is to get a commitment before finding their match; otherwise they will feel it is unnecessary to be completely forthcoming with their goals and unnecessary to move forward.

RECOGNIZE THEIR HESITANCY

Please accept that we will never be able to move toward and complete a purchase if we are unable to gain a commitment on their chosen selection. Also, please accept that for certain reasons, such as anxiety and fear, seeking our customers' commitment may be a delicate situation. Our customers may be somewhat evasive in this situation.

Think about it. Your customers will not want to tell you they do not want to buy because they are uncomfortable with you or your company. They know this may produce an uncomfortable situation. They would prefer to point to a more tangible reason if this were to occur, such as not finding an agreeable choice. They know they will feel more pressed to buy if a suitable choice is found, and they would rather avoid an uncomfortable situation if they did decide to leave. Many will avoid stating their exact preferences. They were probably hassled or repeatedly asked or pushed to buy something whether they liked an offering or not in the past, and will seek to prevent this from happening again. Accept it, some salespeople are unskilled and unprofessional. Even most of you reading this book have had to deal with an unprofessional or pushy salesman before and will guard against it happening again.

It is because of this that our customers will sometimes set these certain preset time limits or escape clauses, just in case they decide not to move forward. They will want to avoid feeling obligated by offering a commitment. And in their efforts, some customers will in fact hold their goals tight or become evasive about what will work. They may even change their parameters as they go, just to stay a step ahead of actually revealing a solution. Even though your customers may know it is not the deciding moment, there will often be the hesitations that will appear. This is something we may have to contend with in every step of the process, and we will have to be able to overcome it.

OVERCOME THEIR HESITANCY

However understandable our customer's motives may be, their evasiveness will often place us in a position of not being able to move forward, even if it turns out they would be willing to proceed. They will be less likely to move forward because they have placed themselves in the position of having to save face. They will have positioned themselves out of making a commitment. Because they have publicly manipulated their choices so that they will not be found, these customers will feel they would be losing their credibility by moving forward.

When in this situation, seek to understand your customers' planned source of evasiveness. When you are able to sense the early appearance of this, you will want to investigate a little further to determine their true likes and dislikes. You will want to search out their true goals and verify them. To best accomplish this, try to outwardly establish and define the purpose of their stated likes and their stated objections. Then take notice of any inconsistencies. Analyze each factor for its importance and search for ulterior motives. If inconsistencies come to light, question them. Analyze their stated goals and benefits with a series of questions and match their responses to a second set of similar, yet differently worded questions to see if their answers are consistent. Repeat these steps until their responses are aligned and there are no further inconsistencies. Once you verify their goals, you will then have an accurate path for your move forward. This process will also help to further confirm their desires.

Establishing rapport and creating a comfortable experience will help keep your customers from becoming evasive; however, if your customers start out or become evasive, you must be prepared. This is a common obstacle and very important for us to understand. As far as keeping their agreement, most people will be unlikely to back out of a commitment if they have publicly agreed to it. People will generally follow through with what they say they are going to do, because again, they will want to save their credibility. If someone does back out, it will almost always be in the form of an excuse to save face; but that's okay too, because using the questions we learned about earlier, we will investigate that as well.

Gaining a commitment is a very important concept in sales, and necessary to understand and use if you are to be successful. Please make sure to recognize this and plan for your future. This cannot be overstated. The effect of this is considerable in this stage and in helping to keep your customers moving forward in every other stage. It is one of the many factors that beginning or average salespeople never seem to fully realize. Know what is best to do and then do it. Always seek a commitment to do business if an acceptable solution can be found and always before you complete your search.

FINAL NOTE

The process for you and your customers to select a solution is basically one of elimination. It is one in which you eliminate all choices except one and then focus on that one. It is a step-by-step plan to discover, understand, and identify a solution for their goals, wants, and needs, all while adjusting your approach. It is one in which every question you ask and statement you make is searching for or leading your customers toward their best choice. Although the selected choice will always vary depending upon the criteria of your customer, the process to find their choice should always be the same, depending on which of these three scenarios applies. These unique paths are your best means to accomplish the task of making a selection in each situation, and should be followed every time. Stay focused, remain on track, and become fully determined to commit yourself to selecting an acceptable choice and having a commitment in place for when one is found. Got it? Good! Let's now look at presenting our selection. Let's get ready to roll back the curtain and start the show.

5

PRESENT THEIR SELECTION

Now that you and your customer have made a selection in which they are interested, it is time to start the show. It is time to present their selection. The first thing you want to do is reset your stage. Display and separate their selection from all of your other similar offerings. You do not want your customer to lose their focus with other similar offerings nearby. You want them to concentrate on this one choice, their choice. Be genuinely enthusiastic about the offering they have selected.

The more value we are able to build in our customers' choice, the more likely they will purchase, and the more likely price will not be an objection. If we skip this step or fly through it, we will be limiting our chances of making a profit or even a sale. While in the selection process, we may have lightly presented many different offerings. This was to determine the offering that was most suitable to them. Now that we have chosen a specific one, we do not want to assume that we have presented it; we have not. It is at this point that we have only singled out their selection. Now is the time to confirm their choice and build value in their selection. Now is the time to single out and display the benefit of owning their new solution.

START THE SHOW

Sales is a show. Your offering is your product, and you are its spokesperson. It is now time to gain your customer's attention and create the energy and enthusiasm to attain their interest and focus. The selected offering is the center of your stage. This selection is the solution to your customer's needs and wants. It is essential to believe that sizzle does sell. It creates the excitement that is the spark for their attention and the desire for their ownership.

ATTENTION, INTEREST, AND EXCITEMENT

Have you ever gone to a seminar and fallen asleep? Why? Was it because you weren't involved? Was it because you weren't engaged or interested?

When presenting, you are not merely presenting an offering; you are presenting your offering to a specific individual. It is important to use the proper approach. Each person you meet will be different, and each will have his or her own level of attention. All of your wonderful knowledge will be wasted if your customer is not actively listening or participating. Our first goal when presenting is to attain, monitor, and increase our customer's attention and enthusiasm so that our presentation will be well received. It must be our goal to keep our customer's interest high. We must remain constantly aware of how receptive our customer is and actively seek to increase or maintain their interest with an engaging interaction. Please understand that nothing we say or show will have an impact unless our customer is alert and engaged.

Keep your customers involved with input-seeking questions and involvement actions. Set up your presentation as a two-way conversation. Create and hold their interest as you present your major selling points. Mix in your commitment inquiries when their receptivity is at its highest. Solicit feedback when demonstrating a feature and encourage their participation. Your entire presentation should be keenly reactive to their level of participation. Adjust the pace and rhythm of your presentation to help create a more receptive audience. Start, stop, slow down, and speed up your staging to help keep your customers' attention and involvement. Keep the flow of your conversation and your customers' participation active. Move around when presenting and change your vocal tones to keep your customers mentally alert. Customers' receptivity will vary, and your presentation should be adapted to them. Create a rhythm in your message. Include small stories in your communication and encourage them to share their own with your open-ended questions. Ask ownership-involvement questions. Your customers will be less likely to get bored when sharing their own stories about how they will enjoy their new solutions than when you are just randomly listing features. Their rising participation is the basis for their receptiveness. Think of yourself as a talk show host and learn to keep the communication flowing.

RECOGNIZE THE SIGNS

Our best means of ensuring our customers' interest is observing and recognizing the signs they send. If your customers are bored, frustrated, or confused, you need to recognize and defuse these emotions. If they are alert, excited, and interested, you want to encourage them. By observing their emotions, you can often determine their level of receptivity and react appropriately. Understand that your customers' participation is as important as the demonstration you provide. This is a large part of being successful in sales, and it is often overlooked by the average salesperson.

In the later chapters of the book, we will learn more about how to observe and better understand our customers' emotions, and will take an in-depth look at recognizing and positively influencing our customers' distractions. For now, let's continue with the course of our presentation.

PRESENT THE BENEFITS THEY WANT

A customers' wants and needs, and their perceptions of an offering's benefit, are generally specific to each individual. This being the case, a professional salesperson will focus their presentation's overall theme on presenting and confirming the benefits that their individual customers will deem important. They will understand their customers' interests, solidify those interests, and then proceed to build upon them. If other benefits exist, they will be sure to gauge the level of interest in each before deciding to what extent they will include them in their motivating efforts. Understand that all successful presentations are ones that are catered to each customer's specific needs and will increase their individual desire to take their new solutions home. It is also one that will entice your customers and is adapted to their personal style.

Customers want a presentation that is just for them, one that is centered on the benefits they are looking for and presented in a comfortable manner. This involves presenting to their wants and needs by demonstrating the features that will motivate their purchase, while adjusting your delivery to suit their individual styles of preference.

- Recognize the benefits your customers are looking for.
- Understand how the features of your offering will satisfy each benefit.
- Restate the benefits your customers want to solidify and confirm them.
- Separate each benefit and demonstrate how your offering will satisfy it.
- Repeat this process by continually stating, confirming, and demonstrating each benefit, thus increasing desire and confirming their selections.

If it is important for your customers to know that their choice is one that is proven, let them know of their selection's accolades. If they like the newness or uniqueness of your product, sell the exclusivity of their choice. Determine the different goals that your customers seek, and then satisfy them. Learn to sell the benefits that each individual customer sees as important. These may be tangible benefits, such as safety or performance, or intangible benefits, such as status or sense of style. Use the information that you discovered in the selection stage and enhance your display of the benefits they are interested in attaining. Your "walk-around" and demonstration should be centered on these. The importance of this cannot be overstated. An effective presentation is a confirmation of how your product or service will satisfy the wants and needs that were discovered while helping them to select.

Randomly listing all the features of your offering is not a presentation that you should consider. This will sound pre-planned and similar to any standard sales pitch. These customers will gain the sense that their salesperson does not care about their objectives or did not listen to their requests. Often, when a sale is not made, these salespeople will not understand what they did wrong. Many will think that they gave a good presentation, when actually they forgot to include the most important part: the customer. This is one of the most common mistakes in the sales business and one of the biggest reasons that a salesperson will under-perform. Do not let this happen to you. Understand your individual customers' goals and tailor your presentation just for them.

INVOLVE YOUR CUSTOMERS AND THEIR SENSES

Physically involve your customers in your presentations. Have them operate the features. Let them open the windows of their new home or listen to the bass of their new sound system. Ask what their favorite radio stations are and show them how to set them. Have them adjust the position of their new recliner. Let them try their new diving watch on. Let them model their new sports coat in the mirror. Create all the comfort and mental ownership you can.

The four senses other than hearing are often the most influential in creating an emotional interest. Include them. Let them experience that "new car smell." Let them understand the feeling of ownership. Do not just tell them your furniture has the softest leather; let them feel it. The more senses you involve, the more likely you will create the excitement needed for a sale. Create an image of where and how your customers will enjoy their new selections. Paint them a picture. Help them visualize ownership.

OPERATE THEIR SELECTION

In the businesses where it is practical, it is essential that your customers "test drive" their new selection before you start to discuss the figures. This is where your customers will truly get to bond with their selection and visualize ownership. This is the next logical step in your customers' purchasing. Most customers will want to test their selections eventually, before they buy, so let's do it now. This way we can put ourselves in the position of selling now. Remember, "now" is important in our business. Your customers' interest levels are at a high point now because they chose to visit you now. Continue with the flow and the idea that they will be purchasing now and position yourself to do so by having them experience it first. And remember, always try to be present when they are getting the feel for their solution. It is a good idea to make sure your product performs as it is meant to and for you to be there for them in case they were to develop any questions.

Know your offerings and know your plan. Have one for every customer. Be flexible. You might suggest a curve-filled road for a performance car or a nice peaceful rest for a new bedroom set. Place your customers in the element they have pictured themselves in while enjoying their new solution. Increase their visualization of ownership. Let them experience the emotion and pride of their new choice. If they have their own plan, let them operate or test however or wherever they want. If they want to show their spouse, boss, or friends, encourage it. It is good to involve other people.

If they are hesitant to experience their selection, become creative in your quest. If they are in a hurry, or say that they are, let them know you have a short trial designed for busy people just like them. Whatever it takes, you want them to be able to experience firsthand how their lives will improve. Understand that printing a few sample pages to show the quality and speed of your printer's operation may just be the confirmation they need to feel comfortable in moving forward.

GAIN THE COMMITMENT

When your demonstration is nearing its completion, pause to set the final focus on their selection. As you do, try to gauge their level of interest in moving forward. If you feel good about it, do not hesitate in moving to the next step. Just say, "Come on in and let's talk about it," or, "Now is a good time to have your previous solution appraised."

Please note that the conclusion of your presentation comes when your customers agree to move to the next step. It is when they agree to purchase if all of the terms of delivery are met. If they do not as of yet, then the presentation stage continues until they do. Please understand that without their acceptance, there is no place to go. Be persistent in your support of their choice.

REAFFIRM THEIR SELECTION

If they are still not convinced, look to restart your presentation by rebuilding the value in their selection. Reconfirm that the selection they have singled out is the one they selected because it has the benefits they are looking for and it completes their needs and wants. Influence them, using their own words. Continue to gain the small commitments necessary to move forward. Ask them the questions that will confirm their own decisions.

Your goal here is to state each desired benefit and confirm that your offering satisfies each of them. This is a continuous process that is made fresh by using new words and by altering your delivery. If you are effective at changing your delivery, it is like offering your own second opinion; you are confirming similar information with a new conveyance. Understand that this is very effective in learning and in persuasion. This, of course, must all be accomplished while still keeping their interest at a high level.

HAVE THEM ANSWER THEIR OWN HESITATION

One of the best ways to reaffirm your customers' selection and overcome their hesitation is with an effective series of the confirming questions that we discussed earlier. This is to have your customers answer and thus influence themselves to overcome their own hesitations with their own answers. These are more effective than our statements of satisfaction because the answer or "confirmation" they realize will originate from them.

"Sir, you did say blue was the color of your choice, didn't you?" or, "You like the way the emeralds highlight the center diamond, don't you?" or, "You are aware that the side-impact door beams and the side-curtain air bags will provide the safety you and your husband are looking for, aren't you?"

Have your customers respond positively to their selection. Have them agree to the minor "yeses" that will lead to the bigger "yes" you are looking for. Close your customers with their own answers. Confirm their needs and confirm that their selections satisfy their needs through their own thoughts.

For this particular situation, where your customer is stalled, know there are many different sentence-finishing confirmers that you can add to help engage and persuade your customers in moving forward. Here are some others: "Wouldn't it? Doesn't it? Shouldn't it? Will it not? Don't you think? Don't you agree? Wouldn't your wife agree?" There are lots of them.

Rehearse some of these for your own presentations. Try to include specific knowledge of your customers' ownership plans when presenting these. Simply restate their established benefit and add a confirming request. The level of influence that your confirming questions will provide is immense and should not be overlooked. If you don't want to appear to overwhelm your customers with too many of these, you can switch their location around. You can put them on the front or in the middle of your questions as well. For example, try, "Wouldn't you appreciate the peace of mind that will come with our comprehensive warranty?" or, "Since this model has reclining rear captain chairs and a center console, don't you think your wife will better enjoy the long trips to New England you take each fall?" If you have a good mix of these and use them in different places, your customers won't feel under pressure.

Over the past fifteen years, I can think of no other single means that has helped me provide more solutions than what we have just gone over: the act of closing our customers with their own answers. If you think about it, there is no more effective way. Your customers will always be more persuaded by an influence that was resolved by their own process. It is here that you are not giving your opinion or decision; you are building off theirs. You are giving them the direction and the encouragement that will promote their own answers. This allows them to discover for themselves how they feel, and will help promote their confidence in moving forward. Please understand the power of this, because this is it; this is sales. This is what will give you the ability to keep your customers' forward direction at every stage of the process and will ultimately allow you to close the sale. It will not only make you a better salesperson, it will make you a salesperson, period, because without understanding and having this skill, you will never begin to reach your potential. I cannot emphasize the importance of this skill enough. If you say it, they will question it; if they say it, they will believe. Please make a specific effort to practice this artful ability whenever you attempt to make someone believe. Learn to ask the questions that will produce the answers that will allow their influence to be one from within their own thoughts.

PERSISTENCE

Even if your customers have found the offering they truly want, know that anxiety may sometimes play a role in their ability to move forward. Many customers may stall at a particular point, even if they are content with their choice, because they may not feel that they have the ability to slow down in the future. If this is the case, try to remove some of your customers' anxieties. Let them know that you are not looking to close the deal here; you are just trying to get to the next logical step by agreeing on an offering. Sometimes it may help to explain to your customers the series of steps in selling, and let them know that they are not owners until the final step.

When your customers are uneasy, emphasize that they are only agreeing to move forward and purchase if the figures are on their terms and that they will only be buying if the terms are agreeable to them. Know that many times, an anxious customer will be more agreeable to proceed if they know that they are not at the actual point of the final decision. Most customers will not be afraid to move forward, as long as they feel they have a "way out" down the road. Now, you don't want to offer this explanation if you don't have to, but if you do, know that you will still be in a good position because the more involved your customers become, the more likely they will be to follow through.   Since having a hesitancy occur at this stage is quite common, and our ability to overcome their hesitancy is so important, let's pause here for a minute and try to understand our customers' possible frame of mind. The more we are able to understand our customers' thoughts, the more we will be able to help them want to move forward and continue to the next step. Lets take a look at an example of how anxiety may occur. While envisioning this example, think of your own emotions regarding this and allow yourself to try to feel what they might be feeling.

Here we go.

Picture yourself sitting in a room. Now picture someone walking up and closing the only door. Now visualize them locking the door. You are now trapped in the room with no way to get out. Has your level of anxiety increased? For most, it will.

Now let's take a look at the frame of mind of the person who locked the door. Do you think their anxiety level was raised? Probably not, because it is not them who had the feeling of being trapped.

As salespeople, we must be aware of the possible anxieties that the people we are working with may have, not of our own. We must be aware of how our customers are feeling at all times. We must also be able to recognize the emotions of each and react accordingly, varying our approach with each. If the pressure gets too high for your customers, relieve the pressure. Open the door. Do not make them stay; make them want to stay. You can always start again. To help accomplish this, try talking to them about themselves again. Visually take them to a comfortable place again. When the pressure has been relieved, try again to gain a commitment.

VARY YOUR ACTIONS

Sales is a careful balancing act. You do not want to do more than you have to, but you do want to do all that is necessary. Vary your actions. If your customers are sold, stop selling. If they are not sold, keep selling. If they are anxious, relieve the pressure; when they become at peace again, start your persuasion again. If you can successfully observe, monitor, and react fittingly

6

APPRAISE THEIR TRADE

T hink back to some of the sales that couldn't be made in your companies past. When asked what went wrong, how many times did a salesperson say, "Oh, we just couldn't get enough for their trade." Or "They decided to keep their old system."

Well, I ask you? Did the salesperson complete the proper steps in the opportunities that they couldn't make? Did their customers really want too much or was the salesperson just ineffective in his or her ability to sway them to a more realistic figure or depreciated sense of benefit in their current situation?

INVITE THEIR DISCOVERY

A customer's trade is their previous solution. It is what they are looking to improve upon or replace. It is what they will be selling us in order to complete the transaction. Your customers will probably know that there is a difference between the value of their current solution and the value of a new solution. However, in most cases, they will often need some additional coaching on accepting this difference. To help accomplish this, we need to have a system in place that will help persuade our customers to accept a more realistic expectation of their trade's value.

RECOGNIZE THE OPPORTUNITY

Please understand that although in many of our businesses our customers will not have an actual trade-in, there will always be something that your customer will be replacing. Even if

previous item to the prices others are asking for similar items. However, in most cases, a customer's trade will not be retail ready, and a price comparison should not be made to one that is. There are a lot of expenses that can go into reconditioning and inspecting certain items, not to mention the cost of doing business and commissions for the sale. There is also a value difference. Your customers will know this to some degree, but in almost all cases, your customers will need additional coaching to accept this difference.

If a question arises from one of their answers, pursue it. Put on your serious technician face. It is very important not to draw attention to your motive. If your customer feels that this is a plan to tell them their previous solution is worth less, they will probably argue the point. However, if you are effectively able to have them question its value without directly indicating so, you will have accomplished your goal. The key is for them to come to their own conclusions so they will be more likely to accept them as truth. You have to separate yourself and your expressions from the facts. This step is powerful. Do not skip it or rush through it. Add some questions designed for the trades of your business and use them. Allow your customers to be influenced by their own answers. Allow them to realize that their item is no longer new. We are not being misleading here; most people truly do not understand the cost of reconditioning or making an item sale ready.

For someone to completely see the benefit of a new decision, they must also be able to see the deficiency in their previous or current one. They must also be sometimes persuaded to allow for this new outlook. The reason that we perform this task in a question format is so our customers do not become defensive. Know that a customer will often choose to defend their current position just out of human nature. Some may become very touchy when examining their current state because they will not want to be seen as some who is out of touch or out of style. Since it was their decision to have their current situation, some will always choose to defend it. This is sometimes simply ones human nature. Always seek to first understand your customer and vary your degree of directness proportionally to their level of resistance.

In some cases, you will want to adjust your line of questioning by adding, deleting, or amending your questions to fit the actual condition of an item or the mindset of your customers; however, again, do not skip this step. If your customers are overly sensitive or start to back up, just look to soften some of your questions with your manner or tone.

Please understand the question is the best method to achieve our goal. Also understand the varying actions of our process. For example, different offerings will often require different approaches. If you were selling shoes, your entire questioning process may simply be a look down in the direction of their current shoes and a glance back up. Of course your question was: "is that what your walking around in?" It was also of course silent or just understood. However, if you were representing the benefits of a new corporate web-based network, you may actually assemble a team of engineers to analyze their current system and prepare an analysis for the presentation of your inquiries. The versatility of any questioning approach is always adaptable to your specific audience while still keeping its premise and effectiveness intact.

THE WALKAROUND

The next step is the physical involvement. This is where you and your customers will visually inspect their current solution. Ask your customers to come with you to go over their item. Just say, "Come with me in case I have any questions," and start walking. It is here that you will be completing your observation and confirming their perception of a lower-valued trade.

7

BUILD VALUE

V alue is everything in our business. It is what our customers
must feel a sense of before they will consider initiating
a purchase. Without value, there is no basis on which to state
a fair price for any product. The purpose of this chapter is
to help prepare for the negotiation stage by building value in
yourself and your company.

In any form of sales, value is recognized as being the
measure of a product's worth. This value may be recognized
by concrete factors such as performance, efficiency, and safety,
or by emotional factors, such as enjoyment, status, and peace of
mind. Note that it is these factors that are common to all types
of sales because they are directly related to the product being
offered. Meaning, a typical product could literally sell or not
sell by being what it is and what it has established it offers.
These are the perceived results of the ownership experience for
the product in question. Think of when you go to a grocery
store or toy store. In larger sales, however, understand that
the experience itself will often account for much of a person's
decision-making as well. It is here that the value of a particular
offering will often be additionally enhanced or diminished.

The value that is created in a sales experience is often
measured by additional variables that a consumer will take into
account before making a purchase. These variables are you, the
salesperson, and your company. Please know that it is because
of these two variables that there will always be a different level
of performance amid our varying companies' sales staffs. The
salesperson with the ability to add additional value into their sales
equations will consistently sell more and be the most profitable.
Please understand that it is always the salesperson's abilities that
will either increase or decrease the likeliness of a sale.

While looking through your album, potential future customers will picture themselves in the photos. This will help with your credibility. Start with a small album and move to a larger one as you get more pictures. Start today. When your customers see people just like themselves purchasing the offerings that you sell, they are going to feel more comfortable with the quality of your service and the acceptability of the products you offer. They will also feel further compelled to do business with you, because people like doing business with successful people. Your photos will show that you successfully make people happy, and who wouldn't want to share the feeling your customers show in your pictures? Remember, everybody smiles for the camera.

SELL THE COMPANY

An excellent time to build value in your company is while you are having your customers' trade appraised or after you have demonstrated their choice. This step as well should always be taken before you negotiate the figures. If you do not take the time to add value to the purchase before you present your figures, the offered price will almost always seem too high.

Here is where you will want to establish the bond between your customers and your "family's home." Walk your customers to the concession area and buy them a drink and maybe a snack. Have your customers feel at home. Use your own money for their refreshments. Show your customers that you are willing to invest in your relationship. This will help them to better connect with you, as they will appreciate your efforts. Besides, it is the mentality of most people to return the favor. Have you ever received an unexpected Christmas card and hurried out to get one for the sender? You probably have; it is a natural reaction. People will often look to give something back. And of course the gift we want is their time and attention.

From here, proceed to the service area and give them a tour. Let them know where they will be getting their solution serviced. Show them all the state-of-the-art service equipment and modern tools your company has to offer. Let them know that your company is capable of properly handling their needs and that they will be well taken care of should something go wrong. Show them the waiting area and the coffee machine. Let them see the service awards and certifications of the employees of your company. Let them know how seriously your company takes the satisfaction of its customers. Show them all the nice letters your company has received over the years. Introduce them to the manager, your partners, and even the owner. This is one more step in building mental ownership for your customers. This is also people involvement. The more people you involve, the more involvement your customers will have. This has the same effect as the "neighbor close," in which you let your customers take their pending solution home for a solo demonstration and their friends or neighbors see them. Now that they have met your fellow staff, they too are involved in your customer's ownership. Status and influence are powerful persuaders. Additionally, since your fellow workers will always have something nice to say about their selection, this will be like getting a second opinion or a reaffirmation of their decision. Please understand the importance of this additional value and the need for it to take place before the negotiation.

SELL THE WHOLE EXPERIENCE

You are setting the stage here. You are building value. If you do a good job here, the negotiation will be the easy stage. People will appreciate and will often pay for good service. Understand that the most important option your customers will be getting in their transaction is the benefit of you and your company. Let them know you will be there for them, let them know your company will be there for them, and then let them know your whole team will be there for them. Tell them how long your company has been a part of the community and how

to negotiate. Give them the opportunity to purchase if that is their intention. If they are agreeable to just filling out the necessary papers, we want to let them. The best way to accomplish this is to assume that they will. Many inexperienced salespeople will incur an obstacle here just by presenting negotiation as an option. Do not do this. If they are willing to write it up, then just write it up. Let them bring up negotiating as a condition of the sale. You should always continue as if you were only proceeding to complete the necessary paperwork. Make this your process, rather than asking for their acceptance of the price.

ARE YOU READY TO NEGOTIATE?

Although we should always assume the sale, our customers will often want to negotiate the figures. If this is the case, stop and make sure you are ready to proceed. Analyze your customers' intentions. Find out if you have a commitment and if the possibility of a sale exists before you start to work out the details. Be sure you are not just providing your customers with the information to leverage a figure from another company. If you give customers a discounted figure without a commitment, that's what they will do: shop. It is here that you want to exhaust all avenues in your attempts to influence your customers' commitment before you start finalizing a price. Otherwise, you will have lost all of your leverage to gain the commitment needed to move forward.

It is also at this stage that you will want to know all the parameters needed to make a sale. It is important that you tie up all the loose ends to avoid unforeseen objections or openings that may give your customer the excuse not to move forward later on. Remember, many people do not come in to negotiate to buy; they come in to see what you have, get the figures, and then go to the next company to see if a better deal can be had. It is often their intention to shop around before they commit. However, it is our goal to get them to buy now, so let's prepare.

PREPARE TO SUCCEED

The best way to succeed is to know and meet the conditions of the sale up front and verify a commitment to do business today if the numbers work out to be agreeable. We must always put ourselves in the best position for a sale to occur. In addition to having completed all of the preceding steps of the sale, you must also be able to answer these three questions before a negotiation can take place.

- Is there a trade involved?
- Are all the decision makers present?
- Are they ready to do business now?

Let's take a look at these questions and go over some advice on gaining the answers we want.

KNOW IF THERE IS A TRADE

If your customer were to have a previous solution, they may be looking to trade it in. If this is the case, your customer's trade will be a condition of the sale. You want to include all price-related variables in the figures. If you do not, you will have to renegotiate for every variable added. If there is a trade, we want to know up front.

In some cases, you will have to investigate if there is a trade. Know that your customers may seek to hide their intentions until the last minute. This is often suggested by the consumer buying guides so that they can have a more accurate means by which to comparison shop and so that they can negotiate twice if they desire. However, because it is our intention to make a deal now, search out their plans. Ask about their current solution and their plans for it. Analyze their answer. Make sure it makes sense. Our goal is to find out if they do have a trade or publicly confirm that they do not.

is what the skilled shoppers want. They want to come in, get all the information they can, and leave for the next company to see if they can get a better offering at a better price. These are the customers you need to be able to sell; you must not lose faith in your process or allow yourself to be persuaded.

Understand that price out of place will decrease your chances of making the sale. The easiest way to leverage a commitment is with the promise of the figures, and this of course must be obtained before giving the figures. Always take the path of success, not the path of least resistance. We are not in the business of giving out shopping figures; we are in the business of finding the best solution for our customers and having them purchase from us. Understand that it is pointless to negotiate on price when you don't have a commitment to purchase or the ability to reach a decision doesn't exist. Having the knowledge and resolve to trust and follow this process is the difference between the top performer and the average order taker. Follow the process. Many of your customers will say they want the figures so they can think or sleep on them; however, odds are they will compare your numbers elsewhere and will often make a decision without giving you a second chance. Think this out and understand it. Prepare yourself beforehand because you will soon be in this position. Be strong and always follow the rules for success.

INFLUENCE THE COMMITMENT

To further persuade your customers for a "now" decision, start by reaffirming their choice as we discussed earlier in the presentation chapter. Confirm that their chosen solution satisfies their wants and needs. Be creative in your quest. Since they have successfully made a selection, explain that this is their next logical step.

If you feel your customers are ready and just need a little pushing, repeat that they will only be purchasing if the figures are on their terms. You can usually persuade a forward move by emphasizing that they will still control the decision, because the terms of the deal must still be on their terms. Reiterate "their terms." Reaffirm that they control what is acceptable. This is another example of relieving the pressure enough for them to move forward. If you do not think your customers are ready, revert to the presentation or value stage until they are. To help afford yourself additional time, be sure to continue building the rapport needed to further establish your working relationship. Remember, the more comfortable they feel with you, the more time and credence they will give you.

If a commitment still cannot be reached, and your solution is of such a nature, let your customers "take it home" or try it out for a while. If you know that they are able to buy and are really in the market, offering a further experience is the best way to keep them involved. If needed, let them know that there are a couple of good reasons for them to try their selection. They should feel comfortable with what they are purchasing. Also, if another party does need to be involved, this is a great opportunity to show their selection in a neutral setting. If you reach this point and are still unable to gain a commitment, encourage a further experience. The longer your customers are involved with their choice, the more comfortable they will likely become. The odds are in your favor that they will bond with it. For the undecided customer, this is often a helpful extension of the presentation stage. Depending upon your offering, it may also create the opportunity for the "involvement close." When they are away from you and enjoying their new solution, it may become their own. It may be that they will grow attached. If this is the case, they will likely not let you take "their" solution back. Also, if their friends, family, neighbors, or co-workers see them, they may realize that they like being seen with their nice new solution. This is the "neighbor close." People like the status of having something new and will probably not want to give that status up. I think it is safe to say that many of the

UNDERSTANDING OUR CUSTOMERS

There are generally two approaches that our shopping customers will present when they want to leave and compare our figures. The first group will not want to offend and will say they want to think about or sleep on the figures. The second will tell us straight out that they will be shopping our figures. In either case, however, if they leave with discounted figures they will probably not be back. They will have what they want, or soon realize that they have something they can use, and will be off to compare.

These are basic objections. Most of our customers do not want to buy and later learn they could have gotten a better deal somewhere else. They want to be able to tell their friends, boss, or family that they got a good deal, and shopping around is the commonly taught way to accomplish this. However, most people really don't want to take the time and effort to shop around; they just want to avoid not getting a good deal. So please know that your efforts to persuade will often be received. If you have followed all of the steps to this point, do not be shy; ask for the agreement needed to complete the sale. Do not let reactive objections derail your direction. Know that it is these objections that we must seek to overcome. Fortunately, these are some of the objections that we will be learning how to overcome in more detail in the upcoming chapters.

FINAL NOTE

The art of selling is a progression of actions and reactions, all while staying within the parameters of the plan. This stage of the process involves a series of steps to put yourself in the best position by not giving up everything at once. There is a definitive response for every action a customer may take. The more control we create, the better the chance we have to complete our sale. The closer we follow the path to the sale, the better chance we have to maintain our control. Be strong, be confident, and remain in control. Always take the steps to succeed. Get a commitment to purchase and verify your customer's ability to purchase before you present the figures. Understand that many will be skilled in hiding their true intentions in order to operate within the parameters they have set for themselves. It is up to us to provide the atmosphere and process that will help influence and allow our customers to change their parameters.

Now that we have completed this step, we are ready to present the figures. However, before you do, stop here once again to be absolutely sure you are prepared to continue by having also completed all of the preceding steps of the sales process. At this point, the steps in order are: greet and build rapport, select a solution, present their choice, create additional value, value the trade, and of course, prepare to negotiate. Okay, now let's present some figures.

have already adjusted your figures and eliminated its purpose. You will then also lack the fluidness and control you would have had with your format.

I have visited many businesses and found that most of the forms or processes for the presentation of terms are similar. Most companies will have some type of form or script to present the figures. They will usually include the details of the product or service being offered, followed by a word track that will help deliver the figures in a structured fashion. However, I have also found that in most stores these forms or processes are never used. This is crazy. Set yourself apart and take the best path to increase your profit and the likelihood of making a sale. Always use a presentation sheet or set format to present the figures. If your company insists on following their system, good for them; if not, make one for yourself using the information listed here as a guide.

OUR PROCESS IS UNIVERSAL

I understand that many of the products and services we offer will vary with the specific sales businesses in which we work. In fact, many of our transactions may simply be handled by the cash registers sitting on our counters. However, in many product or service related offerings, there will be additional steps in the transfer of ownership. This of course will involve us in various procedures such as the escorting of our customers into our settlement or business offices. Although much of our process here will not be transferable to each specific industry, as we mentioned before, the purpose of this book is to take the path of additional learning. So let's take a look. If nothing else, it will help to provide an understanding of the benefits that a step oriented process will provide. The key to this process, as with most, is having the ability to transition through the steps without ever exhibiting the existence of a step.

OUR GOAL IS ONE STEP AT A TIME

Our main objective when presenting the figures should be to transition our customers into the closing stage. In fact, this should be our only goal. We simply want to get an agreement on the figures of the sale in order to proceed to the next step. This next step, of course, may simply be asking for the close in the case of a simple product exchange or in preparing for our customers' transition into our settlement office.

When your offering is characteristic of a more detailed process, allow your settlement office to handle the payment options, warranties, and other terms. In this circumstance, we cannot and do not want to wrap up all of the final terms in the present. We just want to continue the process. We want an agreement on the basic figures so our settlement office can prepare the complete terms of the transaction. This is simply the most effective way to ensure our customers' forward move. You can even explain this to your customers. The settlement officer has the relationships with your financing partners and can offer other associated products, such as extended warranties, maintenance plans, and insurance agreements. This will allow your customers to make the final adjustment involving all of their options and will also keep you from trying to determine their agreeability to the payment or other terms.

Another reason for keeping the offering of the final terms relegated to separate steps is to provide a fresh face, one that is not tainted by what the customers may have earlier demanded. This will allow the settlement office to have no preconceived notions and will also allow our customers to change their parameters, if necessary, without losing their credibility. Simply put, your customers may agree to a higher payment or alternative terms with less hesitancy because they will not have to justify their change. They will not have to back down from what they earlier said because a new audience will always better allow for new decisions. In addition, the business managers are

117

usually some of the best closers in the business and will have the ability to take over with a new aura of control. They will be rested, positioned in the comfort of their offices, and very attuned to completing this final step.

In some cases, customers may push for the payment terms, interest rates, or approximate prices on extended warranties up front. However, we are always best advised to keep to the steps of the sale. Keeping their curiosity active throughout each step will always better lead them to the next. Reiterate that only the business office handles those offerings and only after an agreement on the figures. If they persist, reiterate that only your business office has experience with the banks and payment formulas. Be also forthright about the fact that your company takes very seriously the confidentiality of their financial information; therefore, it is discussed only by qualified professionals and only in the business office. Let them know there are no exceptions.

OFFER UP THE FIGURES

When presenting the actual figures, we want to list all of the figures at once. We want to list the full retail price, any manufacturer rebate, the value of the trade, the amount of the down payment requested and the monthly terms that the business office will use to calculate our customers' payments.

Here is an example of our basic presentation sheet. Please take note of this process and seek to adapt its understanding to the offerings that you provide. I will assume your worksheet has the basic offering and prospect information listed, so I will start from there.

List in order

- The full list price of your offering
- The manufacturer rebate, company discount, if applicable
- The resulting sale price

- The value of the customer's trade
- Payoff difference, to be deducted from the sale price
- The amount of down payment or initial investment requested
- The terms your business office will use for payments. For example, forty-eight, fifty-four, or sixty months

Once you add some blanks and include the connecting phrases you are comfortable with, your presentation sheet is finished. You now have a permanent word track that will smooth your customers' transition into the business office. Simply have them agree to do business at the presented figures and let the business office handle how they will arrange payment.

FOLLOW THE SCRIPT

A good idea for newer salespeople or those who are not confident in this stage would be to read the finished script, word for word, right to the customer. When doing so, read it as though you have to read it, as though reading it is one of your company's mandatory steps. What this will do is give you strength. It will keep you uniform and stable. It will take away much of your fear and not let your internal thinking or lack of assurance be evident in your delivery. Know that this is where fear will strike many beginning salespeople. In fact, even the most experienced salespeople will have some apprehension at this stage. Reading it word for word, however, will let the fear out of it. By approaching this step in this manner, you won't have to worry about your memory or your emotions showing. Just candidly read the proposal with little expression. This will also take you out of the equation in the event that the customer is upset with the figures you have presented. You did not set these figures, your company did; you are just completing a step. This will allow you to still be the good guy and keep your position as someone who wants to help them come to an agreement.

ASK FOR THE SALE

After you have presented your figures, pause and ask for their agreement. It might go like this: "Okay, all I need is your okay and we can finish up the paperwork for the business office." Then, with very little pause and while you are casually straightening your paperwork, continue, "Let me get a little additional information and we will put it all together."

If there is no objection, assume there is none and move forward. Hand the customer a credit application or a delivery form and ask them to fill it out.

PORTRAY CONFIDENCE

When presenting the figures, if your customers are willing to move forward, move forward. Note that not all customers are difficult in proceeding; in fact, you should always assume they are not. Go over your figures with complete confidence. The goal of this book is for you to learn to sell the tough deals, but always assume that they will do business and complete the transaction as presented. Be careful not to create an objection where there is not one.

When completing your presentation of the figures and asking for the sale, it is very important to show an even temperament. Do not act any differently. Customers are sharp and will sense any unevenness in your actions, so stay composed. Act as if this is a natural occurrence and everybody agrees to the figures. Also, try to know your paperwork and forms well so that you can continue with small talk while completing them. You want to get as much of the deal written as fast as possible while they are still occupied, so make sure to give them another form if they finish early. Once they consent to an agreement or state no more objections, continue at a calm but rapid pace. Do not give them the opportunity to go backwards. Complete the paperwork and assemble it for your settlement office. Some people close quickly; if this is the case, do not oversell. Do not give your customers any extra reason to raise an objection.

ENCOURAGE THEIR WILLINGNESS

If your customers do not initially agree, but you feel they are close, it may help to portray that this is just a step necessary to complete before going to the next step. Explain that they are not committed, even if they do agree to the figures, if the final terms do not work out. Explain that you simply want their okay to prepare the paperwork for the business office. Again, vary your actions according to your situation or the process your offering requires.

KEEP YOUR CLOSED CUSTOMERS ACTIVE

If your customers do not readily close here, that is okay. Our chapters on closing and overcoming objections are soon to come. If they do close, however, it is also important to keep your customers active during the wait for settlement, not just while you finish the paperwork. Always be sure that your customers' attention is diverted from the decision they just made. Know that it is here, at this often tentative time, that any idle time may offer the opportunity for second thoughts. If left alone or inactive, their anxieties may start to kick in and they may lose their devotion to you and the deal. If you involve them, however, they will more likely feel comfortable and be less likely to rethink their decision. By keeping them involved and engaged, they will be more likely to accept the final terms your offerings may require.

Place your photo album in front of your customers and see if they recognize anyone. Let them look at your happy, smiling owners one more time for reassurance. If the wait for settlement is a little long, reintroduce them to your supporting staff or other parts of your company. The more comfortable they feel in their surroundings and the more support they feel from you, the more flexible they will be if unforeseen issues arise. Keep them comfortable. When the business office is ready, walk them in and introduce them. Then just make sure their selection is prepared as you await their return.

WORKSHEET WITH A PURPOSE

As with the steps in our process, our worksheet has a purpose as well. The goal of our worksheet, or word track, is to give us a structured plan to present the figures in an easy fashion, all at one time. It is also to put us in the best position of influence for some of our most effective future closes. Our first goal in any presentation is to have our customers close on the terms presented; however, we also want to create the best situation to further work from in case they do not. We have to be prepared and best position ourselves if they want to negotiate.

Our first objective in creating these opportunities is to help construct the curiosity needed for them to move forward by leaving the final payment undetermined. As stated earlier, our goal is to have our customers proceed into the business office, and curiosity will always help drive their willingness.

Our second objective is to draw attention toward a specific variable on which to focus as the closing point of contention. This will help to narrow their focus, subconsciously allowing acceptance of the other variables involved. This is simply accomplished by overvaluing one of our listed parameters.

If they are financing and not readily closing, try to steer their focus to the payment. Use this undefined variable as a lead into the business office. Gain their acceptance to write the deal up as it is and submit it for processing. Just say, "Okay, let me get some information for our business office so they can get started determining the payment terms that will best work for you." Most customers will make their decision based on payment anyway, so get them into the business office and one step closer to completing the sale. This will also leave the opportunity to adjust the final terms with factors other than price, if necessary, such as the term of the loan.

If their primary concern is not payment, our backup objective is to single out the remaining factor they seem concerned with the most. This is usually the amount of their down payment, their trade value, or your listed sale price, and is easily accomplished by over- or undervaluing the selected variable. One example would be to set their trade value overly low or their down payment overly high. It is always easier to negotiate and reach an agreement when you have narrowed the number of variables to one. If you can predetermine your customer's variable of concern before you present your figures, leave the most room to play within that variable. If the focus is limited, such as an advertised sale price, or if they have a written trade appraisal from another company, listing a substantial down payment will usually get their attention. In addition to narrowing the field, adjusting the down payment will save adjusting your figures for last. If they are unresponsive to the down payment amount or are paying cash, try to verify their next biggest point of concern and focus on that as the final condition of the sale. Again, this implies consent with the other variables involved. From here, if a negotiation is imminent, we can then focus on negotiating this one last remaining variable.

WHERE IS THE CASH FROM?

Before negotiating any of the variables or trying additional closes, make sure to allow them to let payment be the deciding factor. If they are cash buyers, research how they are obtaining their cash. Is it from their savings, or have they arranged outside financing? If they have arranged outside financing, allow them the opportunity to have your business office arrange a financing plan for them as well. Let them know of all your company's financing sources and the benefits of having it all arranged for them. Explain that you may be able to offer them comparable or even better terms, and that this way all the paperwork can be handled accurately and immediately. Promote the benefit of keeping their source of financing for other needs by using one of your sources. This may in fact actually convert them into finance buyers and precipitate a less resistant path to the business office. It will also be easier to offer an extended warranty and adjust the final terms with their budget in mind.

THE KEY TO THE FIGURES

The setup of this chapter and your ability to double your sales is based upon one thing: having the ability to stay away from price before it is time. It means not discussing a discounted figure before you establish your customers' desires, create a sense of value within them, and determine that an ability to purchase is present. This element is so important to the sales process and yet is the one that most salespeople never master. From my own early experiences, I feel compelled to testify to the impact this acceptance can have on one's ability to succeed. Because it is so significant, I feel it is worth a further look. This time, let's seek understanding from a salesperson's point of view. Here, I will try to explain in more detail the reason we find this so difficult to accept, yet why we always should.

Some salespeople will rationalize not following the steps and discuss discounts before they should because they want to please their customers. They will skip the steps or allow a price discussion because they will let their customers take control of the pace and structure of the sale. They want to satisfy their customers by providing all of the information requested in the progression the customers want. However, these salespeople are unable to separate the early stage of the process, where it is imperative to listen to and understand their customers' needs, from the later stage, the buying stage.

If you want to be successful, you have to do what is best to help you sell more effectively. You have to separate the stages. There is a time to listen and a time to take control. Once you have listened to your customers' needs and selected the best possible solution, it is time to lead, not follow. Do not discuss a discount until it is time. I understand that there may be a temptation for the lesser skilled salespeople to skip this advice; however, you have to realize that in almost all cases, regular customers will only present a limited challenge. Have the ability to recognize this and remain constant in your efforts. Assess their needs, select a solution, and build value first. Allow them and yourself to justify the list price before either of you start to dismiss it. Know that most customers will readily follow your process if properly presented. Only customers who do not care about you or your service and have little or no intention of buying from you will press for your lowest price up front. And it is with these markedly insistent customers that you must be the most aware, because with them, price is your only leverage.

Another common reason that some salespeople will offer a discount too early is that they want to appear knowledgeable of the pricing possibilities or show that they have the power to discount. Their self-image is more important than their desire to make a sale. These salespeople might not even be aware that this is costing them deals. However, if this is the case, they will not excel until they alter their thinking. All top salespeople know that helping to find a proper solution and taking the best path to complete a sale is what really matters. They know that being smart is more effective than trying to appear smart. Your goal should be to help your customers find the most suitable solution and have them purchase from you, not to do all the work of selecting a solution and having your customers purchase elsewhere. Do not lessen your customers' desire or interest and eliminate their curiosity by offering an early, discounted figure.

Do not give in to the requests that will hurt your chances. You have to give yourself the necessary time to build value, and you have to ensure a capability and a commitment to do business every time to best ensure their forward direction. Make them curious. Make them want. Leave the ability to start the negotiation at the full list price every time. In addition to giving yourself the opportunity to make a profit, it will also greatly increase your chances of completing a sale by leaving you some room in the negotiation. In many cases, customers will often expect some degree of give and take. Do not limit yourself by eliminating your possibilities. The surest way to a successful career in sales is to build your credibility with the knowledge of your products and your assessment skills, not your discounting skills.

FINAL THOUGHT

Presenting the figures should be the easiest step in the sales process, and it can be if you always start and end with your process in mind. Take the time to understand how important your consistency is and condition yourself to become consistent. When you fully believe in having your presentation become habit and do not allow yourself to stray from your path, you will soon see how easy it truly is to prepare yourself and your customers to reach an agreement on the terms that you have offered. Now the close.

10

CLOSING THE SALE

T he vast majority of customers are looking for a good deal, or one they deem fair. However, the definition of a good deal is not a constant. It is something that will vary from customer to customer. A good deal is not a specific number or defined set of completions. A good deal is the perception of the buyer and is a result of the value that has been created. It is where the perceived value of an offering is equal to the investment required.

Making the deal, or closing, is everything. It is why we sell. It is the result that is necessary to achieve before your customers will be able to enjoy the solution that you and they have selected. However, even with the best presentation of figures, not all customers will agree to settle right away. It is because of this that we must learn and practice to close our customers on terms that are agreeable. After we have reached an agreement on the selection, we must then come to an agreement on the figures and the terms of delivery. We have to become experienced in successfully persuading our customers and in closing the deal.

UNDERSTANDING THE CLOSE

Closing the sale is the act of you and your customers agreeing to the terms of delivery and gaining acceptance on the figures that have been presented. Closing is not something that you just ask for; it is something you build to throughout the steps. It is where every question you ask and every piece of information you provide is guiding and motivating your customers toward purchasing the solution they have selected. The key to closing is preparing your customers to be closed.

It is a careful analysis of their wants and needs and the path necessary to persuade them to make a decision. It is where you make the best decision for your customers and then influence them to realize it as well.

Closing is building your customers' perception of value, the value needed to make the sale. Closing is an art. It requires having the ability to see through your customers' eyes, to recognize what they are thinking and feeling, and to understand why. It demands identifying their motivations and hesitations and possessing the insight to understand what influences will best persuade them. It is the art of steering their thinking with the information you both offer and request. It is asking the questions that will produce the answers that will help persuade them to move to a decision. It involves recognizing what answers will influence them to maintain, alter, or rethink their current point of view, all after you have established their point of view.

Closing is also tying up all the loose ends. It is the act of isolating the variables of the deal and gaining acceptance on each before proceeding to the next. When closing, you isolate the selection, you isolate the objections, and then you isolate the figures. A top salesperson will always seek to secure the details of the sale before they start to negotiate a figure. This allows them to build to a close on a successful and uninterrupted path. It is also a way to build on the acceptance of the preliminary approvals that will lead up to the big approval, the sale. A positive momentum will be more likely continued because it is already flowing in that direction. It is always easier to encourage a way of thinking than it is to change its direction.

Closing is additionally knowing when to close. It is sensing when your customers are ready to be asked. It is having the ability to sense when their receptivity is high by the signs that their emotions and actions exhibit. It is recognizing the feeling when the timing is right. It is the point in time when you have established value within them and they have accepted that they will be purchasing. It is when you can sense that they are already planning their lives around their new solution.

WHAT CLOSING IS NOT

What closing *is not* is simple. Closing is not just discounting an offering with the hope that someone might say yes to it. It is not solely negotiating the price to be paid; it is the balancing of price and value. For the successful salesperson, the start of the price discussion is merely another opportunity to build more value.

CLOSE WITH CONFIDENCE

The first rule in closing is to understand the importance of assuming your customers will agree to the terms presented. Some customers will close easy, and some will be challenging. In order to position yourself for an agreeable response, it is essential that you portray a clear confidence in your own approval of the figures you have presented. People are very astute in reading subconscious language. They will recognize any insecurity and uncertainty in your beliefs. They will sense your uneasiness if you think the price is too high and conversely feel your surety if your approval is apparent. Your effectiveness lies in your ability to create a presentation that will naturally flow from the security and confidence you have in your product and yourself. If they see you believe in the numbers offered, they will be much more likely to believe and accept them as well. If they see you are uncomfortable with the numbers, they too will be uncomfortable. Your customers will always be less likely to agree if they feel a better price is possible.

When closing, picture yourself from the outside looking in. Analyze both your strengths and your weaknesses. If confidence is your weakness, focus on the reasons for your lack of comfort and readjust your approach. Too many times, a salesperson will give up profit, or even lose the sale, by consciously or subconsciously indicating that a better deal could be had. Once you have a commitment and your customers are sitting down, show confidence in your figures. Assume that your customers will accept the figures you present when you start the process.

In sales and in closing, your success is in doing the right things well and believing in yourself. If you believe in your offerings, believe in your company, and believe in the level of service you provide, you will have the confidence needed to deliver with a new level of success. Show belief in your offerings and others will believe in them as well. Confidence breeds trust, and trust is essential to your customers' acceptance.

IT IS NOT ALWAYS PRICE

Almost all customers will lead you to believe that they only care about one thing. This one thing is price. They want you to believe that their whole decision is based on the bottom line. In fact, experienced shoppers will have inexperienced salespeople jumping through hoops to try to satisfy all of their price questions and demands. Do not let this happen to you. Take control by adhering to the process.

When negotiating a deal, be strong in your desire to close the sale and maintain a profit. Take into consideration the time you have spent learning about your offerings and the time and effort spent in training. Consider the level of service you will give your customers after the sale. Do not lessen the value of you. If you were successful in building rapport, let them know the value of having you as a salesperson. Reiterate the quality of the service you and your company will provide. Do not be shy; billions of dollars a year are spent in the service industry. Why should yours be free? Think of it as charging them X for the offering and X-plus for your services.

Do not impose your own feelings on what a good deal is or assume what your customer will or will not pay. Let this be the venue of underperforming salespeople. Your customer's perception of a good deal is always one of creation. It is also unique and susceptible to outside influence. In sales, a customer's perception of value is directly proportional to a salesperson's ability to build value. So build some value.

The more value you are able to create, the more likely your customer will accept the terms you have presented. This is absolutely true. Value is in the eye of the beholder. This is why there is no unimportant step in this process. Each step is part of a highly coordinated plan to increase the perception of value in your prospect's mind. This is another reason that some salespeople will consistently sell more than others. Some will understand and believe in building value throughout the process and some will not. Focus on the value of you, your company, and your offering as you attempt to close on a figure. Understand that price is often not the determining factor in a purchase.

If you are consistently unable to close on price, are your company's prices too high or are you ineffective in creating a sense of value for your customers? Look at the clothes you are wearing. Can you honestly say that everything was purchased because it was the least expensive stuff you could find? Probably not. In fact, price was probably not an issue in many of your items. Try to recall how much you paid for each. The fact is that the average consumer will remember the experience of a purchase far longer than they will the price, so think in the future.

ALWAYS ABOUT THE VALUE

Your customers' perception of value only has to equal the expense involved, and this can be accomplished just as easily by increasing their awareness of value than by lowering the price. Sell yourself, your company, and your solution. Don't sell price; sell value. As long as they are being reasonable, a little extra value-building will only help.

START FRESH

There will always be difficult customers. However, do not let these customers determine your pattern of thought. Just because your last customer was not swayed by your efforts, do not assume the next one will not be either. Learn from your past to help your future, not to taint it. All customers may appear challenging when first addressing the purchase price; however, not all will continue to be challenging. Do not fall into the belief, as many salespeople have, that it is all about the price. It is not. It is only about price when you decide to let go of your value-building process.

BREAK THE GROOVE

When something starts to move in one direction, it tends to keep moving in that direction. What I mean by this is that many actions seem to be controlled by momentum. If you are unable to close with profit with one customer, and unable again with another, and then another, this trend will soon start to become self-perpetuating. You may then become conditioned to believe that this is the only way you can sell, if at all. You may then start to skip the steps and stop attempting to build additional value, deciding instead to skip right to the price. Unfortunately, this momentum will likely continue because most customers will at least mention some price concern. It may become the case that the only way a deal may actually be made or profit realized is to run into a customer who agrees so quickly that there is no time to offer a discount.

This does not have to be the case. The key to successful closing is to remain focused on your process and only work in the present. Do not let any past negative momentum dictate your future level of success. Start each presentation with a fresh and determined confidence. Learn, practice, and believe in your process and ability. Learn the process, believe in the process, and stay with the process. You may not always succeed, but you must always position yourself to succeed. Successful salespeople will take the time to gain knowledge, develop skill, and focus on every new beginning. They refuse to be tainted or conditioned by challenging customers or the low performers that dwell within their company.

ALLOW THE STEPS TO KEEP YOUR DIRECTION

The best approach, whether you are selling a house or an evening gown, is to proceed through the steps of your sale professionally and politely, all while keeping the blueprint of your forward direction.

ALLOW THE STEPS TO RECOGNIZE YOUR DIRECTION

In some cases, the relative importance of your customer's decision will be obvious. However, in other cases, its importance may not always be readily evident. Keeping to your steps will additionally help provide the proper recognition of your customer's decision as you keep your forward direction.

The importance of one's decision is always a matter of perception. Different people will have different views on the importance of the decisions they face. Although you should never elevate the importance of a decision if not warranted, you want to be careful not to underestimate it either. Depending on your situation, you will sometimes want to adjust the grandness of your approach to adapt to your customers.

Some will want to be recognized if they feel they are making a big decision, and conversely, some will become curious if you over portray their decision's importance. For the new salespeople reading this, it can sometimes be a very rhythmic dance here. Your best plan is to always have your steps present and yet slightly adjust your time and emphasis to each customer. Meaning, you don't want to overpresent a simple item; you might scare them away. However, you also don't want to skip through your steps when your customer is in the middle of what they feel to be a major decision. This is why we have our process; just adjust the time spent on each step. Listen for your direction. Do not slow the pace of your sale by overvaluing their decision and do not lose your sale by taking it too lightly.

NEGOTIATING THE FIGURES

Well, okay. Even though you followed the process to build value first and presented your figures with absolute confidence, your customers are still not agreeing. They are not going to pay the current market value for your offering and they want more for their trade. On top of that, the down payment is too high. Well, let's get to work. In some cases, despite our best efforts, these factors may not be acceptable and we must be prepared to negotiate.

UNDERSTAND THE FLOW

Although there will always be a set process that we should initiate when closing, there will be no set action that our customers will have when responding. Our customers will always have different desires and levels of ability when seeking to accomplish their goals. Because of this, I will try to help you understand our customers' most common actions within the steps as they will likely occur. I am stating this because I want you to still be able to see the overall outline of our process, even if it takes re-reading it, while I take the time to further explain each part of our process. I am trying to allow for both momentum and understanding. Here we go.

START AT ALL THE MONEY

Always start at the list or full retail price. We start at all the money for two reasons. The first, of course, is that they might accept it. And what professional does not deserve to be paid for their service? The second is that it leaves us with some place to go. Most people will want some give and take. In fact, many customers will think of the close as a series of gives and takes. If you have a commitment, leave yourself room.

PLAY IT SLOW

If you have presented the figures and your customers do not initially agree, do not immediately counteroffer your offer or look for their counteroffer before you spend time in justifying your figures. If you quickly discount your numbers, they will expect you to do so again and again. This will leave you with no credibility and will afford them the control in the negotiation. It is also not yet time to ask for or even to allow a counteroffer. We want to be able to analyze how close their offer may be first. Their quick counteroffer may be too much, too fast. They might think of your initial numbers as too high and counter with figures that are too low.

If they do let out an offer, my advice is to not acknowledge it; refuse to even hear it. Your customers will usually use their first offer, no matter how low, as a basis for where they want to be. This difference may be too much to overcome. You want to continue building your rapport and value until they agree, or at least until you feel confident that their offer will be close. Always look to avoid a spoken reference for them to compare with later on, creating an uphill battle throughout the close.

Rather than pursuing a potentially risky counteroffer, we want to make the first attempt to refigure our variable. If you determine that their acceptance is not forthcoming, it is us who will want to initiate the next step to keep the first spoken difference in our control. The reason behind this is simple. Most people will want to keep their credibility, and any alteration from their offered number may be seen as losing face. Some will just feel they have something to prove. I have actually seen people walk away from a deal they really wanted because their pride would not let them accept it. Do not put yourself in this position.

ADJUSTING OUR OFFER

When negotiating the actual figures, seek to keep all but one of the figures on the worksheet a constant. We want to focus on the figure of most contention. We do not want to negotiate on one part of the equation only to have to re-negotiate on the next. In addition, focusing on one figure will create less resistance to proceed because they will still have the opportunity to adjust the movement of the remaining figures. They will also not have the anxiety in moving forward when agreeing to the lesser variables because they will not be at the final point of agreement. Remember, focusing on a specific parameter is what we prepared for by separating the variables and steering their attention to a specific one when presenting the figures.

Once we have successfully isolated our focus and reconfirmed their commitment, we want to test their pricing resolve in a cautious manner. The key to successful negotiating is to start with small increments in a questioning approach. In addition to setting the first figures, we also want to set the first counteroffer.

It is here that we will want to minimally adjust the figure of most concern in their favor. Ask your customers if moving the figure a percent or two would help persuade them to move forward. Of course the amount may be in the hundreds or thousands, depending on the expense of the offering, but our intention here is to move a relatively small amount. This method of negotiating gives us the opportunity to make more profit and to build credibility, and allows us further room to move if necessary. And remember, always remain silent after asking a closing question. Your silence will help yield a response.

If a percent or two more won't do it, it still may or may not be safe to solicit an offer. If you are able to sense from their expressions and mannerisms that their offer is likely to be close to your original figure, allow them to voice it. If not, continue building value, publicly encouraging them to not make an offer.

RAISE YOUR OBSERVATION

If your efforts do solicit an offer, and you feel that it is still lower than they will eventually agree to, question whether they have information to support their offer. Question if they are just going by feel. Know that many times our customers will voice a price objection, disagreement, or give a low counteroffer simply because that is what they have coached themselves to do. Additionally, in many instances, they may just be testing your reaction for what they should request. It is here that you will have to raise your people-reading skills to determine the direction they are leaning. You will have to assess and analyze their resolve. You must be intuitive and creative in responding to the actions and reactions that occur.

If they reveal or force an unreasonable offer, interrupt their request. Please stop and understand this before continuing. If you do not react immediately to an unreasonable offer, the customer may consider their offer acceptable, or close to acceptable. If it is not, be quick to dismiss it. Tell them their offer is unacceptable. If you are not close, do not act as if you are. This is very important and worth repeating. Do not write this offer down, take it to your boss, or even repeat it aloud. You do not want to validate an unacceptable offer, or you may never be able to revalue their perception of a more reasonable offer. If your customer sees any acceptance of their offer, trust me, they will stick like glue to it and you will not be able to close the sale. Always move for a more reasonable offer up front, or you may never be able to work them up. Gauge your customers' level of closeness with each exchange and constantly analyze any potential change in their thinking before acknowledging their response.

QUESTION THEIR EVIDENCE

If your customer states that your figures are too high, ask, "Why do you say that?" They might realize they have no basis for their statement. They may realize they have no relevant information to support their claim or initiate a lower counteroffer. If they do have a competitor's offer, be sure to verify that what you are comparing is the same. Never underestimate a customer's willingness or ability to stretch the truth. Furthermore, if their information is comparable, there is no law that says you have to be cheaper. The quality of you and your company's service is a variable that should set you apart. Also, you must understand that this reaction is often just one's natural response when negotiating. Simply allow for this and then allow for their acceptance. While continuing to investigate your customer's resolve, try to solicit a reasonable counteroffer. Eventually, most of your customers will come around. Remember, due to the rapport and comfort you created earlier in your interaction, they will often look for reasons to agree.

TRY ONCE AGAIN

If you feel you are getting close, try one more time to offer another percent or two off. This second offer is another reason to avoid hearing any offer that is too low, because if the customer senses that you have acknowledged their low offer, they may be insulted by your small move. However, if you work with a clean slate, they will be more likely to see your response as within reason. Once you restate your offer, again seek their acceptance.

NOW SEEK THE OFFER

If again your customer does not close, you must now abandon your discounting approach and seek an acceptable offer. You always want to limit the number of moves in their direction. Do not negotiate against yourself. If they see a pattern developing, they will remain in their current position and just let you continue. You must now involve them. You must concentrate on soliciting an offer and closing on the difference.

CLOSING IS PERSISTENCE

The easiest way to continue closing is to close with your leading questions. Close from their point of view. Stop and re-ask the questions that will remind them how they reached this point and why they agreed to purchase. Keep steady in your efforts to close the deal. Ask the questions that will help restart the flow of "yes" answers:

"Mr. Customer, you did say that this was the style cruiser you wanted, correct?"

"This is the right color, right?"

"You are able to make a decision today, aren't you?"

"Okay, that being said, at what figure would you be willing to sail your new boat home?"

When the negotiations stall, the best action you can take is to repeat your confirming questions, continue to build value in yourself, your company, and their selection, and continue to solicit an offer. Be polite and courteous, but be persistent. You must push for a figure so that the customer will do business.

When encouraging their offer, use your radar to help steer them to the answers you want. Be quiet when you ask a closing question, but the instant you see that their answer is not the one you want, speak up. Ask another confirming question and then re-ask your closing question. Learn to see the words they are about to speak by analyzing the physical movements leading up to their delivery.

When asking your confirming questions, go for the yeses. Sometimes, when starting momentum, you may have to go for the easy yeses just to get the ownership mood restarted. A customer's "yes-saying" mood is important. It is a law of human nature for someone to remain on the same path unless something alters that path. In some cases, you may have to start further back in your "history," or question the obvious, to get your first yes. Go back as far as necessary to get a positive response. "Sir, you are interested in networking your computer system for your local offices, aren't you?" "You agree that our new generation routers will increase your workforce production and profitability, right?"

Sometimes, if your customers cease negotiating because they are frustrated or feel they are not close, you may have to go lower than you want, or even can, just to interest them again. Although you want to avoid this, it may be necessary to jumpstart a stalled negotiation. You cannot build on a no. You can only build on a yes, so keep trying.

CONTINUE FROM THEIR POSITION

When closing, think like your buyers. When you reach this point in your negotiation, put yourself in their position. Try to look at the negotiation from their point of view. Try to envision what they are thinking. Analyze what they are saying with their words versus what they are saying with their manner. Gauge their level of commitment. Does their physical language and facial expression line up with what they are saying? Do they want to own their new solution? How much do they want to own it? Are they negotiating to determine if they will own it, or have they already decided on ownership and are just negotiating for price? When negotiating, always ask yourself,

"Will they close at these figures?" Are you leaving money on the table?

A customer's words may say "discount," but their actions may say they will purchase at or near the figure requested. You have to be able to quickly read your customers and adjust your approach. Depending on the personality of your customer or their negotiating stance, it may be better here to quicken the pace or to slow it down with small talk. Question your customers' resolve to own against their resolve of getting a discount. Do not give up profit if it is not necessary. Always analyze where you are and determine your best approach.

EVALUATE THEIR OFFER

When you solicit their most reasonable counteroffer, take a second to look at it. Write it down on your worksheet, then pause. Look at it, as if to study its acceptability. Learn to control your emotions and expressions. Know your customers will often base their next move according to your reaction. If you jump up and do the victory dance, they might try to take their offer back. Your reaction should be based on the degree of discount their offer represents. Your responses should range from, "Hmm, let me see if I can get this approved," to, "I can't accept that offer."

Depending on the degree of acceptability, it still may be better to talk your customer up to a higher offer or to simply accept it. This of course depends on the feel of the negotiation. Sometimes the tension or anxiety is best relieved. If their offer is reasonable or your negotiation warrants a break, take it to your owner or manager for consideration and let them know that you will work to make a deal happen.

Note that I do not believe in having your customers sign the offer or taking a deposit at this stage in most cases. Working off trust will produce less anxiety. If your customers are going to back out of their offer, their signature or deposit means nothing anyway, so why add to the apprehension? Also, never say, "Sign here," or, "I need your signature." Have them "authorize the paperwork." Now, however, if their anxiety level is low, or if they are of the hard-to-tie-down nature, a little extra confirmation may help. Unfortunately, there is no best method. You just have to play it by feel. You have to be able to observe and analyze your customers' thoughts.

ANOTHER COUNTEROFFER?

There is no right or wrong answer for one last counter. Sometimes, if you do not counter your customer's offer, they may feel they offered too much and reassess their offer. At other times, they might just explode from the perceived hassle and run for the door. You have to assess each customer individually. When in this circumstance, you have to assess the presence of your specific customers intently and accurately at the time. Get all you can, but don't overdo it.

AUTHENTICATE YOUR COUNTEROFFER

If you or your manager decides on a counteroffer, always use relatively exact-looking numbers. Perception matters. Exact numbers sound more believable as a good deal based on a tight level of acceptability where effort and multiple calculations were involved. Let customers know you are trying to save them every expense possible. If you feel that the exchange of offers will necessitate more than one trip, save this method for what you hope will be your last trip. This way it will not lose its effect for the final close.

BE EXCITED ABOUT YOUR OFFER

When you come back with your counteroffer, let your customer know that you have great news. Let them know that you have a great deal for them and that you are excited for them. Be enthusiastic. Let them know that they are just one step away from owning their new solution. Give them the figures and ask for their agreement.

Move to strike a deal here. Move at a fast pace if not quickly accepted. Narrow the gap with a small series of give and take. Time is best not to be wasted here. Have you, your manager, or your owner leave a little room for your negotiation. Reaching a deal at this stage is nothing more than a series of small compromises. Be persistent. Move quickly beyond any objection and get your customer's agreement.

SHARE THE EXCITEMENT

If your manager is a good closer, it may be a good time to get them involved. If your manager or closer is available, introduce him or her and leave. Stay close enough to be there if called but not close enough to be involved. You want to be out of sight because you want to let your customers make a new decision. Your customers will be less likely to change their minds in front of you because they will lose their sense of credibility if they do. So stay in hearing distance, but stay out of view.

If your manager is unable to close them, try some more on your own. Managers are usually good closers and may have softened your customers up for you. Your friendly face may be all they need to move forward with a deal. If they close here, congratulations. However, if not, don't worry; we are not done yet. "My Favorite Closes" and "Overcoming Objections" are up next.

THE FINAL THOUGHT

The closing process is really pretty simple. Reaffirm your customers' selection, create and build value in owning it, present the information to satisfy their hesitations, and ask for the sale. Successfully closing a tough sale is having the ability to repeat the closing process, all while maintaining your customers' level of willingness to remain willing participants.

Whenever I am closing a tough sale, I think about the directions that say, "Complete this step and repeat." Every time you are able to offer new information or reestablish their perception of value, ask again for the sale. Repeat the step. Remember, when customers say "No," they are only saying it as a result of the information they presently have. If you can offer them new information, you should not be shy in asking them to make a new decision. This new information may be more value, an additional option, or yes, sometimes even a lower price. Whatever it is, have the desire and the persistence to find out. Then have the desire and the persistence to satisfy these hesitations and complete the sale. Be a good salesperson; let your customer start enjoying their new solution right away.

11

MY FAVORITE CLOSES

A close is when the terms of a deal are stated and an agreement is being reached. It is when you attempt to lay the final groundwork for your concluding goal. In our business of sales, there are lots of set plans or methods that will attempt to transition our customers smoothly from visitors to owners. Know that within each step of our process, we will often have to close our customers on one parameter or another. Within each step are a series of mini-closes that all lead to the final, most important one: the purchase. I have listed my favorite closes here.

For this list of closes, I have tried to use the most recognized titles and to explain them in simple terms. This is to help you remember and identify with each for when the appropriate opportunity presents itself. Try to envision how and where you may use them, or a similar version of each, for the progression of each step and for their final agreement. I have also included some advice in each to help you get a better feel for when and where each closing will be of use. Please feel free to adjust your presentation as it may relate to your customer's style, the style of your delivery, or the part of the process that may be of most benefit.

Okay, here we go, but before we start, I want to reiterate one major point: persistence. When closing, persistence is essential. Make as many attempts to close as your customers will let you. Use every one of the closes listed here, and more if necessary.

ASSUMPTION CLOSE: If you have completed all the steps in the process and created a desire, this is the easiest one to close with. After you have stated your proposal, continue writing up the purchase order. Just assume your customers are ready to buy. A good lead into this close, immediately following the presentation of the figures, might be to say, "Okay then, to what address will we be delivering your new solution?" Once your customers answer or respond in the positive, consider the deal closed. Just write it up. This close is that simple.

INVITATION CLOSE: Here, you simply invite your customers to take the deal. It might go like this: "Well, what do you think? Would you like to give it a try?" Simple and straightforward. If they say okay, write it up. If they say no, ask why not. Then handle the objection. When you overcome the objection, invite them again.

SECONDARY-QUESTION CLOSE: This close is where you present two questions at once, the first of which confirms the sale, and the second of which prompts an answer that gives information to initiate the transaction. The second question is easy to respond to, and that is what we want. It is human nature for a person to respond to the last or easiest question first. When your customers respond positively to the second question, they have essentially agreed with your first, right? It may go like this: "Okay, all we have to do is decide when a good time would be for you to pick your new travel trailer up." And continue right away with, "Do you have a copy of your license handy for the paperwork?" Then just casually extend your hand to receive their license. When the customer hands you their license, use it to start writing up the order. They have agreed to take delivery. Continue with your paperwork and involve them as well. Do not worry about an answer to the first question, because it is not specific to actually making a deal. Keep moving forward, knowing it will fall into place as you continue. This close actually assumes the sale without being too direct.

With this close, as with any form of the assumption close, it is imperative to keep your customer busy. Give your customer something to do upon receiving a positive response to your second question. Have them fill out a form or two. If you ask for an insurance card and they do not have one, offer another task. Start them with a credit application or even a purchase order if they are paying cash. Do not let them go to far to retrieve anything or let them have any alone "thinking time." It is a very delicate time between them agreeing and finalizing the sale. Any idle time at all here, and your deal will be at risk.

AGREEABLE CLOSE: "Mr. Customer, does all of this sound agreeable to you?" If he says yes, proceed with, "Okay, all that's left is a little paperwork." Start writing it up. This close is a combination of the invitation and the assumption close. I like this close because I think people want to respond to it positively. Many people have a sense that being agreeable is the acceptable way to interact. Have your paperwork procedure down pat. Top closers proceed with no change in emotion and the ability to carry on an idle conversation while completing paperwork. It is very important to keep your composure if the customer responds in the positive; act as if this is just the next step. Again, try to avoid any victory celebration. If your temperament changes, you may make your customers uneasy. Do not bring attention to the implied acceptance. Just proceed as if you expected their positive answer, and never look back.

IF-THE-PAYMENTS-WORK CLOSE: This close should always be the next attempt to keep your forward progress if the customer does not agree to the terms as presented and is financing. To help with this close, indicate that what really matters is the payment and that they should determine what that is before they consider acceptance. Persuade them to make their decision based on the terms of the payment. It may go like this: "Okay, sir, let me ask you a question. If we can somehow adjust these figures and work out the financial terms to where your monthly payment is acceptable to you, is this the bike you want to own?" If he says yes, simply write it up.

You did not discuss a discount, so write it up at list, and prepare the paperwork for settlement. If the deal has to be adjusted a little to fit in his parameters, that's okay. It is still better to write it at list and try. If you don't try, you won't get it. This is the close we made available by leaving the payments undetermined while presenting the figures. We want to balance our information to maintain interest and curiosity. This close is simply the easiest way to have your financing customers proceed into the settlement office, and this is the forward direction we want.

ANSWER-THE-FINAL-OBJECTION CLOSE: This is where you have your customers agree to move forward contingent upon the resolving of one last variable. This is a transition close, and it can be used at any stage of the process. Steer the close and acceptance to moving forward to one last objection and then isolate it as the last point of contention. This may be price-related, such as negotiating the figures, or may be related to any other parameter of the deal.

An example in the closing stage may be: "Okay, Mr. Buyer, if I can agree to your last request of $_ on your trade and keep all of the other figures as presented, we can write up the paperwork, right?" Get your customers' commitment before you give them yours. Remember, like the payment close, we look to set up this close when presenting the figures in case we have to negotiate.

An example for the presentation stage may be: "Let me ask you a question. If I could find an open parking lot with little or no traffic, you would want to take a small test drive, am I right?" Determine the objection and then overcome it.

In the first example, you might not know you can accomplish their last request. That is okay. Your goal is to get a commitment off which you can work. This helps to put them in a yes-saying mood. It gives them the feeling, and sometimes relief, that ownership is accepted. Once people commit to a deal, they are much more likely to be flexible to ensure that they keep their feeling of acceptance. If it is reasonable, and you can accomplish it, do it. If you cannot, counter with your own offer. When closing, always work off your customers' commitments.

SUMMARY CLOSE: It is here that you seek to sum up all the variables for the customer and ask for the deal. Tying up the loose ends will help both you and them feel good about moving forward. An example for this might go: "Okay, so what you're saying is, if I can get your payment to $400 per month with $500 down, pay off your current loan, and repair that scratch, we have a deal, right?"

Again, we are seeking a commitment we can build upon. Now that you have a commitment, accomplish it or negotiate an acceptable settlement. Concerning the summary above, where we summarized and settled a payment, just say okay upon acceptance and start to write it up. You do not have access to the payment screen. This is fine. You have not committed; they have. Your job is done. Here is where you say, "Okay, great. Let's write it up and give it to the business office for the monthly numbers." That's it. Start writing. Do not try to tackle everything at once. Let things proceed one step at a time. Remember, our intention as salespeople is to facilitate our customers to the next step. We should never assume what our customers will or won't agree to in our settlement office. The settlement officers are usually very strong closers. They are fresh faces for our customers and skilled at going the last fifteen yards. If you get this type of commitment, write it up and pass it on.

NO-MONEY-DOWN CLOSE: Just as it sounds: "What you're telling me is that if I can get you approved with no money down, you will wear your new watch home, correct?" That's it. When they agree, write it up.

Help your customers say yes by nodding your head with an expression of approval when you are closing. At this point, you are confirming the request and confirming the close. This keeps the negotiation open and encourages the yes-saying groove. This close is another example of the importance of the "saying yes pattern." It is essential to stay away from questions that will produce a "No," and it is just as important to continue with the questions that will produce a "Yes." Make no mistake; the little yeses will lead to the big yes. This is what momentum does. Sometimes, if they are in a no-saying groove, you may have to dip below where you want or even can just to get them to start with the little yeses. Using "if" builds on what you have. In most cases, it is far easier to bump them on a yes than to change their direction from a no.

LET'S-PROCEED-ANYWAY CLOSE: Don't laugh. This has worked for me many times. When you simply cannot come to an agreement, you might set this close up like this: "Mr. Customer, you want this deal to work, right? Well, I do too. Let's continue writing up the order, and I'm sure we will get something worked out. Okay?" This does three things. One, it gets customers into the "yes-saying" groove. Two, it involves them with more of an investment. And three, since you are completing the paperwork, there will be little time for them to change their minds when they do say yes. Any opportunity you have to increase their investment, with either time or information, will usually work in your favor if your customers are on the fence. Remember, as long as they are still sitting in front of you, you have the green light to keep on closing.

BEN FRANKLIN CLOSE: This is a great close for the indecisive customer. This close starts when you draw a line down the center of a blank sheet of paper and list all the reasons to do the deal on one side and all the reasons not to on the other. Help your customers with the reasons to do the deal, and then help with the reasons not to do the deal. When completed, count the reasons and ask for the sale.

This is a very well known close, so some customers may see it as a technique. If this is the case, agree with them and admire their perception. However, let them know that the reason it is so popular is because it makes good sense. Let them know that many wise decisions have been made because of this analysis. Once they agree, help them start.

NOT-FOREVER CLOSE: I like this close. It helps relieve the pressure by putting things in perspective. When your customers can afford it and are on the fence, let them know that this probably won't be their last decision. Just say, "This won't be your last phone, right? Okay, then try it for a while." When you are in the late stages of a close, sometimes people are just afraid of making a mistake. They feel that making a decision will limit future options and decisions. Let them know that this is not a lifelong decision. "Go ahead and give it a try. You will have plenty of opportunities to make other, more important decisions down the road. Let's get past this one so you can get on with the more important things in your life." I know this close sounds far-fetched, but I have seen people agree almost immediately. Lots. If you think about it, it really does put things in perspective. It relieves the pressure by taking the importance off the decision.

If your customers are still unsure after a couple of these closes, pause for a minute and try some of the confirming questions we learned about earlier. An example may be, "You did say that your wife liked the sunroof and that your kids will be excited about the DVD, right? Okay, let's go ahead. You deserve it." If necessary, stop and give yourself some positive momentum toward their acceptance. With the example listed here, note we took it back to an emotional decision and involved other people. We provided an image of our customers enjoying the benefits of ownership. It is much more likely that customers will close based on an emotional decision, one that satisfies their wants, as opposed to a logical one. Close on the impending shared enjoyment, not the price. Insert your offering in the text of this and similar confirming questions and gain momentum. Use the time between your attempts to help set up and encourage their approval.

EMPLOYEE CLOSE: In most companies, there is usually a person you work with who either owns or has use of an offering similar to the one you are showing. When your customer needs a little extra encouragement, introduce them to this person for a testimonial. This is a strong second opinion. Your customers know that in most cases an employee in the business would not choose a product that was not a good choice. The word of another who owns or has chosen to enjoy the selection your customer is considering is often the affirmation they need to move forward.

FREE-STUFF CLOSE: Offer to give your customer something if they agree to the deal. Offer or agree to include a free cleaning, a complimentary service, a pinstripe, an additional cartridge, or a discount on the matching sofa. Find their hot button. Think of something they may have mentioned earlier.

This is one of the most used closes and one customers will often look for. It is effective and in many cases is the final piece of the deal. Just remember to leverage a commitment as a condition to receiving the stuff. It might go like this: "Okay, if I throw in free floor mats, we have a deal, right?" This close is one more reason to start the negotiation with all the money. Leave yourself some room.

BOTH-SIDES CLOSE: This close is where you present and argue both sides of a decision. This is my most trusted and successful close for when the more assumptive closes fail to initiate a forward move. This can be used when your customers are deciding between offerings or financial options, or even whether to agree to a deal or not. It is here that you will represent both the positives and negatives of each option in an open discussion in which you ultimately sway your customers by presenting one side a little more eloquently. Most customers internally weigh their decisions anyway. This allows you to become a part of their decision-making processes as well. It will bring their thought process out in the open, where you will be able to help them move to a decision.

The key to this close is to place yourself empathetically in their position and verbally help them balance the options from their point of view. It is best presented in a discussion type manner with the restating of the known facts, involving and encouraging your customers' input with your questions. This close both has and shows concern for your customers' decisions and creates the influence required for your guidance. It solidifies your credibility in the arguments you present and the understanding of the pros and cons of each. It also demonstrates that you care enough about their decision and their best interests by helping them see the pluses and minuses. It is like having a debate in which your customers are both participants and audience. It is like the Ben Franklin close, without the paper and in an open forum. This close, along with others here, will take a great deal of understanding of your customers' motivating factors and the facts involved; however, it is effective and achievable if you are observant, creative, and forward thinking. Learn where your customers may be leaning with your discovery questions and help them realize it with your leading questions. Take the time to envision this close, realize its effectiveness, and practice it with upcoming decisions.

AVAILABLE CLOSE: At some time in the past, most people have wanted something that was unavailable. The item may have been sold out, not yet built, on back order, at another location, or in some way limited in availability. In this close, simply inquire, "If the offering you requested were available, would you be interested in owning it today?" This close will work in most stages of the process, and its directness can be adjusted to fit your customers and situation. Another example for earlier in your process might be, "If a yellow gold setting were available, is that the style you would prefer?" This close can offer both a commitment and a forward move.

SWITCH THE SELECTION CLOSE: This one should be reserved for when several attempts to close have failed. Sigh, sit back, and say, "Mr. Customer, it just doesn't look like the figures are going to work on this offering. Maybe we should step down to another model." If the customer says, "No, this is the model I want," keep closing. He has just furthered himself toward a commitment. If he says, "Okay," then show him another model. He might like it, or he might bump himself on price and switch back to the first. In either case, this will validate your figures as the best possible deal. Remember, sometimes all people want is some sign that they are getting a good deal.

TAKE-AWAY CLOSE: This close is a little risky and only recommended for customers with certain demeanors. This works best with non-agreeable or opposite type thinkers. It is based on the same premise as the available close, only in reverse. This technique will challenge their ego. Take the offering or deal away; they might want it more. It may go like this, "Sir, maybe this just isn't the right truck for you; besides, I think another salesperson has a customer interested in it anyway." Remain silent. Odds are he will open the possibilities back up.

Picture two kids in a sandbox. One is playing happily with his toy crane and loader and paying no attention to his truck. However, let his friend come close to the truck and watch the fight ensue. Many people never outgrow this way of thinking. Many of your customers will develop a newfound desire if they feel that they no longer have access to their choice. They might not miss it until it's off the table. Try it.

REDUCE-THE-EXPENSE CLOSE: This, like the Ben Franklin close, is a very well-known and commonly offered close. Here too, if they see it as a technique, admit it. Just say, "Okay, but it makes sense, right?" This is for customers who state that your bottom line is higher than they would like. For this close, simply take the difference between where your numbers are and where they want to be and spread it out over time. Reduce it to an inconsequential amount. For example, if you are at $14,000 for your customer's solution and he wants to be at $12,500, you have a difference of $1500. Ask him how long he plans to keep his solution and add a little time for safe measure. For argument's sake, let's say he will keep it for five years. That is the same as $300 a year or about $25 per month. So your final step of this close may be, "Sir, the difference is less than a dollar a day. You wouldn't let pennies a day stop you from owning the solution you wanted, would you?" Pause. If he says no, write it up. If he says yes, appeal to his sense of reason. Let him know that this minimal amount is not a valid reason for not moving forward. Ask if pennies a day will affect his budget. If he says no, write it up. If he says yes, verify it. Then ask him again.

It is here that this may not be the real reason. Your customer may be working you for every nickel, or he may be unsure about something. If you suspect the first, maintain your course and appeal to his sense of reason or fair play. If you have good rapport and he can afford it, tell him to stop being so cheap while you smile or laugh. This might break the ice and complete the sale. If, however, he is unsure about something else, continue to search for the objection. A good test here would be to say, "Look, we know it is not the money, so what is it? What is keeping you from enjoying your newly landscaped backyard getaway?" From here, just pause. Pressure for a response with your silence. Then take his answer and proceed to overcome his objection.

PUPPY DOG CLOSE: This close is usually left for one of the final attempts and should be offered when almost nothing else works. You want to do all you can to wrap up and lock in a "today" signed deal first. But make no mistake, this is a very effective close to follow up with if a deal cannot be reached. Let your customer try their new solution, even without a commitment. They may fall in love with it. Most of the time, they will. If you can get them to take their solution home, the odds are overwhelmingly in your favor. Agree that this is an important decision and they should do all they can to make sure.

If they are hesitant, try asking, "Did you try that shirt on before you bought it?" They will probably respond, "Well, yes." When they do, your response should be, "If you tried on a $20 investment for comfort, wouldn't it make sense to make sure you were comfortable with a $25,000 investment?" Pause. Persuade them. In this situation, to justify your offer, you want them to feel the importance of the decision. Another suggestion for this close would be to have them agree to do all the paperwork now, with no obligation, to lock in today's offer. Just state that if they choose not to further enjoy their solution for any reason, you will not activate the paperwork. Be persuasive. Stress that this is good because they will have the feeling of ownership without the risk. Let them know that this is the ultimate "test drive," and then allow their experience to do the work for you.

OKAY-I-GIVE-UP CLOSE: No, we're not really giving up. We are just acting like it to relieve the pressure, since it might just be the stress or pressure keeping them from saying yes. This close goes like this: first, admit that maybe this deal is just not meant to be. The terms are just not lining up. Apologize that you were unable to put a deal together. Take the deal off the table and let the pressure fade. Let the subject change to something other than the deal. Resign yourself to the fact that at least you tried. Agree that there are no hard feelings, and that you will keep in touch. Note that it is very important to portray that you have completely given up trying to put a deal together. Now, once you are sure that they believe they will not be making a deal, put your plan into action.

"Sir?" Pause. "Just out of curiosity, if there were one parameter of this deal that you could have changed, what would that have been?" If he responds at all, it's back on. Work it from there. If he cannot come up with one, or this new angle leads to a dead end as well, it is time to do what all good closers do. Jump up with enthusiasm and say, "Wait one minute, sir." Then go get a better closer.

FINAL NOTE

Picture a chess player carefully making move after move or a mathematician using various formulas until both sides of an equation add up. Now ask yourself, "How often does a chess player accomplish victory with one or two moves?" Skilled closers deliberate in the same manner as those who solve problems. They visualize the result as fact and seek only to adjust the means that will end in an agreement of the terms. They analyze and attempt many courses of action, all with one goal in mind: allowing their customers to start enjoying their new solution. Much as with the chess player or mathematician, salespeople will often have to accomplish their goal of closing through creativity and persistence. They will have to understand their customers' needs, be intuitive in finding their best solution, and be creative in their path to a decision.

Please understand that most customers will accept your advice if presented properly. They want to start enjoying the benefits of their new solution; that is why they are there. Accept that you are the expert. Allow your advice to persuade and have the confidence that it will. During the closing stages of each step, think of yourself as a consultative technician who only acts and reacts with precision, steering your customers to the close with each confirming action, question, and response. If you have followed the steps of the sale and committed your time and knowledge in helping them find the best solution for them, have the creativity and persistence to follow through. Help your customers get the new solution they really want.

12

OVERCOME OBJECTIONS

P roper objection handling and the ability to move forward is essential in becoming a top salesperson. There is the probability of customer objections in every part of the sales process, and these objections will have to be handled in order to proceed. I think that new salespeople start to round the corner on becoming experienced when they realize that an objection will not in itself stop a deal from occurring. It is when they understand that an objection will only impede their forward direction until they are able to understand and overcome each one with an acceptable solution.

A top salesperson understands that an objection is similar to a problem, and overcoming an objection is having the creativity and persistence to solve the problem. To effectively move past or overcome the objections that our customers present, we must first look to understand them by accurately analyzing and discovering their concerns and intentions.

ANALYZE THE OBJECTION

In learning to overcome an objection, we must first analyze the different aspects of the objection. We must understand why the objection occurred, its true purpose, and its degree of importance. Only then can we go about deciding the best answer for each of the questions or objections our customers may have. Let's now take a look at analyzing our customers' objections and go over some advice on how best to overcome them.

WHY THE OBJECTION OCURRED

When you accept an objection as it is stated, you are potentially misunderstanding your customer and missing out on a sale. In most cases, an objection is merely a request for more information. Your customers want to know why they should move forward. An objection may also be just a temporary stall to slow the process a little. To move past or overcome an objection, you must first determine why the objection occurred.

An objection is basically an obstacle that your customers will present as a reason not to move forward. These obstacles are typically derived from one of two possible scenarios. One is where a concern is not lining up with their goals, and the other is where they have manufactured a concern to create leverage for their position. Sometimes customers will realize an obstacle and sometimes they will fabricate it. Before we can respond effectively, we must determine our customers' motive. We must determine whether their objection is a true concern or just a diversion.

An objection that is realized is one where your customers have noticed that some parameter of the offering or deal does not conform to their wants or needs. For example, the seating capacity of a vehicle will not accommodate the size of the family, or the monthly payments do not fall within their budget.

An objection that is fabricated is one that they feel will establish a result that will somehow aid them in what they seek to accomplish. For example, your customer may seek to introduce a concern to better negotiate a discount. They might say: "The roof hasn't been replaced since the home was built." Now, the roof might not be brand-new, but they may just be presenting a reason for future concessions. Another example of a fabricated objection is one of the temporary stalls that your customers may present to slow the process down. Here they might say, "I am just not sure."

Whether our customers' objections are real or fabricated, each of them will inevitably slow or stop our movement toward the sale. Each objection will have a different purpose and a different level of importance. Each must also be analyzed for its true purpose before we decide how to proceed.

THE OBJECTION'S TRUE PURPOSE

When analyzing your customers' objections, think about whether they make sense. Compare them with past experiences. Before we can accurately react, we must be able to identify our customers' purpose in stating their objections. Look at their expressions, their actions, and their voices to help determine any motive. Analyze their level of anxiety. Try to anticipate the reaction they want you to have and understand what this may accomplish for them. Analyze the timing and manner in which they present each objection to help in your determination. The hurdle that we will often face in our determination is that any occurring objection could be the product of any result, so each must be examined uniquely.

In the initial part of your meeting, you might encounter what may appear to be lots of small objections, when in fact they are actually small defensive reactions. These objections' true purpose is to allow an out, and are typically just precautionary interjections your customers have coached themselves to say. They are small insertions that are meant to slow things down or to provide a possible escape route. Note that these objections are not based on the parameters of the sale or the features of the offering. They are only a diversion. To understand the veracity of this, ask yourself this question: How many times has a customer stated that they only have ten minutes to spend, only to leave two hours later with their new matching set of imported, woven lawn chairs? They actually had more than ten minutes; they just wanted to set themselves up with an out if they felt things were not going well. Similar objections may occur near the completion of the sale as well. However, again, this "temporary no" is just a reaction, and we should continue to move forward.

If our customers point out a negative, they might just be setting themselves up for a discount. Recognize this as a negotiating tool and not a lack of interest. This objection's purpose is to set the scene for their negotiation. It is here that you must recognize and use this objection as a lead to the sale. This customer is not necessarily indicating that a feature or expense will stop them; they might just be angling for a discount.

Now, if your customer comes back and states that the utility vehicle she was considering does not fit in her garage and she has no street parking, you might want to show another model. There are minor and major objections in sales. Listen to the objection being raised. When an objection cannot be overcome, it is not an objection; it is a circumstance. At this point, you must change directions. This objection's true purpose is to provide you with new information.

Other objections may occur because you still have not established a desire or provided a sense of value. This is an objection that does not have a set basis. Your customers may feel that although nothing is stopping them from moving forward, there is not enough reason established to do so. This objection is a request for more information and will often appear in a nonspecific manner. They will say they want to think about it or they are not sure. Its true purpose is one that may lack a defined motive and therefore is more of a temporary condition. You must search for customers' reasons before you can overcome them. When this pause occurs in the presentation stage, focus on increasing their desires. When this pause occurs during the close, you may want to stop, reconfirm their selection, and rebuild their feelings of value.

Question. Question. Question. Although many of our customers' objections can be avoided with a proper needs assessment and by adhering to our process, many will just have to be overcome. Our customers' objections will always be real in the sense that they will, at a minimum, slow us down. Many will also have some ulterior motive or form of disguise involved in them.

For the disguised objections, we may have to search a little more thoroughly. In some cases, your customer may hide their true reason for not wanting to move forward. For example, the gentleman you are speaking with may be embarrassed that it is his wife who makes all the decisions, or that he does not yet have the money he said he had for the down payment. He may seek to cover his true reason with something much more obscure, like, "I want to think on it," to avoid being found out. Some customers will even put effort into their objections by coming up with things that are impossible to overcome or disagree with; and if we take their words at face value, we will not be able to move forward. However, if we investigate each objection, as we should, we might uncover the true reasons and overcome them. In the example above, the customer may be able to call his wife for permission and may not need to put any money down.

In almost all cases, for all objections, we have to question. We have to search, inquire, and investigate before we can solve many of the objections we will face. We must thoroughly investigate our customer's purpose. To succeed, we cannot be shy in asking the questions to uncover what is really holding the customer up. Understand that if you do not understand the real reason for your customer's objection, you will never be able to move forward.

One of the biggest reasons a sale is not made is that the salesperson was unable to overcome their customers' objections, and the reason they were not overcome, in most cases, was that the salesperson did not recognize the real objection. Ask your questions and unlock your answers.

THE DEGREE OF IMPORTANCE

Giving credence to something of little or no concern will only stall your forward progress and draw the focus from the real objections down the road. Do not take action on what is not a real objection or overemphasize one of little importance. To help determine the relevance of an objection, it is initially best to pay no attention to it. Do not allow a non-issue to become one. Always measure your customer's anxiety before you act. Look at their facial expression and mannerisms to determine the seriousness of each stated objection. As you proceed, covertly examine the context and manner in which the objection was stated to determine its validity. If it is a valid concern, they will show the signs of their concern. If they do not repeat it, proceed with the process; their objection was of no importance. If they do repeat it or show indications of true concern, you will have to satisfy their concern before moving forward. That's up next.

When an objection is a diversion, treat it as such and lead your customers to the sale. When it is a concern, overcome it with new information. When it is a concern that cannot be overcome, find a new direction.

THE OBJECTION PROCESS

Just as there is a "step by step" program for the sales process, there is also one for handling the objections that will occur. When your customer presents an obstacle that has slowed or diverted their direction, and your initial attempt to let it sit was unsuccessful, you must now look to overcome it.

When this occurs, the first step is to fully understand their objection. Let them completely finish stating their concern. Do not interject your opinion before you know where they are going. Learn the complete objection so you can better analyze it for its purpose and its validity. Next, clarify the objection. When your customers state an objection to you, restate it to them. Clarify what it is that they are saying. Next, confirm it is a true objection. Question their objection for its true intent. Some example questions may be, "How do you mean?" or, "What exactly are you saying?" Sometimes your customers may actually answer their own objection. If they do not, it will certainly give you more information on how to proceed. Next is to answer their objection with the appropriate action or response and then verify that you have answered it.

With each step of the sales process comes a new stage to complete and new variables to overcome. Although each step may be different, the process involved should remain a constant. Here now are just the steps.

- Let them finish stating their concern.
- Clarify what they are saying.
- Confirm that is a true objection.
- Question it for its true purpose.
- Answer the objection.
- Confirm that you have answered it.
- Move forward.

When you have completed your objection process and can confirm that you have answered their objection, move on quickly. Change the subject and proceed with the sales process. You do not want to let them linger with the objection still in their minds. A great way to do this is to ask them an unrelated question. This will clear their mind and persuade them to focus on your new question.

HANDLING A TRUE OBJECTION

Objections will occur; we know that. Therefore, knowing this, we should prepare for them. Your best start is to build the relationship with your customers that will allow you to overcome them. Prepare yourself by having good product knowledge and good people skills. Allow your early connection to help prepare your later influence. Your ability to search for the answer to their concerns and influence them to rethink their position will always be enhanced by having a trusting and comfortable relationship in place. Many of the objections you face will be unique to each customer and each situation, and you will need to be prepared. Although there will be certain patterns that you may recognize, certain influences will still always differ with each individual. It is up to you to develop your own creativity and level of influence to overcome each one.

CREDIBILTY

Your ability to overcome an objection is directly related to the credibility you have created. To overcome a concern-initiated objection, you must be persuasive. What you say must be accepted and believed before you can influence them to alter their position. Your connection will give you your customers' time and attention. Your credibility will give you the persuasiveness needed to influence their decision. This is why it is so important to start building early on, with your assessment questions, concern for their needs and accurate information. Your customers must feel that you understand their goals before they will feel you are qualified to help them. You must have built a level of trust and expertise before they will allow you to influence their decision. You must be able to understand, analyze, and present your case to receptive customers who will listen to the information that you provide.

WELCOME THEIR OBJECTIONS

In many cases, an objection should be welcomed. The lack of any objection may be a sign that your customers are not seriously interested. In fact, an objection is often the first sign of interest. It is here that we must recognize this and encourage their desire, not accept their objection as a lack of interest.

PROVIDE NEW INFORMATION

The key to altering a current belief is new information. Inexperienced salespeople will sometimes push for a decision using the same established facts. A top salesperson, however, will determine what is missing with a series of investigative questions and offer new information. Research your customers' concerns, supply new information, and ask for a new decision based on the new information. Do not push for a decision based solely on the information your customers have. Please know that with the use of some well-thought-out questions, you will often find the information necessary to overcome their objections.

PERSISTENCE

When trying to solve each objection, be persistent. Persistence pays off. Many new salespeople lack persistence and will take their customer's objection at face value. They do not know how to read into what their customers are really saying.

To be successful, you have to understand that sometimes your customers' motives will be disguised or misrepresented. You must have the persistence and tenacity to uncover and overcome their objections before you can proceed. Remember being a kid and seeing your favorite candy bar in the checkout lane? No objection was going to stand between you and that candy. There was no objection you couldn't handle. Reach for that same level of persistence.

Let's say that 5% of the people you talk to will agree to purchase on the first attempt to overcome their final objection.

Another 5% will agree on the second attempt, 10% more will agree on the third attempt, 10% more will agree on the fourth attempt, and another 10% will close on the fifth attempt. According to this chart, you will be closing half the people you should by only making three attempts. Be persistent. Be successful. Make as many attempts as it takes. Help them overcome their concerns.

PART TWO

THE THREE MOST COMMON OBJECTIONS

In our business of sales, there are a few specific objections that you will hear over and over. This business will generally produce some of the same objections no matter what or where you sell. The ones you will hear most often are "I want to think about it," "the price is too high," and "I want to check with other companies." It is these objections that you will have to become comfortable with and successful in overcoming in order to perform at a high level. Let's take a look at these objections and go over some advice on how best to handle them. Use this guidance as a source to help create your own responses. Make a list of them and practice answering them. There is no better way to become better at something than to practice.

Please note that these objections, although common, are still subject to some variations in appearance due to the influences that will shape each as they appear. The style of your customer, the relationship that has developed, the desire to acquire your offering, and the timing of the objection will all influence the nature of each. In addition, the same verbal objection could be the result of different reasoning. The information regarding each objection can only be so specific and loosely tied to any objection. You will still have to adapt the knowledge you gain to fit your experience. You will still have to develop the traits to aid you in your success, increase your curiosity, become proactive in your discoveries, and institute persistence. Your ability to overcome these and other objections must be supplied by you and derived from your experience. To be successful, you must become aware of the importance of overcoming your customers' objections and of the qualities needed to succeed. Once started, you will have to fine-tune your abilities continuously as you incur more experiences.

I WANT TO THINK ABOUT IT

This objection is typically due to a concern where your customers will not be completely forthcoming with the reasoning behind their concern. When a customer states, "I want to think about it," there is likely some reason holding them up, but they have chosen not to disclose it. Meaning, something has occurred or exists that is stopping them from buying, however, for some reason, they have instead opted to state a more obscure and harder-to-overcome objection. It is here that we must investigate.

DETERMINE THE TRUE CONCERN

The key to overcoming this objection is to first verify that there really is a concern, and then determine where it lies. Search for and find the real objection. Uncover and satisfy their underlying concern. We should always attempt to find a valid reason first, and that is what we will do here. We must examine our customer's reasoning where it specifically relates to this particular objection.

If their objection is a real concern, it could literally be anything, the color of the siding, the waiting period for delivery, · the terms of the warranty, the coffee machine was out of sugar, or they could even be waiting for another company to call them back. Seriously. It could be any of these or a number of other reasons. You will have to clarify and investigate to uncover what is actually impeding them from moving forward. It is here that you will have to have the perception to realize there is an underlying concern and you will have to have the persistence to uncover it.

What makes this particular objection even more difficult than most is that you not only have to determine their "reasoning," you have to get them to admit it. This of course is while they may not want to lose their credibility and admit that there really is an underlying or ulterior reason. Remember, it is here that they are saying there is no reason; they just want to think about it. However, we know the odds are greatly tilted in the direction that there is a reason, and we must find it before we can begin to proceed. I know this might be a little confusing or even far-fetched for the beginning salesperson to understand, but it is an everyday reality in the closing process. Take the time to work this out for yourself and try to rationalize it.

Start and finish your discovery with a series of questions. Search for their reasons, one question after another. Ask your customer what they will be thinking about. Look inquisitive. Ask why they wouldn't move forward. Ask why they would. Ask if there is any other reason they may have, other than wanting to think on it, for not moving forward. Try to get them to agree on certain aspects of the deal to see what is not yet agreeable. Be persistent. Imply that they should let you know because you will eventually figure it out anyway.

If they are still not forthcoming, be upfront and ask what is holding them up. Be candid. "Mr. Customer, I have found that many times, when a customer wants to think about it, there is usually some underlying reason holding them up. Is that the case here? Honestly, what's bothering you? Is it the color, the deal, the options? What is it? Is it the trade value? Is it your down payment? Is it the wrong time of day?" Pause.

Stay silent. Will them to answer with your waiting, helpful, curious, silent expression. Look confused. This usually does it. If not, continue with, "Is it me? Did I do something wrong? Is there something I haven't explained?" Pause. Stay silent. If your customer likes you, they will usually say, "Oh, no, it wasn't you. Well, to be honest with you, the..." And they will proceed to tell you what it is. This method usually works as it did here. Try it. If it does not, do not give in. Be persistent.

When continuing, always be sure to monitor your customers' level of anxiety so you can judge when to turn up or down the "heat." Keep them willing with your rapport and humor. You may be able to go from one question to the next, or you may have to add some additional rapport time to help open your customers up. Show that you care and are concerned. Let them know you want to help, and the best way for you to start is for them to help you determine the origin of their concern. Look concerned. Show empathy that they will not be able to start enjoying their new solution. Look disappointed in yourself because you were not able to help. Look confused. Continue to ask about specific possibilities as you replay the last stages of the process in your mind.

If you still have no luck, try this approach: "Sir, let me ask you a question. I understand that you are not making a decision today and that you want to think about it, but if you were to make a decision today, what one parameter of this deal would you change?" Pause again. Stay silent. Silence will usually lead him to answer. Note that this question is easy for your customer to answer because the first part of your question takes the pressure off.

If their reasoning is still unclear or they are unresponsive, look perplexed. Stare into space while you concentrate on what it might be. Let them know that there must be a reason and that you want to help find it. This is not a timed effort. This investigation is not over until you uncover the true reason. If you need to or the situation warrants it, take a break back into your common ground and then try some more.

The only way you can overcome this objection is to find out what the true objection is and why your customer is not moving forward. Again, ask specific questions regarding each parameter of the deal. Pay attention to their body language while introducing each variable. Try to tell which one produces a reaction. Eventually you will touch on the one that is of concern. While searching, think back to if or when they appeared unsure or anxious. Try to recall any less than positive reaction to the variable you were discussing at the time. Was it the options on the selection, the cost of the airfare, the added expense of delivery, or the down payment? There is no set answer; you just have to keep searching until something shows up.

If they need to sleep on it, let them know that's okay, your pillow is in your car. Continue to use your wit, charm, and creativity, and they will hopefully fill you in. It is by now that you will have to have some rapport built up. So from early on, make them like you. Tell them you like them and want to be their salesperson. Have fun with them. Make them laugh. Wanting to think on it is rarely a valid objection; however, with creativity and persistence, you will eventually determine what is standing in the way.

If your attempts fail to find an underlying reason, there might just be another explanation. In other, less likely cases, your customers may not have an understandable reason. They may just have a hard time making a decision. It may be that your customer is not good at making decisions and there may not be a valid reason. However unlikely, this is a possibility. I was hesitant to include this because I do not want you to think that this is common and give you an excuse to give up too early. You must always exhaust all other possibilities before you even begin to entertain this line of thinking. However, because this explanation is a reality in some cases, I will discuss it further towards the end of the chapter. But first, let's look at our second most common objection.

THE PRICE IS TOO HIGH

Many times, when a customer says your price is too high, it comes from instinct. It is a natural reaction. For the typical customer, this is just the easiest response to open up with to best accomplish their actual motive, which is to either leave or start positioning for a discount. It is here that your customer's reasoning is usually well-defined. They may be saying they can get it cheaper, they can't afford it, or they are just not sold on the value. The positive part about this objection is that it is usually a sign that they are open to purchasing if you are able to work out the terms. This is an objection that can often be overcome in the present.

Your first response to this objection should be to ask your customer to explain. Try, "What makes the price seem high?" or, "High in comparison to what?" Pause for their answer. If they can get it cheaper, ask how much cheaper. If they say they can't afford it, help them with their budget to verify. If they really can't afford it, switch offerings. Adjust as necessary. These are acceptable questions, and they will usually give you an answer. If they are taking a shot at a discount, and most of the time this is the case, just work your deal.

ESTABLISH THEIR MOTIVE

The key to this objection is to establish their intentions and motives. The key to overcoming this objection, as with most similar objections, is to question it until they come forward with their specific concern. In this case, they will either want to leave or they will want to negotiate. Usually, if they have made it all the way through the sales process and all of their other goals are lining up, the motive is price, meaning they want a discount. Even if the motive is just an excuse to leave, it may be that they don't think an acceptable agreement can be reached. So as long as you have a commitment to purchase if the terms are agreeable, continue your negotiation process. A lower price or the perception of additional value will often counter the reason for them wanting to leave at this late stage.

Note that if they do want a discount, it does not necessarily mean they will not buy without one. In many cases, they may not know what a good price really is and this might just be their attempt to find out. They may just be trying to read your reaction. Many will think to ask, but many will also lack the resolve or desire to make it a condition of the sale. Now is not the time to discount, it's the time to establish the value. Know there is always a risk in discounting your offering too fast. Your customers might be concerned with why you have chosen to discount the price. Makes sense, right? This is why you must always follow the process.

I WANT TO CHECK WITH OTHER COMPANIES

This is the one of the toughest objections to work against because in most cases, this is what they really have in mind. The advice to "shop around" is the most common advice given to anyone looking to purchase. Some people take this to heart.

APPEAL TO THE CUSTOMER'S SENSE OF REASON

The best approach here is to appeal to their sense of reason and fairness. Let your customers know that retail vendors pay about the same on the wholesale market, so the deal here could be as good as anywhere. Even for pre-owned merchandise, the market value is somewhat stable. Establish that your deal is a fair one, then persuade the customer that it is. Let them know that you have given them a great deal. Let them know that you will be there for them after the sale. Reiterate the value of having you and your company as their support. Let them know that their goal should be a great deal up front and great service afterward.

If your emotional responses are not well received, try to reason with them logically. Let them know that even if they went to a hundred companies, they still might not get the lowest price, because one of the thousand other companies would likely beat their deal. Let them know that their goal should be to get a good deal, because the possibility of getting the best possible deal doesn't really exist. The parameters of any deal are subject to change as time goes by, and lots of time will go by as they check with other companies. If their goal is to save money, ask them if their time is worth nothing. Let them know that they can and should be happy with the great deal you have given them and that you will take care of all their servicing needs. Remind them of the value you already have given them with your knowledge and efforts. Remind them of the value of your service department and supporting staff.

To help overcome this objection, here is one more question that may work well. Ask: "If all parameters of the deal were equal, including price, where would you rather buy?" Now ask why. Separate that fact and build value in it. Be persuasive. For this particular objection, you will often have to be diverse in your approach. Analyze your customer for the response that will work the best. Try to persuade them both logically and emotionally and then follow with what appears to be working the most.

If you are still not getting through, you may have to verify if this is really their intention. Although it is not typical here, it may still just be the case. Here again, investigate. Use the exploratory methods discussed in the previous objections, because you must always be sure of the true objection before continuing.

In all circumstances, though, be thorough and persistent, because it is here if your customers leave, they will probably not be back. Someone else will provide these customers with their new solution. This is especially true if you have given them too much information. You can bet your price will never stand as the lowest. Your information will only become leverage for their negotiations elsewhere. If all fails and you are unable to persuade them, at least leave them with some curiosity. Suggest that a better deal or program may come out. However, save the details until they come back. If you can't persuade them, your only hope is their curiosity. If you are able to develop this, they might come back. In any case, always follow up with your customers promptly and try to create or regain their interest in a new visit.

Note that this is often an objection that you can avoid by giving a great presentation, bringing your rapport to a high level, and building the value of purchasing from you and your company. Please know the real overcoming of this objection starts when you say hello.

ALWAYS REVERE THE QUESTION

As you by now may have figured out, it is the question that we rely on as our most important tool in overcoming our customers' objections. Leave no stone unturned in your efforts to understand their concerns and never, ever be afraid to ask. Allow your questions the opportunity to work. When seeking an answer to a resistant question, one of the most effective approaches is to remain silent after you ask. This silence will help pressure an answer. This is never more evident than when seeking to understand an objection. It lessens their ability to evade an answer.

Trust me when I say that your customers really will want you to ask. If they have made it this far in the process, it should be obvious that they really are in the market for a new solution. As long as you make the effort to increase their willingness to participate and keep their receptivity high, your questions will always be welcome. Although some of your research methods or your approach may produce some tension, do not be shy. Just relieve the pressure when necessary. Always look to position yourself to be best received. Understand that having a credibility and a rapport established before reaching this stage is essential in ensuring their willingness to let you continue. If, while proceeding, your rapport starts to run low, be sure to bring it back up. Question, pause, and return to rapport as necessary. Now just add in the persistence to repeat this step as often as it takes, and you should eventually be able to uncover their concern so you can then go about trying to solve it.

WHERE IS THE OBJECTION?

The hardest objection to overcome just may be when there really isn't one. What I mean by this is that there may not be a tangible reason that is stopping your customer from making a purchase. As we stated earlier, this may be the reason for your customer stating, "I want to think about it." I wanted to separate this section a little because I think it is important for a salesperson to be aware of this and understand that different people operate differently. However, I do not want you to feel that this is the norm.

Having no real objection is hard for most salespeople to understand. This is because most people will simply think there is a standard habit in buying. Most people will only believe the level of indecisiveness someone can have will stop at the level that they themselves have. They believe at this point their customers will either want it or not. However, for many people, this is not the case; for many it is just hard to make a decision. Think about how many people go through the whole process and still say, "I want to think about it." Even after multiple attempts to search for the reason behind them not buying, they still leave. Well, please understand that the reason they leave isn't necessarily because they don't want to buy; more likely it is just that they are not able to feel comfortable enough to buy.

These are the people we need to understand. How much more would you sell if you sold to everybody who wanted to think about it? Am I safe to guess probably a lot? Please understand that some people are just uncomfortable with making a decision, any decision. Maybe it was a bad purchase in the past or maybe they were just raised not to spend money. Maybe your customer is the victim of his or her own eccentricities. There is always the possibility of many underlying reasons for the decision-making process that these customers have. These reasons may make no sense to you; however, to excel you will have to become aware of them. Seek to broaden your understanding. Recognize that there isn't always a real reason.

If you are not aware of these possibilities or cannot identify them, you will not be able to influence these customers. Open your mind and accept that people's thoughts or actions do not always make sense.

PROVIDE A LEVEL OF COMFORT

Since these particular customers are uncomfortable with making decisions, our logical initial response should be to make them comfortable. The key to selling these customers is to provide an understanding of their decision process and enable them to feel comfortable with making a decision. Have empathy with these customers. If you open up and share a story about when you had a hard time making a decision, they might lose some of their anxiety. They may find common ground with you.

Understand that these customers will usually want to make a decision, however, they may just need to be persuaded; they may just need some help. Have patience. They want to know they are making the right decision and they want to feel comfortable about it. Slowly confirm and reconfirm that the offered terms are agreeable and that their selected solution fits all of their wants and needs.

For the fearful customer, let them know that their fears are unfounded. For the pattern-driven or ritualistic customer, let them know that their actions do not make sense. They are not logical. Know that these particular customers will typically recognize that their internal halting or persuading factors don't make sense; they just need help in overcoming them. Actually, in many cases these customers probably wish that they could overcome their obstacles and proceed with the purchase. These customers will usually want to buy; they just have to be at peace with all of the loose ends and all of the possible scenarios that may result from their action. Rushing these people will not help. Helping them to patiently visualize, work out, and come to terms with these resulting possibilities will. Too many salespeople give up here. This is because they will only use their own buying steps as a comparison. To be as successful as possible, you cannot do that. You have to realize that different people have different decision-making abilities. Your customers at this point may be having their own internal battles. They may be literally going back and forth in their own minds on what to do. Understand here that it is sometimes difficult for people to make a decision, no matter what the decision is. So work with them. Try to understand them. Put yourself in your customers' state of mind and visualize with them how best to help. Examine what they are saying. Learn to recognize the minor ploys that these customers will self-fabricate to put off the decision and understand them. Know that their self-limiting "ploys" are often just internal mechanisms and are not based on tangible information. In some cases, it may possibly be their self-realization of the possible downside of their decision. In other cases, it may be their wanting to avoid reliving any anguish that may have been caused by previous decisions. They may want to avoid making a mistake. However, because these fears are generally non-specific, they usually can't logically tie this decision to a specific feeling in the past; and this is good, because with the proper show of concern and the proper conveyance of assurance, you can persuade these customers. You can complete your job.

Please know that at this late stage in the process, these customers really want to buy. Their pause or indecision in no way definitively means that they do not want to buy their selected solution. It also does not mean they do not want to buy it now. In fact, it is usually safe to assume that if they went through the whole process and made it to this point, they really want to start enjoying the benefits of your offering; they just want and need some help. They want someone to make them feel comfortable and confident first, but ultimately they want to buy. Allow them all the comfort and opportunity you can.

In some cases, your customers also just might not want to let go of the decision process. Some will simply feel that making a decision now will negate the opportunity of making a decision in the future, and sensible or not, some people will always want to have a decision to ponder. To help overcome this in a light or humorous way, let these customers know that not making a decision is in fact actually making a decision, a decision not to act. If they want to take their new solution home and there isn't really a reason not to, this may just bring their lack of logic to their attention.

Have you ever gone into an electronics store or a home-tool store and come home empty-handed? Did you walk in hoping to come home with a big-screen TV or digital camera, and yet come up with some excuse not to? You put it off. You wanted it but couldn't justify it. Some people may want to buy but cannot. They need help allowing themselves to bring it home. They may want and need someone to give them credible buying advice and steer them in the direction of a good product and a good deal.

180

Try to think of a specific time when you had a hard time making a decision, and see if you can use your understanding to help in your future persuasion attempts. While thinking of a time when you did not act on a purchase for yourself, place yourself in the position of being your own salesperson. Now, as the salesperson, picture yourself as someone who always makes the sale. Your listening, understanding, and problem-solving skills are so good that you have the best qualities of the top five salespeople in your dealership. Well, guess what? You made the sale. Congratulations. How did you do it? How did you convince yourself? Seriously, how? Take the time to visualize your process here and then save it. Use it the next time you get a challenging customer who you can see really wants to buy.

Please understand that in most cases, when someone leaves, they will often move on, at least in the short term, because there are too many other distractions in life. In some cases they may decide to make a similar purchase, however, it probably resulted from a trip to another place of business or a conversation with another salesperson. The moral of this story is that you have to take action when the opportunity exists. You have to take a current interest and develop it into a "today" buying decision.

FINAL THOUGHT

Let me share one fact with you. People do not come into your store or agree to meet with you to get their clothes dry-cleaned. They do not come in for a loaf of bread or some milk. Most people do not even like to enter a sales environment. If they are there, they are there for a reason. They are there for a solution. They will, at some time, invest in one, and you must believe that they want to now.

To be successful in sales, you have to recognize, understand, and be able to overcome your customers' objections. You have to have the understanding, the patience, and the ability to make your customers feel comfortable about you, your offering, your company, and the terms of the deal. It is your job to help and believe in them. Please believe that your customers want to be helped. Give all your customers all the opportunity in the world to own and enjoy their new solution. Give them the status, style, comfort, protection, reliability, and enjoyment they want. Do not let their reactionary, defensive actions or solvable objections stand in the way. Seek out their concerns and hesitations and answer them.

13

STILL CLOSING

E ach time we ask a customer to move forward, we should be sure we have supplied sufficient new information for them to alter their position. Closing certain customers will often take more than one attempt. In fact a close may take many attempts, using many different approaches. Different approaches that will afford new opportunities to raise their offer or lower their demands when negotiating; different approaches that may also establish what is keeping them from moving forward.

ERASE YOUR MEMORY

When closing a complex customer, you want to plan your approach and convey your offering in a way that will best allow your customer to enhance or alter their previous line of thought. This is best accomplished by a new approach. What I mean is that you should always make an effort to restart with a clean slate. Every time you are able to add value or offer new information, you want to ask them to move forward again while showing no memory of their previous demands or the reasons for their hesitation. It is here that you will have to selectively lose some of your memory. Understand that the reason many people do not close is that they cannot let go of their previous demands. However, this is exactly what must happen before you can move forward.

In order to start fresh, you will have to disregard your customer's previous demands or offers and erase them from your memory. Clear your memory, attempt to clear theirs, and then offer them a new opportunity to make a new decision. You do not want to be influenced and do not want to influence them by allowing their previous offer or demands to be present in any form. Take them to a different topic before you reattempt your approach. Leave your closing aside for a moment and go back to your rapport-building stage. Create a gap in their train of thought. Allow your customer to distance their future thoughts from their past thoughts.

Conditioning yourself to believe and act on this line of thinking is very important if you want to be a good closer. You have to understand and trust this to be consistently effective. When your customers' requests are unacceptable:

▪ State that their wants are unacceptable.	Decline
▪ Let them know why.	Enlighten
▪ Bring the conversation back to a personal level.	Erase
▪ Rebuild value or supply new information.	Re-setup
▪ Ask for a new decision.	Re-attempt

You can, and may have to repeat this process many times before your customer's reason for not moving forward is resolved.

In many cases, when a negotiation stalls, you will want to bring in your manager or a skilled closer, but if one is not available, it is up to you to reset the scene and close the deal by yourself. The key here, again, is to erase your recent memory or history and pretend you are meeting your customer for the first time, just as your manager or closer would be. After you have reset your scene with a little rapport, it is usually better to separate yourself from your customer before your new attempt. Get yourself some water or something. When you come back, come as a new person with a new demeanor. Come back with a straight business face. Let them know through your verbal and physical presence that you are there for one reason and one reason only, to close the deal. Remember that at this stage, we have already gone through the whole process and our only goal is to get them to agree to the final figures.

The script that you are about to read is your best approach when re-attempting a close, so learn it and follow it every time. This script is question-based and will engage your customers. This script will allow you to take and keep control and to lead them, step by step, to the sale. I understand that they have already answered all of these questions in the past, in fact, this is part of the key.

If you are an assigned closer, it might start like this:

"Hi, how are you doing? My name is J.B., and I just wanted to take the time to meet you and see if we can put this deal together." Pause. "Is that okay with you? Great."

If you are making another attempt to finish, it may start like this:

"Hi. Okay, I'm back. What I would like to do, if it is okay with you, is go ahead and attempt to work this deal out. Is that okay? Okay, great. I would like to take a second to reconfirm a couple of facts and then get into the details of how we can accomplish this. Is that okay with you? Great."

Reconfirming that this is okay will start the momentum of their yes-saying mood. Trust this.

Restart here.

"Let me ask you a question." Pause to get your customer's attention. "If we were able to work out a deal that is acceptable to you, you would be in a position to move forward, right? Okay, great. Is anyone else involved in this decision? Okay, great. Are there any other questions you have about this offering? Okay, great. If you wanted to, and if the terms were acceptable, you could take this home today, is that correct? Okay, great. If you were to purchase this offering, would you be paying cash or financing? Okay, great. And that cash is available or your credit is of good standing? Okay, great. So what you're saying is that there is nothing stopping you from making this deal, if you want to, right now, right? Okay, great." Slightly nod your head to encourage a positive response to each of your questions. This questioning process is business like and fast paced. It is meant to start the groundwork for your reconfirming agreement.

It is now time to further confirm or reconfirm what you already know is acceptable to them. This may be the terms of the deal or the established benefits of the offering's features. Continue to ask your re-confirming questions until you feel them start to take ownership. These questions will often lead them to realize that they want to, are able to, and emotionally and logically should take ownership.

"You like the cut of the diamonds, right? You like the matching set of earrings, don't you? You are okay with the return policy of our store, aren't you? You feel comfortable with our service so far, don't you? The down payment is agreeable, correct? You can afford them if you choose to, right?"

With your encouragement, your customers have answered in the affirmative in a steady manner. You have now set yourself up to re-close. They have essentially taken ownership by now, so it is now that you should re-attempt your close. If this questioning turns up a non-positive answer, that is the objection that remains. Upon answering it, back up a couple of questions to get the flow started again and then continue.

"Okay then, let's go ahead and agree to our offering. Let me have the address for delivery, and I promise not to delay you any further." Pause while gesturing your approval. Do not speak. Allow for their agreement. Once you have set up your close, the final close can be the one above, any of the question closes from the My Favorite Closes chapter, or any other that caters to them.

What you are doing here is tying up all the loose ends and escalating the flow of their approval. You are first resetting and then rebuilding for your close. If again they do not close, try repeating the whole process, however, this time slower. Look bewildered after every one of their positive responses. Portray that their final answer just isn't making sense. Again, look confused. Show that you want to help with the decision but that you need their help in understanding their hesitation. In any case, if your customers are still there, they are there for a reason, so keep closing until they're closed.

ONE LAST CLOSE

In the spirit of never giving up, I like to have one final close. For this final close, because nothing else has worked, I think it is okay to be a little different. With this close, it will be our intention to wake our customer up a little. This close will challenge them, while also pointing out how their indecision does not add up. Of course you still want to vary your delivery to match up to your customer, but I think it is okay to push a little harder and with a little more personality. Most of the time, I try to deliver it as one of their friends would, kind of like when a person pokes fun at a friend's lack of action when they both know it is best to take action. Here we go.

"Okay, look. The people around us might not know it and you might not be acting like it, but you want to own this. You can fool them, but you can't fool me. I have been doing this for a while and I can feel it. You did not get in your car, drive across town, spend two hours with someone you don't know, give out all your personal information, and go through all these steps not to want to own your selected choice. You said you don't even like shopping. So let's get it on. I didn't drag you out of bed, so let's get going. All I need is your agreement and I will take care of everything else."

FINAL NOTE

Never give up. Seriously.

14

SENSE OF UNDERSTANDING

How we understand someone's needs is by the answers to the questions we ask. However, sometimes people's thoughts, emotions, and concerns will not be readily evident in their answers alone. They may only come out in their facial expressions, body language, or tone of voice. It is here that we will be learning how to observe this nonverbal language and start to develop our sense of understanding.

The purpose of our understanding is to gain an overall image of our customers' personalities and emotions so that we will know how best to interact with each. Our customers' expressions and mannerisms, when combined with other observations will often give us an accurate picture of how to best communicate. The purpose of this chapter is to learn how to quickly and accurately read our customers.

The business of sales involves us in interacting with a wide range of people, all with their own unique emotions, personalities, and preferred styles. In order to transition your customers smoothly through the steps of the buying process, you have to become able to interact successfully with each of your customers on their level. Your ability to quickly read people and adjust your approach to best line up with their individual presence and preferred style of interaction is essential in being able to sell as a top salesperson. Your awareness of this, and the observation skills that you attain, will help develop your ability to understand your customers and determine how to best promote a buying atmosphere for each.

AWARENESS

The first step in developing our sense is to become aware of the importance of recognizing and adapting to the people we meet. Having one's personality and style line up with the customers' and properly reacting to individual emotions is more important than the average salesperson may think. In fact, it is just as important to develop our people knowledge as it is to develop our product knowledge.

Would you communicate with your friends from back home differently than you would with your child's teacher? Do people interact differently at a backyard barbeque than they would at an opera? The answers to these questions should be easy because of the disparity of the scenes. However, in a sales setting it may be a little more difficult to understand your customers' preferred style because you are meeting them out of their typical environment. It is here that you must rely on the available clues. This is why we must raise our level of perception through our observation.

PEOPLE SKILLS

There are three key factors that we will be seeking to learn about here. They are our customers' *personal style*, their *individual emotions*, and their *overall personalities*.

PERSONAL STYLE

One's personal style is what they have chosen to be in the world. It is the manner and style of their behavior. It is the environment they have chosen to exist in and how they have adapted to fit in. It is their job, home, dress, choice of activities, and associates. It is how and where one feels comfortable. It is their hobbies, choice of vacations, and favorite restaurants.

It is important to understand your customers' style to help determine common ground and build rapport. This is the information that is needed to provide comfort for your customers. Your ability to read, understand, and get a feel for your customers' unique styles of interaction is essential to being able to work with them effectively. For example, a priest, a construction worker, and a business executive will probably vary in the style that they have and the manner in which they prefer to do business. To become a top salesperson, you have to be able to work successfully with a diverse range of customers. It is my opinion that our customers' personal style is an intricate part of their buying personality.

INDIVIDUAL EMOTIONS

Your customers' individual emotions are the thoughts or feelings that your customers have and will typically exhibit through their physical language. Some examples may be boredom, excitement, attentiveness, or anxiety. Notice that some of these of these are conducive to selling and some are not. It is important to recognize our customers' emotions so that we can encourage or defuse the varying ones. Fortunately, most of our customers' emotions will have consistent and discernable signs that should become evident with an active evaluation.

I believe that our customers' emotions are both the cause and the effect of their temperament and disposition. Meaning, in some cases a person's actions may be influenced by their emotions at the time, and in other situations a person's more natural emotional makeup may influence a predictable presence in their actions. By understanding this and recognizing our customers' more inherent sets of actions and reactions, we will better know when and to what level we should react to the emotions that appear. The emotions we can't change we should seek to adapt to, and the ones we can we should look to so as to create a more positive sales setting. Some emotions may be innate and part of our customers' overall demeanor; however, with the right approach, certain less innate emotions can often be reshaped to help encourage our customers' receptiveness and participation. A quick example of this would be to calm an angry customer or involve an inattentive customer. Please know that it is a customer's emotional status that will often influence the atmosphere of the sale.

PERSONALITY

One's personality is the totality of their behavioral and emotional characteristics. It is how someone both chooses and reflexively acts and reacts in a setting. It is the person's overall image influenced by his or her temperament, disposition, and behavioral style. It is the person's overall behavioral pattern. It is this personality that we will have to be able to understand and work with to excel as a salesperson. To help accomplish this, we must prepare ourselves to be able to understand our people from the clues that are available.

OBSERVATION

By recognizing our customers' personal style, we are better able to make our customers more comfortable. By recognizing their emotions, we are better equipped to maintain the sale's forward direction and keep them on the right path by reacting with the proper response. By understanding their overall personality type, we are more likely to know what traits to expect and can better prepare ourselves to adapt and respond appropriately. The salespeople who excel in these areas are skillful in observation. By closely observing our customers' actions and reactions, we are often able to read the conscious and subconscious messages they send.

In the first step of our process, we will use our observation skill to establish a proper greeting and help develop common ground. In each of the following steps, we will continue to observe and analyze to help guide our process forward. In the upcoming chapters, we will learn to work with the various emotions and personalities our customers have, but first let's look at increasing our observation skills.

GETTING STARTED

There are different skill levels in a salesperson's ability to observe. These may range from oblivious to ultra-perceptive. If you feel that an ultra-perceptive salesperson will be more successful than one who is oblivious, you have to feel that increasing your ability to observe and effectively read people will help you succeed. Since this is the case, it makes sense to better your observation skill. The process to gain your sense of understanding is something that you will start with and continue to add to throughout your interaction. With each observation, you will be one step closer to being able to read and adapt to the people with whom you will be working.

To get yourself going, start paying more attention to people. Look at their expressions and listen to their tone of voice when they are conversing with others. Think about what you are seeing and hearing. Start with a blank chart and an open mind. Involve all of your senses. Gather information about the people you are observing to help gain clues about the person with whom you are working. How someone dresses, what someone drives, and the jewelry one wears can all help establish the kind of person your customer might be. Ask yourself, "Are these accessories a reflection of their style?" Take these observations and combine them with body language, verbal tone, and mannerisms. Try to recognize the similarities. See if you can package your customer's overall appearance and actions to help form a starting image of their personality type.

ONE'S CHOSEN APPEARANCE

While you cannot definitively state that someone is conservative, flashy, or care-free by the car they drive or the clothes they wear, these characteristics can certainly provide potential clues. Do flashy clothes indicate an out-going personality? Does a conservative dresser indicate a more reserved person? Does a cluttered car or home indicate a busy person? Well, not necessarily, but when taken in the combination of other patterns and the context of their actions, they can certainly give you a basis for your analysis and an idea of how to calculate their character traits to determine how best to interact with them.

The key to bringing this picture into focus is to continue adding to your information as your interaction progresses. Would you greet an outgoing person differently than you would a reserved person? Would you be more direct and informative when presenting to a busy person? Although there is no perfect answer, and this is not an exact science, your observations and ability to read someone quickly are useful early in your interaction and throughout your meeting. As your communication increases and your customer's style becomes more evident, adjust and adapt your presence to theirs. Creating an amicable interaction will always better allow you to have and maintain the control necessary to keep your customers moving towards the sale.

THEIR CHOSEN VEHICLE

The vehicle your customer is currently driving will often offer a host of insight. The color, the size, and the style are just some of the clues available. How your customer has chosen to accessorize their vehicle may also be of aid.

Does their vehicle have personalized license plates? How about an alarm? What is their sound system like? Is there a bumper sticker or a club association sticker on the bumper or windshield? How has it been maintained? Is it old, new, expensive, economical, or flashy?

Take the answers to these questions and match them with the commonly exhibited traits in your previous experiences. Ask yourself, will these items give us a hint into our customer's expressive or personal styles? Is there a basis available here for common ground or insight on how best to line up with their personality? For example, might there be a style difference between the person with a bike rack and the person with a ladder rack? Would these people typically have different interests? Can we use the clues obtained in our observations to help us realize certain interests or gain common ground? Is common ground important in building rapport? Is understanding style important in helping us to offer a comfortable atmosphere? The common answer to these questions in most cases is "Yes." A person's choice of possessions and accessories will often be good indicators of their style and personality; and are also possible topics of conversation.

PLACE OF EMPLOYMENT AND RESIDENCE

The environments that your customers choose to exist in are often an extension of their personality. The type of work that a person does and where someone chooses to live will often give you an indication of certain preferences or even the acquired traits he or she may have.

Would a production foreman of an assembly line likely be less leisurely when selecting a solution than an artist? Would an engineer or accountant be more likely to need logical reasons to help justify their impending purchase? Would a financial advisor be more concerned than most with the investment required for a solution? Does one's work influence one's personality? Would your initial personal style of approach be distinct when attempting to adapt to each preferred style?

Again, an accurate answer to these and other similar questions is likely to be "Yes." Although you cannot conclude a particular buyer's style from this source alone, you should be able to use this information to become further aware of how your customers may conduct themselves in their buying process. The impression of our customers' varying work environments will often be a telling sign of how each will typically prefer to communicate.

Where someone chooses to live is also a good indicator of the atmosphere that they will find comfortable. Learn where your customers live and learn about where they live. Do they live in a sailboat town, a gated community, an industrial town, the inner city, the suburbs, or the country? Has the influence of their neighborhood affected the way they see, approach, or interact with people? Could this be an influence on their level of outgoingness? Their driver's licenses are needed for most identification purposes, so this information is readily available. Their car also may have a community or parking sticker attached.

Understanding your customers' chosen environments may give you the information needed to help you better relate to them. Do not ignore signs that are readily available to you. Always take every opportunity you can to understand and better relate to your customers.

THEIR FRIENDS

The best example of one's preferred style of contact might be found in how they relate with their friends. If your customer is with another person, maybe a coworker or relative, pay attention to how they interact. Use what you see and hear as a reference. Try to recognize the common patterns of their mannerisms and emotions. See if you can gain some insight of your customer's personality type. Are their children with them? How do they relate with them? How people's children act in public is often a good indication of their expectations of others. How they communicate with their kids will often give you an example of what they deem appropriate or acceptable behavior.

COMMUNICATION

Focus on people's voices when they speak. Understand that in many cases, it is not what a person says that conveys the true message but how they say it. Where they put an emphasis in the sentence, the pitch of their tone, and the rate of their speech will all offer insight into their thoughts or intentions.

Does a loud voice indicate someone who needs to be in control? Does fast talking indicate nervousness or anxiety? Should you seek to respond uniquely within these various individual patterns or emotion-driven responses to aid your ability to stay on a positive path?

There are many messages that people will knowingly and unknowingly send when communicating. Determine if there is motive in their voice or if they are even aware that they are altering their voice. Is their tone simply a result of the emotions they are feeling? Add the context of the situation and the variations in their expression to help answer your questions. Know that their tone will often be the projection of their intention. Investigate these questions and more, and you'll begin to understand how effective this information can be in helping you better understand your future sales experiences.

INCREASE YOUR EXPOSURE

The fastest way to increase your ability to observe is to observe. Start watching people. The more people-watching you do, the more information you will have. The more data you have to draw from, the more likely you will be able to make the correct decision on how to proceed. Go out into the world where people gather and prepare to observe. Grab a glass of iced tea and sit down right in the busiest area. Focus on people's actions, mannerisms, and speech and then try to envision their common emotions and personalities. This is enlightening. People-watching can be fun. See how often you can accurately gauge someone's next move or action by watching his or her previous one. Think of this as building your base. Keep watching. Once you can consistently anticipate a person's next move, you will be well on your way to increasing your sales ability.

Please believe and understand that this is not more than is needed to help you sell more effectively. In fact, your perception and your ability to quickly read people is exactly what is needed to sell more effectively. If you can envision a person's typical response to an action or reaction, you will be more likely to influence or persuade their responses and actions. Our ability to observe is the source we must draw from while creating the actions and questions that will produce the responses we seek.

FINE-TUNE YOUR ABILITY

Some good settings to further your people-reading skills are places where a commissioned sale may take place. Other sales-related environments will often give you direct insight into how others interact in the sales process. Some examples may be an electronics store, an appliance center, a furniture showroom, or a franchised clothing store. When you are at work or in another place of business, put yourself in training mode. Learn from the interactions that are taking place. Learn from others. When you are personally involved in the sale, it is hard to be an objective learner. Your own involvement or anxiety will often cloud your ability to observe. Sometimes an outside view is the best when learning.

I have visited the showrooms of many companies, and I can say firsthand that this will often provide a priceless learning experience. While watching and listening to random customers milling around the products, see if you can gain insight into their style and try to formulate an approach that would be comfortable for them. Watch and listen to their expressions, mannerisms, and voices as they are approached by the salesperson. How were they approached and how did they respond? Were you accurate in your estimation? Was the salesperson? How would you have adjusted your own selling style to better complement their likely preferred buying style?

Watch for the patterns of your customers' actions and reactions and prepare your response. Please understand that your ability to read people more effectively will require a continued perception and understanding of every sound or move they make.

SENSE OF FEELING

Have you ever thought a certain way but just couldn't explain it, or had a feeling about something but couldn't put a finger on it? Well, this was probably your subconscious telling you something. During the course of everyday life, too much happens for us to be able to absorb all that we see in our conscious memory. Much of it gets put away in our subconscious memory. As we observe, our subconscious memories are filled with random pictures that will often help guide us in the future. We begin to create an internal file of information that will allow us to start assessing accurate views almost instinctively. This is called our sales intuition. Our intuition is a powerful tool to have in guiding our actions and a large reason why we should always look to increase our exposure in observing people.

When dealing with a particular customer, you might not see or recognize all the signs, but you might get a feeling at some point that something is not quite right. When you feel uncertain, investigate. Many times, the information provided by your subconscious is accurate and should be acknowledged. If something doesn't feel right, stop and seek to understand your best direction. Do not let your sales relationship take a bad turn. Adjust your actions if necessary. If you sense something is wrong in your customers' behavior, inquire. It is often that your customers will appreciate your concern and openness and fill you in. Sometimes your awareness and concern in itself may be enough to defuse it.

Your intuition is an important benefit when becoming a successful salesperson, and one that can be forever improved upon with increased exposure to people. Make sure you listen to your "inner voice" and always look to fill your information file.

REFINE YOUR OWN GROUPS

As a continuation of developing our people skills, we will be taking a look at our customers' emotions in the next chapter and listing some common buying personalities in the following chapter. This is to further our ability in recognizing the differences in the people we will meet and will help form a basis to identify and anticipate our customers' most probable future actions and reactions. However, before I list these, I want you to know that there is no set standard for categorizing emotions or personalities. The realizations of this science are not restricted to anyone's clear measure. There are no defined specifics when it comes to type or classification. There really can't be because of all the variations possible and the fact that this science is based on a premise of opinion and theories. There are no rights or wrongs.

This being the case, you are welcome and encouraged to set up your own learning guide. You can refer to each emotion or "style" as you prefer. For example, your profiles may be named differently than someone else's, depending on the criteria that you have used in narrowing one's characteristics. The more you expand your people-reading abilities, the more experience you can draw from. The further you refine your profiles, the more accurate you will be in relating to each person you meet.

The profiles that I have included in the upcoming chapters are those I have run across the most. In presenting them, I have tried to use the most often referred to or recognized titles so that you will be more likely to relate to them. This is an approach that is designed to aid you in accurately recognizing the signs and patterns available. But again, you are welcome to arrange them in any way that works for you. Emotion and personality headings are not important; what is important is to actively develop a means to better relate to and interact with each of the individual people you will be meeting.

FINAL NOTE

Have you ever heard someone described as having a unique ability to connect with other people? It can't be explained, but people just seem to naturally take a liking to the person? Well, I think this is easily explained by the essence of this chapter.

People skills are important. They are important in our regular everyday life and they are important in our profession of sales. Do not let someone tell you that they are not. Sales is not just presenting an item; it is understanding how to best present an item. Sales is a rhythm. It is a creation of balance between you and your customers. It is a harmony that is created by your ability to react to each physical and emotional move your customers make. It is having the advanced ability to observe, understand, and adapt to people in a way that instantly creates a rhythm or harmony.

Yes, to be successful in sales requires you to have more than one skill and a deeper understanding than most. However, this understanding is achievable and these skills are attainable. Most of what is needed to be successful can be attained merely through your desire to be successful and an open mind. Start now and seek to develop your understanding. Create the ability to interact with your customers in a manner beneficial to each. Allow yourself to start effectively observing and understanding each of the varying people you will soon greet. Once you get started, your ability to interact successfully with others will become second nature and you will soon be well on your way to a more successful career.

15

RECOGNIZING THE SIGNS

T hink of your drive to work in the morning. Try to visualize all of the devices that keep you headed in the right direction. There are lanes, curbs, and an assortment of signs and signals that all lead the way. In order for you to arrive at work, you need to know when to steer left or right, when to slow down, and when to speed up. You rely on being able to understand the signs and signals available to help you reach your destination. Now imagine you didn't notice the signs or were unable to read them. Would you easily find your way?

It is the same when you are trying to sell. If you do not recognize the signs your customers are sending, you will be less likely to complete a sale. Many times, when you were unable to make a sale and couldn't understand why, you were probably missing the signals your customers were providing. However, by developing your ability to observe people's actions and read their conscious and subconscious messages, you will be better prepared to keep your customers on the right path and move toward the sale.

OUR UNDERSTANDING

The importance of our customers' signals lies in the emotions that prompted their emergence. As a salesperson, it is our goal to read and interpret the signs and signals our customers send so that we are better able to recognize and effectively react to each to better promote a buying atmosphere. Now that we have increased our level of observation and developed an understanding of how it will aid in our success, let's focus in on recognizing and responding to some of the specific emotions that will soon present themselves.

In sales, there are both positive and negative emotions that will occur. It is these emotions that will influence the direction and pace of the sale. Some negative emotions may be boredom, frustration, confusion, or impatience. Some positive emotions may be attentiveness, excitement, or interest. To be successful, it is our goal to encourage our customers' positive emotions and yet also defuse their negative emotions. This is how we will both control the path of the sale and keep its forward momentum. However, before we can respond accurately to any of our customers' varying emotions, we must first be able to recognize the signs that indicate an emotion exists and identify its origin. Only then can we respond appropriately.

The most effective way to respond to our customers' emotions is to observe, analyze, understand, and react. We need to *observe* the signals they send, *analyze* them for the emotions involved, *understand* why the emotions occurred, and *react* appropriately. To perform this sequence effectively, we must be both vigilant and perceptive. As salespeople, we must act as emotional screeners. We must be able to encourage, shape, dissuade, or defuse each differing emotion to help keep our customers on the correct path.

As each positive emotion emerges, we must seek to encourage it by responding with positive feedback. As each negative emotion emerges, we must seek to dissuade it or buffer its impact. With both actions, we are looking to keep our customers on track and moving forward.

EMOTIONS, THE SIGNS AND SOLUTIONS

A customer's non-verbal language is a large part of their communication and often a telling sign to their true feelings.

People can choose what they say, but it is hard to disguise the immediate signs of an emotion that will come out in their expressions and movements. These are usually reflex reactions, and are more often than not quite genuine. To help recognize the signs and emotions that you may come across, I have included the more prominent ones here. This listing, along with your observation skills, will help you understand this form of communication. Once you become skilled at recognizing the tell-tale signs of a person's emotions and understand how or why they developed, you should have a more accurate sense of direction for your response. To start, read each of the listed emotions and try to picture them in your past. Try to recall and recognize the signs that existed. Pay close attention to future interactions and try to match up the varying emotions with the signals you see. The more people you interact with, the more aware you will become of the predictable relation between people's outward appearance and their internal thoughts.

Please note the difference between a specific reactionary emotion and a personality type. An emotion is a reaction to a specific cause, whereas a personality type is more of a recurring theme. Adjusting to one's personality requires a continued, flexible state of complementation, whereas an emotion will often require immediate and direct attention. Lets now take a look at some of the more difficult emotions.

DOUBTFUL

Possible signs: focused eyes, squinting, tilted head, one eyebrow higher than the other.

Solution: Verify the facts. Back up to your most recent statement and offer verifying data. Support your presentation with information that will clarify your assertions. If unsure of the reason for doubt, ask if there are any questions. Measure your interaction and seek feedback. You cannot move forward until this is resolved. Credibility is crucial in sales.

BORED

Possible signs: sighing, wandering eyes, twiddling, yawning, stretching, shifting positions, rocking, looking at watch.

Solution: Involve your customer. Stop talking and include them in your presentation. Try involvement questions or physical activity. Listen to their responses and input. Engage them. Turn up the enthusiasm. Enough of the facts; involve their emotions.

FRUSTRATED

Possible signs: exaggerated moves, hand gesturing, shrugging shoulders, repeating themselves.

Solution: Frustration is usually the result of another emotion that was either not recognized or not acknowledged. Identify and alleviate the issue. Once you have found the origin, seek to diffuse their frustration directly by solving or clarifying the issue or concern. If you cannot diffuse it completely, try to lighten it or divert the customer's attention. Take them mentally back to a place they enjoy. The longer this emotion exists, the worse it will get. Understand the source and immediately amend it.

INATTENTIVE

Possible signs: lack of eye contact, swaying, diverted focus.

Solution: Your customers may be preoccupied or losing interest. Determine their source of preoccupation. If they are losing interest, involve them with some open-ended questions. Try to energize them. Turn up the volume. Show empathy and compassion. Put yourself in their position. It may be best to reschedule, depending on the effect their distraction is having. Use your best judgment here. If you have to reschedule, be sure to follow up.

IMPATIENT

Possible signs: heavy sighing, aggressive watch-looking, shifting quickly from side to side, turning flush.

Solution: Stop the process and gain the customer's attention. Apologize for the pace and provide an immediate course of action. This way, they will see the progression as it takes place. Impatience is often caused by uncertainty. Chart your agenda completely and assure them that you will be moving forward. You may even quicken your tempo; however, do not let your customers force you to skip the steps of the sales process. You are always more likely to make a sale by following the process.

ANXIOUS/NERVOUS

Possible signs: erratic movements, pacing, fidgeting, tapping, hand wringing.

Solution: Take your customer's thoughts to a different place. Provide a mental image of a place they enjoy. Guide the conversation back to one of the activities, experiences, or associations learned about in your rapport-building stage. Engage in small talk. Revisit the common ground you have established. Get them to talk about themselves and what they enjoy.

DEFENSIVE

Possible signs: arms folded, closed mouth, backing into a stable stance.

Solution: Defensiveness is usually a direct result of your questioning or interaction. Ease up on your intensity. Use a more empathetic approach. Develop a more thoughtful or caring manner. When questioning, use a softer, less repetitive style.

CONFUSED

Possible signs: hand to forehead, focused look, repeating movements, hand through the hair.

Solution: Clear up the issue. Try to narrow the scope of your presentation by eliminating items of least importance or concern. Identify the source of the issue and then analyze and clarify it. Explain your position. Separate relative issues and provide understanding for each.

INSULTED

Possible signs: focused look, head moved back, pointed eyes.

Solution: Some people are more "touchy" than others. If you accidentally insult someone, ease off quickly. Depending on the context of the situation, you have one of two choices. The first option is to laugh it off as if you were kidding. If you choose this option, try to react quickly with a joke aimed at yourself to balance it out. Self-directed humor will usually help defer most negative feelings. If successful, act as if they too are good sports. Keep the situation as light as possible. The second option is to apologize. Take the blame for your miscalculation and assure them you meant no ill will. You will probably have to convince them that it was not your intention to offend them before they will be receptive to continuing.

EVASIVE

Possible signs: looking away, facing in another direction, less communication.

Solution: It is here that your customers are either hiding something or feel that moving forward will uncover something. It may be a response to a direct question or a result of something they foresee in the future. In either case, either make no notice of it or investigate it, depending on its relevance or importance. If questioning them will not scare them away, search for the reason why. One example would be avoiding something they think is embarrassing, such as not yet having a down payment. Try to determine the reason without putting them on the spot. Use the context of the situation. Vary your approach to balance their anxiety. Be careful. Once you have determined the source of their evasiveness, show understanding or move on quickly, depending on the situation. If people are embarrassed, they will look for the exit, so quickly engage them in another topic. This emotion, if of importance, will usually hinder your ability to move forward until it is resolved.

GUILTY/ CAUGHT IN LIE

Possible signs: looking down or away, turning flush, talking fast, hand over mouth, looking for the nearest exit. Similar to being evasive.

Solutions: Be careful not to press too hard or overemphasize that you caught them. Your goal is to provide a solution, not prove you are right. Most people need credibility. Try to change the subject. If it is really obvious or a conversation stopper, admit your own mistakes or "fibs." See if admitting some of your own miscalculations helps diffuse their discomfort. Try admiring their technique. Laugh it off. Remember, if you embarrass them, they will probably want to hide or leave.

INDECISIVE

Possible signs: moving or looking back and forth, tilting head side to side, focusing and unfocusing.

Solution: Separate the issues and try to clarify the points. Help weigh the positives and the negatives of each. Evaluate the situation, determine the best response, and then seek to influence a resolution. Do not be too aggressive on the decisions you deem beneficial. They may be skeptical of your motives. Portray both sides, presenting the most beneficial side with a little more eloquence.

AGITATED

Possible signs: becoming stiff, turning red, aggressive movements, tenseness.

Solutions: Calm them. Determine the source of their agitation and eliminate or explain it in a compassionate manner. This will often separate them from their current thoughts and help them to relax. Offer sodas or other drinks. Ask if there is anything you can do for them. Try to recognize the reasons for their uneasiness and resolve them before reentering the sales process. Once the situation has been successfully defused, move on.

REACT PROMPTLY

When something comes up that you deem out of place with the usual character of your customer, you should take notice. These are probably emotions that you should address. If, in the course of your presentation, your customer shows signs of boredom or inattentiveness and these are not consistent with their overall personality, immediate action is necessary. Change the direction of your approach to reestablish their interest. You have to become able to recognize and interpret the initial signs of your customer's emotions so you can correct the problem before it becomes more serious. Please understand that just because people are sometimes not forthright in their feelings does not mean that a source of discontent does not exist. Nor does it mean that they would not be open to reconciliation. However, it is often required that you initiate the aid.

THE HIDDEN MESSAGE

As stated earlier, your customer's non-verbal language is often a source of information that will provide a very accurate picture of their true thoughts and feelings. This is because people's reactionary emotions are often less planned or rehearsed. Their immediate reactions will usually portray exactly what they are feeling. However, if given time to think, it is also a form of communication that we may sometimes have to decipher to best understand its true message.

Sometimes your customers' emotions will be hidden or disguised. Some people are better poker players than others. Some will be more skilled in the process of purchasing and will have conditioned themselves to be very controlled in this situation. When people have time to think out or plan their reactions, their true message may be less obvious or even a diversion. We may need to search further for what they are truly feeling. It is here that we need to recognize the inconsistencies in our customers' behaviors and analyze their subsequent signals for any possible underlying motives.

People will sometimes choose to hide or alter their emotions, depending on what they seek to accomplish. For example, in some instances your customers may look to temper their excitement or signs of interest to lower your expectations before negotiating. If you were unable to recognize this, you would probably lose profit. In other instances, your customers may try to hide certain feelings because they will not want to confront you with their concerns. Some customers will feel it is easier to look for the exit than to continue in an uncomfortable experience. Many people will naturally have a very low tolerance for anything not going exactly as planned.

In any example, these are the signs we cannot afford to overlook or misunderstand. These are the customers we need to be able to figure out. As salespeople, we need to be constantly aware and vigilant of the true meaning associated with the signs that our customers will present. We must be able to interpret the information that our customers are trying to provide us versus what they are actually feeling. To be able to handle all of your customers' emotions successfully, both hidden and not, you have to set yourself up to succeed. You must become skilled in analyzing and searching out your customers' true thoughts and emotions. You must always look to optimize your observation skills and further your ability to recognize the signals your customers will provide. Do not underestimate the value of this skill.

SELF-AWARENESS

As salespeople, we too are constantly being watched and read. Our customers are observing our own body language for the thoughts and motives we may have. They are evaluating our own signs and signals to determine factors such as openness, honesty, and concern. Look in the mirror. How is it that you are presented? An important part of being able to communicate effectively is being aware of the emotions we may have and the way they may influence our customers. Become aware of how you look to your customers and establish their perception of you. Understand the effects that your emotions may have on others. Is your expression one of warmth? Is your body language one of openness? Is your tone of voice one of consideration? Are you aware of both the positive and negative qualities you have when interacting with people? Before you can ever seek to grow as a salesperson, you must first recognize your strengths and weaknesses. Only then can you go about eliminating the negatives and increasing the positives.

FINAL NOTE

Although there may be an unlimited number of variations of emotions, the ones that I have listed for you here are the ones you will come across most often. Take the time to study these emotions and their solutions and then apply them in your real life experiences. Understand the cause and effect of each and look to develop your ability by increasing your observation of these and other recognizable emotions in your future. Seek to develop a response ability that will allow you to better understand and react to each of your customers' emotions and use it effectively to help keep them on a forward path. Become aware of how powerful one's emotions are and how significantly they can affect the direction of your sale.

All too often, your customer may feel the easiest way to reclaim a level of comfort is to search for a new salesperson, one who can promote a pleasant interaction and a smooth process. Do not let this happen to you. Be observant, understanding, and prepared. Develop the concern and the reactionary instinct needed to help keep your customers headed in the right direction: the ownership of their new solution.

16

BUYING PERSONALITIES

Have you ever heard someone say, "We just didn't hit it off" or, "They rubbed me the wrong way"? Have you ever walked away from an uncomfortable encounter and had someone else say, "Oh, he's all right; you just have to get used to him"?

The reality is that you probably have and probably will again. So will your customers. To them, their visit is not about you, and they too will walk away. The customers you meet are there to satisfy a need for themselves and will always want to work with someone with whom they feel comfortable. Your customers will not feel the need to adapt to you. It is up to us to make sure we adjust our actions and reactions to them. Please understand that your customers will always naturally respond better to someone who is able to relate to them on their level. If you want to sell with more success, you have to be able to adapt to your customers' preferred styles of doing business. This includes recognizing and understanding your customers' overall personal and emotional presences and then establishing the best approach for each. It is knowing when and how to act and react to your customers' buying personalities.

AWARENESS

If we are able to understand how our customers will likely react to specific actions, we will better know what to do or say in each situation. We will better know how to motivate, influence, and ultimately involve them in purchasing. The first step in improving our abilities is to become aware of the different personalities we will soon meet. It is then that we can go about better understanding their most typical actions and reactions so we are able to interact with each in an effective way.

Would you approach a shy person differently than you would an aggressive person? Would you be more likely to persuade an emotional person with information or enthusiasm? What is the best approach when closing a defensive customer?

You are losing sales if you expect your customers to follow your own personality lead. It is you who must recognize, understand, and adapt to theirs. This is to set the selling scene; it is to put yourself in the best possible position to influence them by increasing their acceptance of you. You must understand that different approaches will work better with different people. Your awareness of this, and the observation skills that you have learned in the recent chapters, will soon allow you to instinctively know your best course of action for each person and situation. Once you become skilled at identifying certain personality traits and recognizing their various typical actions and reactions, these answers, and even the less common ones, should be easily resolved.

BUYER TYPES

Each customer we meet will usually have a guiding theme. This theme will be determined by the sum of their individual traits and will influence their actions and reactions in the buying process. This theme is their buying personality. It is the entirety of their personal style and emotional characteristics.

Although there are probably more than a hundred different variations of buyer types, I think most buyers will fall into only a handful. The subtle differences in each trait and the influence of additional traits will often produce a defined group of buying personalities. In the last chapter, we went over how to handle our customers' emotions. In this chapter, we will learn how to work with our customers in their entirety by recognizing and adapting to their buying personalities.

Please note that as with our customers' emotions, there is also no exact science to understanding one's personality. There is only a reference created by common patterns of behavior. The examples that I will give you here are the ones that I have found to be the most common. Here again, I have tried to use the most recognized terms so that you will be able to identify with them. However, again, feel free to add to your learning by observing and taking note of what works best for you. My goal in this chapter is to help you gain a basic understanding of the communication and buying styles preferred by different people. It is to help become aware of your own personality and to give you some helpful advice on how best to understand others. Let's take a look.

CUSTOMERS' GUIDING FACTORS

I have found that one's outward emotional presence consists mainly of two factors. The first and most prominent is one's level of outgoingness. The second is to what degree one is positive or not. Their measure of outgoingness will set their tempo, and the degree to which they are positive will set their attitude and degree of amiability. The combination of these factors will be the overall image of the more prominent traits exhibited in the customers we meet.

Take some time to picture the people you have interacted with in the past. I think it is important at this stage for you to agree that these are in fact two of the most acceptable dominant traits, to best allow my upcoming reasoning to be effective in helping you. Think about a person's most recognizable trait. What stands out most when first meeting someone? Isn't his or her level of outgoingness the most noticeable? Isn't it also one of the first characteristics mentioned when describing somebody?

Think of all the adjectives used to describe a person's degree of outgoingness: shy, loud, reserved, aggressive, quiet, obnoxious, passive, forward, docile, pressing, timid, uninhibited, controlled, explosive, yielding, and more. Wouldn't you agree it is a person's most noted attribute? Isn't it also a factor that we should be appreciably aware of when talking to or working with someone? Isn't it also a factor that could easily sour a relationship if misaligned?

Similarly, wouldn't you say that one's positive or negative demeanor is the likely next candidate for describing someone's outward characterization? Think here too of all the commonly used descriptions when describing someone's overall demeanor: nice, mean, easy-going, nasty, optimistic, indifferent, cheerful, happy, dismal, pleasant, polite, rude, enjoyable, and on and on. Isn't it acceptable to believe that one's positive or negative approach is a major factor in deciding the effectiveness of an encounter? Isn't this also an attribute that should be noted before you try to adapt to the person attached to these descriptions?

I believe the answer to these questions is reasonably "Yes." I also believe that by recognizing these factors and effectively adjusting to complement them, we will better be on our way to becoming skilled and effective salespeople. Let's now take a look at understanding the outgoing and the reserved customer, and how each is influenced by our secondary factor, and the most suitable approach for each.

```
/-------------------------------*---------------------------------/
        NEUTRAL
        OUTGOING
        RESERVED
/-------------------------------*---------------------------------/
        NEUTRAL
        POSITIVE
        NEGATIVE
```

OUTGOING

A person's most obvious characteristic is whether he or she is outgoing. His or her approach and style of conversation will quickly tell you this. Your first step in working with an outgoing customer is to determine whether they are more positive or negative. Since they are outgoing, you will find out quickly, which is good because there is a very different approach that will work best for each. Here is a look.

Outgoing/positive: Outgoing/positive people are your ideal customers. They are confident, upbeat, and able to make decisions. Present yourself in a similar fashion. Greet these customers with enthusiasm. Inspire their dreams and encourage their visualizations. It is safe to present your ideas. Although they may have their own plans, they will often be receptive to yours. Seek to build your credibility early. Share and explain your beliefs on what would be their best choices and then initiate action. Keep the energy high and the mood positive, and move forward.

Outgoing/negative: The negative outgoing person is usually the most difficult to work with. Expect an abrasive person. Because they are outgoing, they will usually act on each negative feeling. If they are doubtful, they will interrogate you. If they are impatient, they will rush you. If they are unengaged, they will dismiss you. They will force their opinions, attitudes, and moods on you. They will seek and expect a confrontational experience. The best approach is to stay positive and friendly yet keep your focus. Do not let your emotions get involved. If you remain positive and stay away from the actions that will produce negativity, you can sell these customers. Lean more to a business approach in the early stages. Keep your composure. Allow your customers to work away from their negativity with your credible information and pleasant demeanor. Let them release their energy. It is good to be confident here but not overly assertive, as this may cause conflict. Listen more than you talk. Stay away from statements. These are the customers who will be best influenced by your amicable questioning skills. When questioning, do so slowly, allowing them to be more receptive. Do not let them rattle you. They will be less likely to argue if you refuse to argue. Present your ideas in an open manner and allow room for their additions. By involving them, they will feel that it was their idea. Their credibility is important to them. Let them take the credit and roll with the decisions that will take you toward the sale. Compliment them on their ideas and proceed to realize them. Because their nature is negative, this customer will often get a negative response from the people they meet. If you do not return their negative nature, they will soon see you as different from everyone else. If you can withstand their abuse with a smile, you will sell them their solution. You will then probably have a new friend for life.

RESERVED

Reserved customers are more difficult to understand. It is here that you will have to investigate whether they are also influenced by being positive or negative. Your best approach is to take it slow in the beginning to let them open up. With an approach that is too outgoing you will quickly send these customers to the door. You want to ease them into a more outgoing position with a calm, amicable approach.

You will have to engage these customers at their level before they will become receptive in following. Think of how a magnet works when you are with this type of customer. Understand that you will have to move close enough to their style and comfort before you will be able to influence their direction. If you too move in a reserved manner, you will attract them. Once you are connected, it will be easier to encourage a more open and outgoing presence. Let's look at the best approach to both the negative and positive influencing factors.

Reserved/positive: Reserved/positive customers are often agreeable to your ideas, but they may need some encouragement to get them to take action. My first advice here is to start with the process that will increase their level of outgoingness. The key to these customers is to mildly encourage them to open up. Start with an approach that is complementary to theirs and then slowly look to increase their energy. Because these customers are also positive, they will often want to open up; they will just not be good at it. Small, common-ground questions are your best choice here. Search for their interests and encourage them to share them with you. Gradually seek to increase their level of enthusiasm with your interest in them and their activities. Transfer the resulting atmosphere of your rapport into your sales presentation. Just because they are slow to open up doesn't mean they won't. Get them started, and keep them rolling. Because they are already positive, focus on their emotions. Once they feel comfortable with you, they will buy from you.

Reserved/negative: Okay, here we have some work to do. These customers will not be receptive to your ideas or help. These customers were usually satisfied with their previous solution and are often there only to fulfill a need. These are the customers who have often done their own research and will look to you only as someone who is there to handle the paperwork. Be cautious in your attempts to get them to open up or become more positive with an approach that is too outgoing. Your best approach here is to start slow and take it one step at a time. Do the best you can to accommodate their personality and transition through each step. Be informative and professional. Treat them in a business-like manner. If you move too fast, you will lose them. They will look for reasons to leave. Do not give them any. Ask questions and stay away from statements. Seek to have them alter their own views with the answers to your carefully structured and leading inquiries. Gradually look to increase the impact of each question as they begin to move in your direction.

These customers are a challenge. They are also a great learning experience. Although it is always recommended to attempt to influence your customers' buying attitudes, it is not completely necessary to accomplish here. These customers' decisions are usually based on need and logic, therefore they will not feel it necessary to have established a connection with you to buy from you. If they are in the early stages of looking, it may be difficult to promote a "today" purchase. However, after you create the best atmosphere you possibly can, ask for the sale. Always ask for the sale. However, if it is to no avail, do not give up on future possibilities. It is often this customer's nature not to allow himself or herself to move forward until ready. Put yourself in a favorable position and follow up with them respectfully, as most competing salespeople will not.

KEEP YOUR FOCUS

In sales, you will meet many different personalities. Some will be a combination of several types. Some will be pleasant and some will be difficult. The most important point to realize when working with a challenging personality is never to involve your own harmful emotions. Keep your feelings in check. Think of yourself as a skilled professional who only responds in a manner that is productive for the sale and for gaining you and your company a future customer. Many of your customers will have different wants and desires and different styles of interaction. You must learn to work with each to be successful.

A SALESPERSON'S APPROACH

The most likely determining factor in our ability to complete a purchase is our customer's receptiveness. Even if we completely understand our customer's needs and effectively establish a favorable direction, our advice will mean nothing if they are not receptive to our approach and influence. Our goal is to create an atmosphere in which we are best able to persuade our customers to move forward.

The most successful salesperson is one who is able to develop an outgoing and positive interaction with his or her customers. This approach is to create an optimum performance in our sales ability and also to encourage maximum receptivity in our customers. Although some of our customers' traits are innate and will not be easily altered, I believe that many can be with a positive and outgoing presence. If we are able to have our customers open up and respond, they are more likely to be receptive to our persuasion and more likely to purchase. We want to be able to interact where we are knowledgeable, informative, and persuasive, and where our customers are interested, receptive, and motivated. This is best accomplished by an outgoing and positive personality. This is the temperament and disposition that will create our best possible selling atmosphere. An obvious first step in becoming more successful is to become aware of your presence and acquire these qualities.

KEEP YOUR PERSPECTIVE

For the new salespeople reading this, I want to take a minute to make clear what may be possibly a confusing objective. The reason we seek to understand and adapt to our customers is not to follow them or their lead; in fact, it is the opposite. It is to better have them follow our lead. It is to increase our ability to set and control the pace and the direction of the sale by aligning our personalities to best complement theirs. It is to effectively influence the resulting actions of our customers to better create a more positive selling atmosphere. All too often, new or inexperienced salespeople get so caught up in adapting to customers that they unknowingly allow their customers to take control of the sales. And, depending on their customers' intentions, the control they seek may not lead them in the direction of purchasing from them. Understand the effect of this before proceeding. Different customers will always operate with different agendas. Remain positive, but be aware of the underlying motives of some of the customers with whom you will be working. It is okay to love your customers; just be careful. Some people are genuine and naturally good people. However, others will need encouragement to show these qualities. This is why we adapt; this is why we seek to help them adapt.

Always look to keep your sales process moving forward by providing a comfortable experience for each customer without losing sight of your sales-related plans. Understand that our ultimate goal is for our customers to proceed through the steps of the process with little or no personality resistance at all. Look to adapt and adjust to your customers' personality to better allow and keep the forward path of your sale, not to allow them to lead you. Please work this out, because understanding this is very important to becoming successful. If people are comfortable in their surroundings and in working with you, they are much more likely to be agreeable in their move toward the sale. Always seek to adapt both for and before control of the sale.

UNIQUE BUYER TYPES

To get a better feel for the personality types you will meet and better ways to handle them, I have included some of the more challenging ones here. Now that we have examined how best to interact with the general style of buyer types, we will now take a closer look at how to effectively interact with some common variations. Before we do, though, I would like to qualify this as well. During the buying process, many customers, if not most, will adopt a different personality than their usual selves. A sales setting is often a place that may produce a greater anxiety than other environments. My advice is to not be offended or discouraged by your customers' actions. Learn to maintain your composure and always seek to balance their presence.

THE AGREEABLE AND THE NON-AGREEABLE

I think that to some extent, all customers are either mostly agreeable or not. Where one person will typically agree with what is said, another will typically state the other side. One will see the similarities in an item and the other will see the differences. Picture yourself saying something to a customer as random as, "This is a nice truck, isn't it?" About half the time, a person will respond, "Yes, it is." This would be your agreeable person. Another, however, will introduce the counterpoint. This person, from the non-agreeable group, will introduce the negative. Their response might be, "Well, sure, but not as nice as others I've seen" or, "It's okay, but not as nice as they used to make." Where one person will agree, another will debate or argue every point you make. It is important to recognize early on which type you are dealing with because you will need to proceed very differently with each. It is best to know how each individual customer will likely react to your actions so you can best adjust your approach to receive the desired response.

With agreeable customers, you want to be consultative and provide credible information. You want to present knowledge and advice that will lead them to a buying decision. You want to be confident and move at a good pace. Do not hesitate or look for the objection that is not there. Many salespeople actually falter with this style of customer because they get stalled waiting for objections that may not be coming.

Non-agreeable customers must be handled with greater care. You have to be careful not to present information that will produce a debatable response. The easiest way to do this is to present your information and carry on a conversation that is question-based. If you think about it, it is hard for people to state the opposite of a question. Instead of saying, "This is a nice truck," try, "Do you think this is a nice truck?" Or you could also phrase this question to encourage a positive response. You could ask, "What do you like about this truck?" Since you asked what they liked, their response will be structured toward the positive.

Another example is using the reverse. Lead in the opposite direction. For example, if a potential model has the options they like, you might say, "I do have a blue one with similar options, but it might be too dark for you." Where the agreeable will accept your advice, the non-agreeable will want to see it.

Please understand the importance of this. A sale has its own unique path. Customers will not usually take the lead or keep us moving in the right direction. Sometimes it is in your best interest to encourage a certain direction, and sometimes it is best to discourage one. In any case, it is always important to understand how best to encourage each of your customers.

THE EMOTIONAL

Emotional buyers will respond to your enthusiasm. They are outgoing people who will share their thoughts. They are often excitable and open to new ideas. It is with these people that you will want to be positive, upbeat, and agreeable. Keep your conversations personable and your presentations energized. Create a show, and they will gladly follow. Try to move along at a steady pace right into the paperwork and assume the sale.

THE UNEMOTIONAL

Unemotional buyers will move methodically. They usually try to satisfy their needs with logical reasons. Provide these customers with information. Try to raise their enthusiasm by

224

slowly bringing them along. Have patience. Try to motivate them; however, do not get frustrated if they do not respond initially to your energy or enthusiasm. Some people are just less emotional. Be professional, business-like, and informative. These customers will eventually buy, so simply follow your plan.

THE INDECISIVE

These customers are not able to make up their mind. Generally, these people want to make a decision, but can't. They need and want help. Patience and gentle persistence is the approach I recommend here. Most salespeople will have a hard time selling these customers because they are unable to understand what motivates them. This is because I think the goal may be better placed on what is hindering them. Search for their concerns. Validate their selection. Confirm that your offering satisfies their wants and needs. Reiterate that their selection was chosen based on their criteria. Confirm the value of your offering and then confirm that they are making a good decision.

Think back to a decision you had a hard time making. Empathize with your customer and support them. This customer wants to make a decision; they just need help being convinced. Patience and persistence are the key factors in closing these sales.

THE LOGICAL THINKER

This is your practical buyer. This person will usually buy only to accommodate their needs. It is important to be knowledgeable and credible with this customer. This customer will seek information for the basis of their decision, and you must be able to provide it. Pushing this customer will not result in a sale. This customer has to determine all the angles in their own mind before making a decision. Your goal should be to help sort through the information and then point out how and why it makes sense. Help confirm that everything adds up. Once you have confirmed this "type," ease back on the buying pressure and stick with the facts. This style of customer will typically not be interested in fancy options and will not even discuss discounts before they have accepted their pending solution. They will methodically move from one aspect of the sale to the next, completing each before advancing to the next. Try to emulate their form of thinking when discussing how the facts line up, and then try to satisfy their goals. Although it is rare that you will sell this customer on their first visit, with the proper investment and the right answers, you may. If not, follow up. Like unemotional customers, logical customers do buy, just in steps. Logical steps.

THE ANGRY BUYER

This customer will be very demanding and will usually have to get their way. To sell this customer, you must first let them work out why they are upset. Listen to and acknowledge their reasoning. Do not fear the angry customer. As long as you are able to defuse their anger, they will buy. Let them vent. Acknowledge that they are upset and empathize with them. Show concern. Do not try to sell them until they release their anger. Know that most of the time, their demeanor is a just precautionary front. Kindness is your best resource. True empathetic listening and understanding will always help them to open up to you. You are a professional; do not let yourself get caught up in their hostility. Your goal is to sell a solution, not to fight. Control your emotions, and you will control the sale.

THE IMPATIENT BUYER

This buyer may cause you to skip the steps. This is one of the hardest customers to work with for anyone new in the business. Many times, this particular customer will look to increase their level of impatience just to further take and show control. Which is fine, but only if they are on the path to purchasing from you. If they are not, you will have to take control before you can sell them.

The key to selling this customer is determining the direction of the sale, not the pace of the sale. Most of the time, a customer's impatience is just their own state of mind. They are in a hurry because they feel they are in a hurry. If they are headed in the direction of making a purchase, share control with your own fast pace. Don't skip or rush your steps, just eliminate the downtime. Keep them on the move and mentally busy.

Although they may press you for it, do not let them rush you into giving them a discount before you can present the figures. You will lose this customer faster than most if you give out pricing information too fast. Confirm their commitment before the negotiation. If they are there just for information, take control and slow them down. They will generally give you the time as long as they feel you are not wasting their time. A skilled salesperson will be able to present the value stage and still keep them engaged. When you do get a commitment, proceed with the sale. This customer will buy; they just don't want to be bothered with the little things. Close the deal and let them know that you will make certain that everything is handled properly.

THE ARROGANT BUYER

This is the customer with the big ego. With the right approach, this customer could be one of your easiest sales. The first step is to position yourself as one of the top salespeople.

Act with strength and confidence. This customer will not want to work with the average; they will only want to work with the best. Their opinion of themselves requires this. Let them know of your sales awards or achievements.

Once you have positioned yourself as the best, try to feed and challenge their ego at the same time. Listen to their stories and admire their power. Let them be the center of your attention. Create a show just for them. Give them the experience they are looking for and then ask them to buy. If you set this up right, they will purchase without hesitation. They will not want to seem indecisive or unable to buy. Your confidence will pay off. The key is to recognize these customers early and not react negatively or confront them. Remember, your goal is to make a sale and not get caught up in an emotional battle. Think of yourself as a technician. Respond appropriately without involving your own emotions.

THE SHOPPER

This customer wants to stop at every store in town and compare prices. The only way to sell this customer is to slow them down. If you give them a discounted figure before you have an established commitment to buy, you will have a very short future with them, because they will leave to meet with your competitor. Your resolve to build value in yourself and your company will be tested against their resolve to get a price and leave. It is that simple. If you give in to their demands, you will have lost any chance of making a sale.

This style of customer may also appear within many other personalities. It is with this customer that you will have to adapt to their personality while still taking the steps to best influence a decision. Keep your personality attuned to theirs, but keep your resolve as well. These customers are usually very skilled at making you believe that the only way to sell them is by giving them a price. However, you must trust your process. Do not

228

allow this customer to intimidate or influence your actions. No exceptions, never offer up discounted figures before you have taken the time to create a bond, built the appropriate value, and received a commitment to do business.

FINAL NOTE

Many customers have come to expect a lack of compatibility with salespeople and will often set up excuses upon their arrival. I think the most popular is "I'm just looking." Well, yes, they are just looking, unless they happen to find a salesperson who they feel is open, receptive, and capable of handling their needs, someone who will be pleasant to deal with and complementary to their style.

The people you meet will often be willing to work with you; however, they will not feel the need to adapt to you. Think of some of your own experiences. Have you ever come up with an excuse to leave because you didn't feel comfortable with the person you were with? Selling is not just handing over a cheeseburger and some fries. People know that they will have to spend some time with you. Most will only want to proceed with a transaction that is pleasant. Please know that most customers will not tell you that they are uncomfortable. They will not want a confrontation. They will just humor you with some questions and ask for a card and a brochure. However, could this result be different if the salesperson's personality complemented theirs? Yes. People will want to interact with you and will want to purchase from you if they find comfort in working with you. Believe this, and success will be yours.

17

TRAITS OF A TOP SALESPERSON

C haracter traits are something that we all have. They are the habits we have formed over time, which guide us in everything we seek to accomplish. They are the patterns we have developed that shape both the way we express ourselves and the way we interact in the world. Our set of traits is our unconscious guide. They have an impact on everything we do, including the results we are able to accomplish.

Certain habits are conducive to being a successful salesperson and certain habits are not. Picture the difference in production of someone who is proactive versus someone who is inactive. Picture the objection-handling ability of someone who is persistent versus someone who is easily dissuaded. It is easy to understand that the person with the better habits or traits will make the most sales. Now, take a minute to picture some of your own traits and the effect that they may have in your sales efforts. Seek to understand the influence that each will have to offer. Analyze your current presence and determine the traits that you may need to keep, add, or adjust. In order to be successful, we have to be able to align ourselves with the proper traits and look to eliminate or diminish the traits that may be holding us back. We must understand the power of our traits and the importance they have in influencing our ability to succeed.

Our traits are our control pattern. They are the parameters that create and influence the functions we perform. Our set of traits is our guide, much like a program on a computer is its guide. For the computer, its scope of production and its depth of effectiveness lie in the program in which it operates. The computer only has the ability to perform as it was programmed to perform. Similarly, we as salespeople are only able to perform as our current set of traits, or program, will allow as well. In order to obtain a different set of results or more enhanced results, we, like the computer, must be reprogrammed or rewired.

Fortunately for us, we have the ability to rewrite our own program. By adding new traits or amending some of our current ones, we can improve ourselves and increase our sales. Developing the proper character traits needed to increase your ability in sales takes the same two ingredients involved in reading this book. They are desire and initiative. For example, you have the desire to become a better salesperson, so you took the initiative to read this book. In order to redefine your character and achieve success in sales, you have to be able to search for and further attain these factors. You must identify and examine the traits or habits that you have and then establish an effort to adjust them to better succeed. You must understand the strength of their influence and then develop your own strength to amend them. Understand that your traits or habits were not formed overnight, and it may take considerable energy to alter them or develop new ones. However, if it is truly your desire to achieve higher results, search for the initiative. Find the strength within yourself and strive to take control of your own success. If you have the initiative and strength to get started, time and momentum will aid in your goal. Your positive traits will only become stronger and more dominant.

OUR TRAITS DEFINED

Here are some of the traits, habits, and philosophies that successful salespeople share.

MOTIVATED

The number one trait of a salesperson comes from within. It is the desire to succeed. While we all have some measure of desire, only those who are able to define and utilize theirs will become the best. To help develop your own personal motivation, you must first realize what inspires you to want to succeed. Only then can you go about working on how best to achieve your success.

The profession of sales is a business for performers. It offers us the freedom and opportunity to achieve any level of success we want. If you have chosen sales as your career, there is probably something within you that desires to succeed. To help further establish your driving factors, choose what you most want to accomplish and use it to aid in your motivation. Look at yourself and at the other people involved in your success. What factors in your life will further encourage your success? Do you owe it to yourself or your family to be successful? Do you owe it to your place of employment? Search for what will jumpstart your initiative. There is usually some stimulus in one's life that will trigger this. What is yours? Determine what will motivate you. Is it status? Money? Security? Achievement? If competition is a motivation, track previous sales results and strive to surpass them. If money is a motivation, reach for that next level of bonus.

Determine what drives you. I cannot say this more emphatically. Find your own direction. Before you can ever be successful in any career, you must first look within. Upon finding your motivations, keep them active and present in your mind, allowing them to influence your production. This will set yourself up for success and will take the work out of selling. It will keep you active in successfully enacting your skill, not just in performing a task. Please know that the people who excel in their fields are the ones who are motivated to succeed, not the ones who feel they are just working a job.

GOAL DRIVEN

One of the most inspiring factors in one's motivation is often found in the quest of achieving a goal that you have set for yourself. A goal is an accomplishment that you wish to attain. It is something that is desired and set to encourage your motivation. It is the prize that you will enjoy when you are able to accomplish what you have set out to do. Whether you are new to the sales business or just looking to restart your career, you can help increase your motivation by setting yourself up with some specific goals.

When setting your goals, take the time to think about the things you want. Imagine some of the items or rewards that will motivate you. A goal can only be effective if it is something that you truly desire. Goals should be meant to challenge you, to push you further than you would normally go. Your goal is the achievement; your motivation is to attain the reward tied to it. To help get your motivation started, look to set the goals that will encourage your actions and reward you in the near future. Enjoy your reward and use it as motivation for your next goal. Then start to mix in your reachable, short-term goals with some long-term goals to help build for your future. Once you set your goals, build the framework to achieve them. Position your goals to influence your actions. Build one step at a time. Soon the achievement will become part of your reward.

An example of a long-term goal is to create your own customers. To achieve this goal, become your own business and do your own marketing. Stay in contact with your previous customers and ask for referrals. Do not let your success be based on how many people come in the door or on current market conditions. Goals such as this will help keep you focused in the present and ensure your future success. Use the mix of your goals as a basis for long-term success.

If you take pride in sales as your profession and look at it as your future, take the time to set your goals. You will not be able to release your energy or completely reach your potential without first understanding your motivations and establishing your goals.

PROACTIVE

Being proactive means harnessing the power of your inner motivations and taking action. It is to act or react when an opportunity arises. It is having the ability to generate your own self-determined opportunities. This trait, when combined with persistence, is the difference between success and failure. This is the one trait all successful salespeople have in common.

Successful salespeople are opportunity focused. When you see an opportunity, move forward. Learn what it takes to be a top salesperson and then develop the skills needed to become one. Take control of your actions. Do not let your dreams and goals pass you by. Prepare yourself to succeed, and then take the initiative to succeed. Create your path and take it. Start with the principles and steps in this book. Learn the proper selling skills, develop your people skills, and put yourself in motion. Do not fear your mistakes. Use them to learn and grow. Once you are in motion, you will always be able to adjust your actions to better succeed.

CREDIBLE

Credibility is the key to being persuasive. You have to be able to present yourself as a credible salesperson before you will ever be able to influence your customers. If your customers do not feel you are capable of providing the proper information, they will not be open to your influence.

Credibility requires two elements. First, you have to demonstrate understanding of your customer and their needs. This is accomplished by asking the proper discovery questions and listening to their answers. Your customer has to believe that you understand their needs before they will feel that you are capable of helping them. Secondly, you must be able to give accurate advice. This is where your product knowledge will come into play. Know your line of offerings and know how their benefits relate to your customers' wants and needs. Position yourself as an expert. You must be able to portray a belief in yourself and in your product line before you can ever expect a customer to believe in you or be influenced by your advice. A top salesperson will always seek to establish their credibility by asking the proper questions, and will solidify their credibility by providing the proper guidance.

PERSISTENT

Selling is a series of steps in which you may find resistance to proceed with each. Successful selling is having the persistence to amicably overcome resistance. Being successful is finding the answer to the question. Being persistent is having the drive to find the answer. The salespeople who are willing to try different solutions and refuse to give up are the ones who will sell the most. Understand that having the persistence to solve your customers' needs, concerns, and hesitations will often lead you to the sale.

There is a philosophy in our business that it often takes several attempts to close a deal, however, without persistence, we would never know. Do not deny yourself the benefit of persistence by not wanting to feel too forward. Persistence and being too forward are not the same. Let me explain. Being "too forward" is asking your customer to make a move without offering new information. Persistence is creatively searching for a new direction and then asking your customer to make a new decision based on the new information. Understand that your customers are there for a reason and may just want to be persuaded. Always have the perseverance to help your customers achieve what they came for: a nice, new, shiny solution.

AWARE

Become aware of what it takes to be successful, aware of yourself, your customers, and your process. Aware of your customers' actions, emotions, and personalities. Aware of your plan, where you want to go, and the obstacles along the way. Become aware of the training and practice needed to be successful, and aware that the process is your best path. Aware of your projection, their projection, and the best response for each. Aware of the possibilities.

Perception. I'm really not trying to be too philosophical here; I just believe that for some it is essential to increase their awareness. You would probably not cross the street without looking, so don't do it while selling. You might not make it across. Allow yourself the ability to realize any and all possibilities.

Picture yourself walking down the beach, carefree and oblivious to the world. Now, picture yourself walking down a dark street, late at night, in a bad part of town. Take note of how your awareness will increase. Different circumstances will always require different levels of awareness.

When you are selling or preparing yourself to sell, become aware. Allow yourself to recognize your setting. Think of yourself as a quarterback dropping back to pass. Don't be oblivious to the charging defense; scan your perimeter when looking down field, and afford yourself the opportunity to bob and weave. Don't let yourself be tackled.

CURIOUS

Curiosity is having the desire to understand what it takes to make a sale. It is what will drive the top salespeople to question and search for the answers to each obstacle presented. Discovering information is crucial to gaining insight on how best to proceed. A successful questioning process is the key to success, and curiosity is its driving factor.

While we all have some level of curiosity, some of us will just need to develop ours a little further to be completely effective in sales. Start by asking why and why not. When you are in a selling situation and face an obstacle, make sure there are no unanswered questions. Leave no stone unturned. Develop the interest to understand why things are the way they are. Do not accept resistance, yours or theirs, or failure, without trying to understand what happened and why it happened. Make a commitment to yourself to understand what will motivate and persuade your customers to move forward. When you know why or why not, you may have the right answer. Without knowing why, you will not know why. Use your curiosity and persistence to search for the answers.

VISUALIZING

Visualization is the act of creating an experience in your mind before it actually happens. It is preparing your path and recognizing the obstacles you may encounter before they occur. It is understanding how to better act and react in your future experiences. With your imagination and creativity, you have the opportunity to visualize the sale ahead of time. Visualization is a powerful tool in the sales process. It will help prepare your path and allow you to recognize the obstacles you may encounter. The actual sales process will become more fluid because it will be a re-creation of your visualization. This will often give you the comfort you need to better act and react in each situation.

Before your appointments arrive, picture the process and the direction you will take throughout the sale. Imagine your greeting and how you will build rapport. Think of the questions you will use to identify the customers' needs and imagine the responses they may have. Play the different scenarios over and over until you can feel them. This will give you the opportunity for a practice run and enable you to feel more comfortable and better prepared for the real thing. Practice makes perfect. Isn't it easier to do something a second or third time? Try this and you will instantly see the results. Your visualization will have a positive influence on your sales ability.

DRESSED FOR SUCCESS

As the saying goes, first impressions are everything. Take the time to increase the quality and credibility of your clothes. Look the part. Dress professionally. Salespeople who are professionally dressed are more influential with their customers. Understand that this is your first available offering of credibility. Think of some of the people you see for services in your life. You would not want your business attorney to be dressed as a plumber and you would not want your plumber to be dressed as an attorney. They would both lack credibility. If your plumber showed up wearing a suit and tie, you would question his ability to handle the service you had asked him to accomplish. It is the same in sales. You have to look the part to be credible. You should look successful without overdoing it. If you are selling Swiss watches or diamond rings, a suit and tie may be recommended. If you are selling commercial roofing materials, a clean pair of slacks and a pressed company shirt may be a more suitable choice.

POSITIVELY PRESENTED

Have you ever heard the expression, "He has a magnetic personality"? If so, try to picture the person they were talking about. This may be an actor, a politician, the leader of a country, or the salesman next to you. Their nature is such that anyone can identify with them. Well, examine what enables them to be so liked and accepted. Is it their smile, their charm, their character? Study the compassion they share with other people. Recognize the traits in them that you can adapt to your own self. Learn to create a level of evenness and consistency when you are interacting with different people and situations. Work with people in a way that is comfortable for them. Be a person of the people. Create a presence. The ability to radiate your good nature will increase your ability to persuade.

PROPERLY INFLUENCED

There are many different qualities of salespeople. It is important to emulate the top salespeople and not the underachiever. Where one will help you, the other will drag you down. Watch and learn from the best. How do they greet people? How do they carry themselves? What is their presentation style? What questions do they ask? Take note of the successes of each and analyze their actions. How does each manage his or her time? How do successful salespeople get their prospects? Different people have different levels of success for a reason. Search for these reasons and examine the qualities that may aid in your success.

UNDERSTANDING

Understanding is the result of knowledge and experience. When giving advice during an active deal, I notice that it is more likely to be followed when an explanation of why you are giving it is attached. If you think about it, this makes sense. Without having the knowledge, your confidence will likely be less represented. If you understand why, you will be much more likely to react better.

Become understanding. Investigate what you do not know. Investigate before, during, and after the sale. Successful understanding requires knowledge and schooling. Understand that you were not born with all the learning and training you need. The better educated a person is, the more likely they will be a positive part of society. It is the same in sales. The more knowledgeable you are, the more understanding you will be and the more successful you will become. Understanding. The word itself is so deep that it is hard even to know where to start. First of all, accept this: Understanding is the basis of all agreements. If you think about it, this makes sense. All things that go wrong usually do so because of a misunderstanding.

Understanding takes knowledge, experience, and an open mind. It necessitates a willingness to allow for a new view. For ourselves, we have to realize that we are not all-knowing. We can't always impose our way of thought on the people we meet. For our customers, we must look to open their understanding. They must understand how they will benefit.

"I don't understand."

"Well, let me explain it to you."

Please understand that this is the start and continuance of the most productive conversation possible. Understanding is the reason for the need for higher education. It takes an understanding to provide an understanding. We need an open mind and a willingness to learn what we do not yet know. One of the most negative qualities a salesperson may have is a closed mind, the unwillingness to further their learning. The biggest handicap of any underperforming salesperson is the lack of understanding; the lack of understanding that they might be doing something wrong and the lack of understanding or belief that they should even look to improve.

I often see the same frustrated salespeople at the month's end. I even get frustrated for them. Month after month, some will try to help. Some will try to teach them how to be better. Still, month after month, some will not improve, and this, I think, is due to understanding. They do not understand the need or even their ability to improve. However, they should. They have to recognize that there is a reason that certain salespeople will always outsell them. Successful salespeople will always look to increase their understanding. They will open their mind and allow new information to enter. Understand that learning and knowledge will provide the tools and your ever-increasing understanding will provide your success.

When most people improve, and I think all successful people reading this will agree, they improve all of a sudden, seemingly overnight. The reason for this is that they have found their understanding. They have accepted that there is more than one perspective. When you find it, it is like a switch. Bam. On. Please take a minute and analyze where you are at in relation to your field. Take off your blinders and allow yourself the possibility of a new outlook. Find your understanding.

EMPATHETIC AND COMPASSIONATE

Empathy is involvement. It is being so close to your customers that you can actually feel what they are feeling. It is a deep form of understanding. When they are mad, you are mad for them. When they are happy, you are also happy. You feel their pain and you feel their excitement. You share their emotions as if they were your own. Our business is one that will often produce an atmosphere of anxiety. The better you are at defusing this anxiety, the more success you will have. There is no greater bond or feeling of trust than that of someone who is willing to make an emotional investment in someone else's needs.

EMOTIONALLY IN CHECK

Like it or not, people are judged more by their outward emotions than their inner character. How we appear is how we are seen. How we are received will often be influenced by the nature of our current emotions. Understand that it is the disposition of our emotions that we will be judged upon, not how we are thinking or feeling inside.

In sales, it is important to be able to diminish the signs of our negative emotions and be more open and expressive with our positive ones. To present a more positive and outgoing presence, we must understand our projection and learn to control the reactions that our emotions exhibit. Although we may not have a choice in our capacity to feel an emotion, our reactions can be one of choice. Accept your emotions, but control your reactions. Understand that a positive presence will have a positive impact with your customers and a negative presence will have an adverse effect. In a sales interaction, is it more important that you are confident or is it more important to project that you are confident? Understand that even the most successful salespeople have the same emotions and capacities as others; however, they have learned to keep their emotions in check. How we portray ourselves will ultimately decide the effect that we will have in our interactions. Become aware of your presence, and always seek to adjust your actions to form a more open and positive image.

COMPETITIVE

Motivation, desire, drive, ambition. All good qualities. In fact, in sales, all essential qualities. In any successful performance, an energy of some sort is needed. All successful flights will have to be powered.

We are all capable of performing better if we want to. We are all capable of learning more and practicing harder if we want to. Well, some of us just need to want to. Have you ever heard: "You have to want it"? Well, you have to want it. Find the spark that will ignite your desire and energy. Become competitive. Compete with yourself by comparing previous results or line yourself up against your fellow salespeople. Competition. Think about it. Just place it in front of you and see if it will entice you.

I'm not exactly sure what it takes to become competitive. For some, I think that they just hate to lose, and this hatred of losing requires them to search for the reasons of why they lost and to further investigate how they can win. This will push them to further their learning and practice harder. Well, see if this works for you. Think of a competitive exercise and see if you like winning. When creating your competition, publicly announce your intention, as this will often encourage victory. Winning really is better than losing, and it is often quite addictive. See if it will drive you.

Think of running a lap around a track. If someone were to take a certain time to complete the course, they may be satisfied. However, if their partner were to complete it faster, there might be an incentive to run faster next time. Please recognize that without competitions or measured performances, we would not have the accomplishments we have. There would be no book of world records. If we didn't keep score, there would be no practice. Why would there be? No one would have to wake up early and train. There would be no drills, no laps, no time trials, and no eliminations. There would be no training, no guides, no special shoes, or special gloves. No one would have to pay extra to have their golf club balanced. There would be no aspirations in sports or in industry. We would not have the quality we have in our current products or even be able to afford them. Without competition there would be no incentive to improve. There wouldn't be a Super Bowl or a Stanley Cup. But you know what, there is. There is because people like to compete and they like to win.

When someone sells more than you, let it bother you. Understand that it is okay to win and to want to win. Finding the drive to improve your abilities is the key to all future success. Whether it's an internal motivation, a goal, a sense of accomplishment, an obsession, or an inspired competitiveness, allow yourself to be motivated. It's okay to be a winner and it's okay to be driven.

OBSESSED

The ultimate commitment. Everything has a time and place, and most of the time, moderation and balance are qualities to embrace. But I think this should be mainly for our obsessive people. For normal people, a little of this trait may be of some good use. The focus that this trait requires could be of benefit.

I understand that it is not healthy to obsess over anything, but it may just provide the determination that is needed to excel.

Any Olympic athlete, award-winning actor, or doctorate-level student has, you can believe, been a little obsessed in their learning and training. You have to believe and understand that a natural ability will only take you so far. There will always be different degrees of performance, and yet there will often be a shared level of drive for those who excel. To reach a higher high, you will have to increase your ability and keep increasing. Please recognize that even the pros practice and drill every day. If it takes a little extra practice and focus to increase your skill, go ahead and focus. If you get a little carried away in your training, don't be too quick to look for a change. Being obsessed requires a certain degree of perfection. It mandates a focus that requires a determination you may not ordinarily demand. This may just be the right trait for you to investigate. This trait will often allow your other positive traits and your success to better emerge.

IN CONTROL OF YOUR FEARS

Do not let fear limit your success. Fear is the biggest reason that most people do not accomplish their goals or fail to succeed. This may be the fear of rejection, fear of failure, or even the fear of the unknown. Fear may stop you from asking for the close and making the sale. Fear may also limit your level of persistence. You may be the most courteous and knowledgeable salesperson around, but if you do not have the courage to ask for the sale, your efforts will be wasted. Recognize and conquer your fears. The best cure for fear is knowledge. Knowledge will give you the confidence you need to perform at a high level. If you learn your product, learn your process, and understand the best way to work with your customers, your fear will always be surpassed by your natural confidence.

Examine the worst-case scenario. Picture the worst result that could happen because of your action and then think of your response. If you rehearse positive responses, you will always feel more confident to proceed. If you do not try for something, you will not achieve it. This is equal to not having tried at all. So, when you think about it, you have nothing to lose.

FINAL NOTE

There is such a slight difference between being able to sell in the top of your field and selling with the average. But it happens every month. In the same time period, one salesperson will consistently outsell another. In our business, a deal is measured in inches. It is the little things that are imperceptible to most that make the difference. For those of you who have been in the business for even a little while, I have a question. Have you ever looked at the leading salespeople and wondered how they do it? What is it that they are doing? Well, I'll tell you. It is attaining qualities and traits such as these. It is creating a connection with their customers that exceeds the circumstance of their meeting. Do not doubt the effect of aligning yourself with the proper traits.

18

QUESTIONS ANSWERED

B eing successful in sales takes a lot of self-acceptance and pride. It is essential to have a clear mind and to be at peace with yourself and your profession to perform at your best. Whether your customers are aware of it or not, they have an innate ability to sense your credibility and confidence. This is the same credibility and confidence needed to influence and persuade your customers to make a purchase. In order to have this belief portrayed in your sales interactions, you must be free of doubt and have a clear focus.

I want to take the time now in the hopes of clearing up some of the questions you may have regarding your own perceptions of the sales profession. Here are some of the most frequently asked questions that I have heard from beginning salespeople, and some advice regarding those questions.

SALES IS AN HONEST PROFESSION

The whole business world revolves around the salesperson. Without sales, there would be no business at all. Without salespeople, no one would ever enjoy any of the wonderful products that are available. Have you ever asked yourself, "How can I be comfortable being a salesperson with all of the less-than-positive references people will make?" Well, my answer to this is simple. Be proud of yourself and your profession.

Being a good salesperson is not a compromise of your principles. In fact, all truly successful salespeople rank high in honesty, integrity, and compassion. Refuse to let anyone think of sales as a dishonest profession. The goal of a successful salesperson is to bring a solution and enjoyment into his or her customers' lives by helping them get what they need and want. Learn to care for your customers, and you will soon have plenty of them in your future.

SINCERITY

Many new or unsuccessful salespeople have a difficult time understanding their values and principles and the roles they play in our business. For many, it is not just how our business is sometimes viewed from the outside; it is also their internal set of morals or conscience that they may question.

Many salespeople will ask themselves, "How can I be sincere when my goal is to sell?" The answer to this is simple as well. The more sincere you are, the more offerings you will sell. The more needs you understand, the more solutions you will provide. If your goal is to push your customers into something you know doesn't suit them, you will fail in this career. People are perceptive, and they will sense your intentions. The lack of trust you exhibit will limit your ability to persuade. You can only expect to build a truly productive career if you establish yourself as a person with a solid character. Please believe that it is the person who wants to understand people and their needs who will sell the most. Before you can succeed in any field, you must first set yourself up to succeed. Write, rewrite, or enhance your values. Become the person it takes to be successful, and you soon will be well on your way.

INCOME

Money is an important factor in our world. It is a product that will often be attained and thought of in many positive and not-so-positive manners, justifiably or not. As a result, many of you will ask, "How can I justify making a profit when my goal is supposed to be to help people?"

This is a good question, so let's reason it out.

Think of yourself as a problem solver, someone who seeks a solution for the needs of the people. You provide a service. You are a professional. You have studied your offerings and practiced your skills. If you can help your customers with a solution, do you deserve to be compensated? If you can accurately assess their goals and use your knowledge and understanding to help find an offering that is right for them, should your time and effort be rewarded? The answer is, "Yes."

Our company is a business, and there are costs and incomes associated with running a business. Think of other professionals who provide a service. Would you expect a doctor, a lawyer, an agent, or an accountant to accurately solve and complete your needs for free? When they handle your task, are they compensated? Yes, they are, and you should be too. Any successful company in the world is probably that way for a reason. In our business and in most businesses there is a high level of competition. We are in an open market. Staying profitable and in business takes quality production and sensible pricing. If all good companies gave away their products or services, there wouldn't be any good companies left. In the business world, the companies that perform the best are also the most successful. Shouldn't we, if we perform well, be compensated well?

The key to becoming and remaining a successful salesperson is to provide a quality experience and a successful solution and yet be profitable for you and your company. This way, you and company can be there for your customers when they need service and when they are looking for their next solution. All successful businesses have created a balance of quality service and fair compensation, and it should be no different for our business. A salesperson's level of profit should always be equal to the level of service they provide and the performance they achieve. The more solutions you provide and the better you are at performing your service, the more successful you deserve to become. Please believe that all successful salespeople are and should be dedicated to providing their services well and being well compensated.

REJECTION

How do I deal with rejection?

There's no way around it, rejection is part of our profession. It is safe to say that not everyone will want all of your offerings all of the time. However, even knowing this, salespeople will still sometimes feel the impact of being rejected and will ask themselves how they can overcome their feelings. Well, the answer to this is not so simple. It is something we must look at and analyze from different perspectives. It is something we will constantly face, and must condition ourselves to understand and overcome.

In the sales profession, there are generally two levels of rejection. There are the small rejections that we will continually face during the sales process, and then there are the more permanent rejections that will occur when we are unable to complete a sale. Let's take a look at each.

During the sales process, you will often be confronted with a show of resistance from your customers. This rejection is often reactionary and usually only temporary. It is impossible for customers to agree with everything that occurs or that is asked of them. Learn to accept this and only proceed in the manner that is best. Do not let this resistance inhibit your ability to proceed. With this rejection, know that persistence, creativity, credibility, and knowledge are the keys to your success. You will have temporary rejections, so prepare for them. Understand their occurrence and follow your process to overcome them.

In the second instance, you may incur a more definitive rejection. When you are unable to complete a sale, your sense of rejection may be a little more difficult to shake. It is here that you will need to look from within and concentrate on the positives. You will need to stop, focus, and start again.

You will need to refocus your confidence and self-belief. Sales is a learning experience, and there is no better way to learn than by facing adversity. Do not get down on yourself or your career. Look at this rejection only as temporary and as a learning experience. Be happy in knowing that you will most likely return to your next interaction more knowledgeable and better able to handle any of the future obstacles you will encounter.

When dealing with rejection, take solace in knowing that you will never truly learn what not to do until you fail, and failing is always only temporary as long as you keep your willingness to learn. It is only when you no longer feel that you need to learn and move forward that you set yourself up to fail. Understand what happened and learn from it. With every new customer comes a new start. If you keep moving forward and retain each experience as a learning one, you will always succeed in the long run.

SALES DOWNTURN

Sales slumps occur. Why? Well, there is no easy answer to this question either. A sales slump is a period of time in which few or no sales occur. The reasoning for this may be, and usually is, due to a combination of cyclical happenings and a negative outlook. As I said earlier, confidence and belief in oneself is important in sales, and the lack of this produced by a slump may help to perpetuate our slide. Make sense? Let's take a further look and start at the beginning.

To help ease the possibility of letting yourself get uninspired, try to understand that sales are just sometimes strong or weak at certain times. Sometimes it rains more often than at other times. We really do not know why. In our case, it may just be the various cycles that occur in people's lives. An example of this can often be found by looking at a typical Saturday. Have you ever noticed that at certain times, there is no one in the store, and at other times, you're packed full? Why? Did everyone get together and time their visit? Well, not likely. Sometimes it just works that way. Now, if you expand this time period to a typical week or month, you will see the potential for slow periods in longer lengths of time as well.

There are also more rational reasons. Other explanations, such as large public events, economic swings, seasonal changes, and even the timely influence of local and national news may also enhance or affect certain patterns of traffic. These reasons, along with a lack of momentum, may in fact produce a period of slowness. However, this reasoning, explainable or not, should not be an excuse for you not to be optimistic about your future. With hard work, effort, and persistence, you will eventually break through any slump and continue to higher ground.

Stay prepared and focused on your future. Use this philosophy to keep from getting discouraged; however, at the same time, always continue to implement the many ways to help lighten any impending slump. Be proactive in your prospecting efforts. Take the time to create your future success and limit your exposure to the downturns. Prospecting will help supply you with additional opportunities and keep you occupied. It will also help you to be less likely affected by any temporary downturn, explainable or not. This is always a sure path for a brighter future.

There will always be factors that are not in your control. However, there will also always be factors that are in your control. Take control of the factors that are and you will be less likely guided by the factors that are not. Understand that sales is not a "sit back and wait," patterned event. Sales is a continual process of production and preparation for production. If production is low, focus on preparing for a more productive tomorrow by being active today. Oh, and always remember, slump or no slump, with one sale you're right back in the game.

FINAL NOTE

There will always be the potential for uncertainties to occur in our profession. Sales is a profession that will constantly be subjected to outside factors and influences. You will often be challenged by the questions that present themselves. However, know that most of your questions can be resolved if you take the time to work them through. Know that your desire and resolve to succeed will give you the strength and the answers to succeed. Learn to look at each question as it applies to you, and search for the understanding that works best. Resolve your questions, overcome your obstacles, and establish your direction. Do not allow yourself to be influenced in a negative way by anything or anyone. Develop your sense of peace and stay determined to maintain it throughout your career.

19

THE TELEPHONE

The telephone has a purpose in our business, and it is a definitive one. The purpose of the telephone is to arrange a convenient time for you and your customers to meet. It is for you to set an appointment. Unless you are in telephone sales, you should not try to negotiate a deal over the phone. Your only motive when calling or answering should be to have your party visit you and your offerings in person.

The first step in becoming better at having your customers visit is to realize that what the salesperson says and does will matter more than the specifics of what your company is offering. Some salespeople are consistently successful at getting people to visit and some are not. So it would make sense that it is the salesperson's ability that will decide if a customer makes a visit more than what their company has to offer. There are too many special deals and choices available to consistently meet with your customers on the value of your offerings alone. You have to create and develop your customers' interest to learn more, and then motivate them to make a visit. Yes, it is true that all of your information may line up perfectly, and they may come in based solely on that; however, the odds are not in your favor. Additionally, in most cases, even if your information does line up, many will still check other avenues first for comparison.

Your customers' desire to learn more and make a visit is best created by both developing your rapport and by leaving some information to their curiosity. If you have not sufficiently created a rapport with your customers, they will have no common interest in visiting. Additionally, if you offer all of the details of your sale or inventory up front and answer all of their questions, they will lack the curiosity needed to visit. They won't need to come in; they will already have the information needed to decide if they should make a visit. They will also have the information they need to make a comparison elsewhere. They will then call the next place to see if there is a better deal there, and there always will be. However, by creating a bond and balancing the answers they give, a skilled salesperson can be engaging and leave their customers' curiosity intact, the same curiosity needed to increase their desire to find out more and encourage a visit.

If you think about it, it is quite evident that the customers who call or accept your call will be some of your best candidates for a sale. They will have somehow developed an interest or question regarding your offerings and will be looking to fulfill a desire. In most cases, they have seen an ad and have an interest in a specific offering. It is your job to take this interest and further create the desire for them to make the trip or meet in person. It is your job to make an appointment.

UNDERSTANDING THE CALL: THEIR OBJECTIVE, YOUR OBJECTIVE, AND THE BEST PATH TO ACHIEVE YOUR OBJECTIVE.

Before we get into the specifics of each step, I want to take a minute to help further your understanding of the call. I want you to understand how to make the call work for you.

EACH OF OUR OBJECTIVES

The most important factor in understanding the call is to recognize the intent of your calling customers. It is to trust and believe that the sole reason for your customers' call is to decide if they will visit or not. It is to decide if your offerings warrant further research. This is why, to be most effective, you should only look to increase their desire to visit. You should not provide them with too much information or try to complete a sale. You must first have your customers visit before you can get them to buy, and this is always best accomplished by increasing their curiosity, not by satisfying it.

It is not yet time for your customers to decide if they will purchase or not. Your customers are calling, not visiting. They are calling to decide if they will visit, not if they will purchase. Move one step at a time. Have them agree to visit before you start the process of your sale. When taking or making a call, you have to believe, have faith in, and condition yourself to focus on one goal: setting the appointment. You also have to be careful to follow your plan, because unlike when you are with someone in person, there is very little opportunity to correct a mistake over the phone.

CONTROL AND RAPPORT: ALWAYS THE BEST PATH

The most important factor in being able to consistently set an appointment is for you, the salesperson, to establish the structure of the call. It is to set and influence the overall mood and direction of the conversation by taking the lead in conducting the call. It is to take control of the call by initiating what questions are asked and to what measure questions are answered, all while being proactive in increasing the customer's agreeability and receptivity in feeling both interested and desirous to learn more. In order to best follow the process of the call and complete our goals, we will need to set the pace, tone, and direction of the call.

TAKE THE LEAD

Taking the lead in a conversation is having the ability to decide what is said and what is asked and controlling the extent of each. The party with control of the conversation can always take the call in the direction they choose. Without control of the call, we will be obligated to respond to our callers' inquires;

with control of the call, they will be inclined to respond to ours. To best position ourselves to set an appointment, we need to establish the lead in the conversation to limit the information we are obligated to give and also to effectively give us the position to receive the information we want.

In most conversations, there is a recognized etiquette of responding to inquiries with an answer, not a question. It is also accepted etiquette for people not to start asking questions or offering an opinion until an opening is presented. This is why we must sometimes look to create an opening for our turn to inquire. The best way to establish the control of a conversation is to be the one who initiates the questions, and the best way to keep control is by promptly following each of our questions up with another. We must always look to open or respond with a question and always look to position ourselves to question. Because our customers will likely open their conversations with a question, we must look to exchange our position. To best accomplish this, simply answer their question and then, without pause, follow your answer up with a question of your own. Answer, then ask. If ignored and asked another, answer again, lightly of course, and politely ask again. Also, never allow a silence or a gap in your conversation when your customers have finished responding. If you do, they will generally feel obligated to ask a question and that will hand over the control. When you set your direction with the questions you ask and the answers they give, you can then start to look for the transitional questions that will help lead you into asking for the appointment.

When answering your customers' initial questions, you may want to respond either directly or indirectly, depending on the finality of the information they request. If you feel their question is unlikely to be followed by another or will offer the ability they need to make a decision to visit or not, do not look to answer in a definitive manner.

MAINTAIN THEIR WILLINGNESS

Achieving control in a sales setting is always best accomplished with skill and finesse. Being effective on the phone is directly dependent on the amiability and flexibility of your individual customer. Our ability to be successful necessitates a balance; you want to stick to your objectives and accomplish all you can, but you also want to acquire their agreement and receptiveness by adjusting your approach.

Our goal on the phone is to keep our customers on the receiving end of our questions to establish control, and yet also to keep them agreeable. If your customers are aggressive, calm them. If your customers are tentative, relax them. In some cases, you may even have to suspend your goals until you are able to realign your harmony. Understand that there is always going to be the possibility of contention in our phone conversations. Because your callers want to gain information to determine if they will make a visit, and we want to limit their information to keep their curiosity intact, the conversation may not always flow smoothly. Some customers will be more demanding and less accommodating than others. Everyone is different, and you will always have to be able to adapt to each.

If your customers insist on having their inquiries addressed first and offer little leeway in answering, you may have to adjust your response. You may have to deliver some level of satisfaction before attempting to find the information you want. Answer their question to the degree necessary to reacquire bliss before again attempting to gain control. Think of a ballet, not combat, when trying to achieve the control you need to receive the information you want. Keep a balance between the information you request and their willingness to give. Sometimes, if you keep pushing, they will keep backing up. However, if you ease off, it may be easier to get them to move forward. They will often become more involved and thus be more receptive.

Gaining the control to set an appointment is going to take some understanding and practice on your part; however, to be successful, this is essential. You will often have to decide quickly between accommodating their approach and furthering their desire. You will have to understand people and be able to read them quickly. You will have to be able to determine when they are bluffing and when they are not. You will have to know when to be flexible and when to seize control.

KEEP YOUR PROCESS

When attempting to adjust, be sure to only adjust your approach and not your process. Your best chance for success is to stay with your process and only act and react to the varying people you meet. Know that the mood of any conversation can still be one of pleasantness even while you seek the completion of your goals, because the nature of any conversation is always more determined by how something is said than by the specifics of what is said. You may have to do more or less adapting, adjusting, and rapport building, depending upon your customers' demeanors, but you always want to maintain your goals and your optimism. Do not become frustrated here; always believe in your ability to master this. Keep your customers' receptivity and agreeability increased by adjusting your approach, yet remain persistent in your goal to increase their curiosity and set an appointment.

In most cases, control is either forced or finessed. One is smooth and one is not. When communicating on the phone, especially in the early stages, the control you seek should always be one of agreeable influence.

Even though most salespeople will understand this best approach, they will still have to remain focused here to succeed. There will always be the temptation to give in to their customer's response, skip the process, and answer all of their questions. Although following the process is the best path to the sale, it is not always the easiest to maintain; it always seems the path of least resistance is the most inviting. Be strong and follow your path.

THE TELEPHONE PROCESS

We are best able to create an interest and increase the odds of having our customers visit by having a set process and following it every time. This process is simple and solely designed to lead our customers to the appointment.

- Answer with enthusiasm.
- Answer initial question lightly if needed.
- Get caller's name and number.
- Create a bond.
- Further caller's curiosity.
- Set the appointment.
- Confirm the appointment.
- Reconfirm the appointment.

That is all there is to it. Do not overcomplicate it or let yourself get off track. Take and keep control of the conversation. Keep it simple. Do not let potential customers run you all over the lot in the search for minor details; this will only limit the possibility of them visiting. Simply let them know that all of their questions will be answered upon your meeting. Complete each step and then move on to the next. Accomplish all of the steps of this process during this one call, while their interest still exists.

EACH GOAL EXPLAINED

ANSWER WITH ENTHUSIASM

Your first goal is to answer the phone right. Clear your mind and turn it on. Eliminate your distractions. Answer politely and professionally, and most importantly, with some enthusiasm. Your attitude and desire are the two most important factors when conversing on the phone. Understand that people want to communicate with people who are bright, cheerful, and pleasant, and do not want to communicate with those who are not. Know that your manner and expression will set the tone of your conversation. Greet your callers with a smile, give them a chance to identify why they are calling, and then set your path. A large part of your ability to sell successfully relies on having the proper phone skills, and these skills start here. Focus on the person you are speaking with and start to create their desire to visit.

THEIR NAME AND NUMBER

Okay, get their name and number. No problem, you might say. I'll just ask. Well, not so fast. It's not always that easy. There may be a lot more involved. Many customers will often not be forthcoming with their information. In fact, you will often have to plan to receive this information and should always take the necessary steps to ensure you are in the best position to obtain it.

When getting our customers' names and numbers, there are three things we should understand. They are: why we want this information, why our customers may not want to give us this information, and most importantly, how to get this information. Let's look at each.

WHY WE WANT THEIR NAME AND NUMBER

Obtaining our customers' return information is our first objective. We want their name and their phone number. We always want to be able to follow up with any potential customer. If for some reason an appointment cannot be set after the first conversation, it would make sense to have a way to get back in touch with them, right? Additionally, there may be times when we do not have access to the facts that will help us create their interest. At other times, we may not be at our best and need another opportunity to try to initiate a visit. Always make sure you get their names and numbers.

Another reason to get your customer's name is so that you can use it in your conversation. Remember, people wake up and respond when they hear their own name. Also, if we have their name and number, they will be less likely to skip the appointment or not ask for you when they arrive. Makes sense, right?

WHY THEY MAY NOT WANT TO OFFER THEIR NAMES AND NUMBERS

Many times, our customers may be hesitant about giving their information out. They will prefer to be in control of how their contact with you is initiated. The customer you are speaking with may have had a bad experience in the past. They may have had an inexperienced salesperson re-contact them too often with no new reason to visit, and will guard against this happening again.

Many customers have prepared themselves for this and have become very good at guarding their information. For example, you may ask, "Sir, can I have your name and number?" And he might respond, "Um, I am at work," "I am in transit," "I'm hard to get ahold of," "I can't be reached," "I can't take incoming calls," "I don't want anyone to know I am looking at purchasing a new solution," "I am leaving town later tonight,"

"I don't have a phone," etc. Who can blame them? No one likes to deal with an inexperienced, pushy salesperson. However, we need this information, so we will have to separate ourselves from the average and become skilled in getting this information and handling it properly when we do. Let's take a look.

HOW BEST TO GET THEIR NAME AND NUMBER

Our best chance of getting our customers' names and numbers is to obtain them before we satisfy their own quest for information. Believe this, this is true. If you give too much information early on, they will be much less likely to give you their information later. We will then be at their mercy to contact us, and they probably won't. Although you may be tempted to start with the information they seek, restrain yourself. The best way to sell is to do what's right to sell, not to blindly do all that your customers ask. Hold on to some of your key points until they give you the information you want. People are generally willing to give something if they want something. However, if they already have what they want, they will not feel the need to give up anything. They will often no longer feel they need your service and will not want to be contacted. So, first things first.

START WITH THE EASIEST ROUTE

The key to obtaining your customer's information is to request it smoothly and receive it without letting on that you are in fact holding onto your information. This is where you must become practiced and skilled. This is the exact point where you must be calm and well-versed.

When trying to get your caller's name and number, we should take a look at some laws of human nature. The first law here is "Give to get." Many people are naturally instilled with a sense of fair play. Although a person may resist making the first move, she or he will almost always be willing to follow your lead. Here's our plan.

GIVE TO GET

Right before you ask your customer for their name, give them yours. It is human nature for people to return the favor. "Hi, my name is J.B., and yours is?" Most people will offer you theirs just to be on even ground. They will feel the need to balance the flow of information. This need for balance is formed with the help of society, peer pressure, and even schooling. This balance is considered playing fair. Also, the pause and silence that follows your request will always help encourage your customer to answer.

If the caller ignores your inquiry and continues with a question, try again. Answer their question lightly and repeat with the question you desire. An example response may be, "Let me get that information for you. My name is J.B., and your name is?" or "Yes, ma'am, I believe that offer is still available; let me check that. My name is J.B., and yours is?" When you are finished, pause and wait for their response. If your customers do not respond as you wish, just calmly and nicely repeat this step. Give a brief answer and again ask for their name. Just be sure to keep the conversation friendly and flowing. In some cases, you may have to take a break with some rapport-building conversation and maybe even offer additional indirect information before you re-attempt. The key is to remain calm and amicable without getting frustrated. Trust that this works, and with a little real-life practice, it will soon be easy.

This step can be easily repeated for their phone number as well. "John, do you have a pen? Okay, let me give you my 800 number. It is…" Then, with no pause at all, continue with, "And your number is?" or, "John, my most reachable number is…, and yours is?" Give information to get information. In sales, we constantly have to play to the laws of human nature.

Another way to get a number is to get them started by giving them what you think is their area code. For example, you could start out by saying: "Great, let me get that information for you; your most reachable number is 410 ..." Then pause. It will be natural for them to finish it for you or correct you with the proper area code and continue with the number. People will generally follow your lead and cannot take the silence you have left. They will need to speak. They are not likely to leave an empty or incorrect blank. They are also not likely to ignore your request and upset you before they have the information they want. Even if they had decided before the call that they would not give out their number, this will usually catch them off-guard.

CORDIAL YET PERSISTENT

If these attempts do not work, it is probably safe to say that they are guarding their information. However, after you have built some rapport or lightened the tone, try again. An additional attempt can be to appeal to their sense of past experiences. Everyone has incurred a malfunction when using electronics, and the phone is no exception. How many times have you been disconnected when being transferred or put on hold? Use this to your advantage. When your customers ask a question in the course of your conversation, offer to put them on hold while you "check on that for them." When you do, just say, "Okay, and your number, in case we get disconnected, is 410 ...?" They will almost always give it to you at this point. If they do not, let them know it may take a while and that you do not want to risk not being able to help them. Explain that it is your job to get them the information they need, and for this, you will need their number, just in case. If they continue to be evasive, continue to maneuver for their number amicably. You could also let them know that you may need a number to call back because the information is not readily at hand.

Another method, if all else fails, or if you accidentally did give too much information, is to ask, "Okay, and in case you call back for additional information and I am not here, your return number is? And your first name is?" Again, it is human nature to want to fill in the blanks. Also, since their obvious goal is information, your request will be more acceptable because you included the promise of information. Even though they have not yet received the information they called for, they will still likely agree to more information. This works most of the time; try it.

If their evasiveness continues and they are still reluctant to give you their number, it is probably time for you to acknowledge their concern and assure them that you will respect their information and not overcall them. Let them know you understand their reluctance because you too have been in their position. Put yourself on common ground. Let them know that you also dislike pushy salespeople. Then reiterate that your only goal is to get the information they have requested and you want to be able to return their call if new information should arise.

NOTE

Many salespeople have been taught to get their customers' numbers by offering to get their requested information and then calling back. If this is the path you have chosen, once you have their information, don't look to hang up and call them back; always continue trying to set the appointment.

If you do not seek the appointment in the present, you take the chance of them cooling off or getting busy with something else. Since they are right there with the phone, they will often call someone else right away and set an appointment with them. Even if your intention is to call right back, it may be too late.

Once you have their return information, continue with your phone process, and ask for the appointment. Encourage a visit and make an appointment without disconnecting your current connection. This is when they are most receptive, because this is when they called. Calling your customer back with more information is not how to set an appointment. Creating curiosity by giving selected information and asking for an appointment is how to set an appointment. Get their name, get their number, and ask for the appointment while on your first call.

MAKE A FRIEND

There is no better way to ease the flow of communication than with a friendly relationship. Always keep your rapport-building skills on hand. While in this step of the process, stay polite. If your customer is tough or combative, slow down and try to build rapport. Handling different styles and personalities on the phone is just like in person. Remain professional, and only react to each situation in the most suitable manner. Search for the common ground that exists and build upon it.

When conversing, slip in some common ground questions with your discovery questions. Try to find the connection between you and your customers. Search for the people, places, or things that will create your bond, your relationship. It is surprising the common ground you will find when you start to search. It can almost be played like a game. How many degrees of separation are there between you and them? Maybe you went to the same high school or maybe your aunt once visited the same vacation spot. Become skillful at casually interviewing your customers and searching for common interests. Start general and then focus in once you sense a match. A good opening may be to ask where they are calling from and take it from there. As your rapport develops, cater your approach to them. Let them take the lead you provide. Enable them and then let them go where they want. The opening common ground you reveal will allow them to be included in the rapport. It will allow them to open up, better relate with you, and ultimately feel more comfortable.

When you learn your customers' wants, you will know how to fulfill their needs. When you develop rapport, they will want you to fulfill their needs. Your customers will be much more likely to visit if you can create a bond with them. If they like you, they will look for reasons to do business with you. Many will actually seek a way to help you help them. People will always prefer to do business where they feel comfortable.

ADJUST YOUR APPROACH

In some cases, you not may need a rapport, and in all cases, you should not force someone to develop one. If a caller appears focused on coming in anyway, and their tone is pure business, allow an appointment based solely on that. For example, if they open the conversation with, "Hey, I am about to head over there and I wanted to make sure my solution is still there," your phone rapport is unlikely to be necessary. Initiating too much side conversation may be seen as insincere or wasteful of your customer's time. Always seek to quickly get a feel for your customer's buying personality and adjust your approach as necessary. If you can be seen like your customer, professional yet all business, they will likely ask for you upon arriving. It is all about being able to read each situation effectively and understanding how to adapt to each. Just be sure to have your customers write down your name and number, in case they get lost or are running late, and be sure to get theirs as well.

KEEP THE FOCUS ON THEM

Your customer's call is about them, not you. Keep the focus on your customer and their benefit in coming to visit. When trying to set an appointment, do not say things like, "Please visit me; I need the sale" or, "Come in and help me with my month." Present the benefit to them, not you. Their impending purchase is for them and their wants and needs, not yours. They did not call with the intention of giving someone a sale; they called to find a solution for themselves. Only when you have a great deal of rapport and shared concern for each other can you bring yourself in as a factor, and even then, in most cases, the perceived benefit of purchasing from you will still have to outweigh or equal the benefits of purchasing elsewhere. Keep your conversation positive, friendly, and flowing, and always maintain the focus on how the visit will benefit the customer.

DEVELOP THEIR CURIOSITY

Now that we have the customer's return information and have started a rapport, it is time to determine their interest and further develop it. It is time to increase their curiosity. The goal here is to give your customers enough information to have them want to come in, but not so much that they will not need to. You want to build on their interests with selective information, not satisfy it by leaving no questions unanswered. Always look to meet them in person. Do not randomly present all the knowledge you have on a particular offering or the details of the sale you are having. Develop your customer's curiosity by controlling the amount of information you give. Seek to answer their initial inquiry and then lead into your first attempt for the appointment. It is here that you must establish the control that we talked about earlier.

If your customer opens their contact by inquiring about a specific offering, a good response may be, "Yes, I believe that offering is still available; we also have many offerings with similar options. When would be a good time for you to come in and see them?" Very little pause here. "Would it be convenient for you to visit now, or would this evening be better for you?"

This sequence is one you should learn and learn well. It answers their question and yet will also increase their curiosity. It also forces them to answer a question of yours, one that will derail their second question, which was probably another information-related question. This is where you will take control of the interaction and can use it to obtain your goals. Remember, in most cases people will follow your lead. Memorize this response and use it every time you are able to create an opportunity. Note that the option we give at the end of our response will make it easier for the customer to answer. When they answer, simply follow up with your next question, which will lead you into your rapport building or your quest for their name and number. Again, follow the lead of their demeanor.

Stay away from specifics like individual stocking numbers or small features as you proceed with your conversation. It is best to be a little imprecise here so that they will be more compelled to visit. It is important to stay focused. Even if you have a similar offering with better features at a better value, you will have a hard time convincing them of this on the phone. Do this in person, not over the phone.

Both you and your customers have a job here. It is their job to receive the information they want to decide if they will visit or not, and it is your job to have them visit so you can afford them the opportunity of investigating all your company has to offer. It is your job to position yourself to make a sale and position them to consider all of their opportunities. It is not your job to be a source of information. Let your customers know that your various offerings all have different features, setups, and purchasing options, all of which you would be happy to go over with them in detail in person. Every time you answer an information-related question, follow up with the exact question we listed above. "Yes, I believe that it is, and when would be a good time to visit? Would now be possible, or would this evening be better?" Your goal is to have your customer visit.

Being vague or limited here is okay; otherwise, you will be limiting their opportunities by having them not visit.

Additionally, never allow your customers to state too many of their goals in the course of their communication. Even though you may not have to address their goals at that moment, many will still hold you accountable for not offering the fact that their goals did not line up when they do visit. Many will state exactly what they want and then wait for your response, basically asking, "Do you have this available?" Many will feel that this is the easiest way to determine if a trip is necessary. However, if you let them build their perfect solution or perfect deal, it will be very difficult for you to be able to say, "Okay, come on in, because we can offer exactly that." Stop them, mid-sentence if necessary, and reiterate that you have many offerings. "When would be a good time for you to come in and see them all?" Divert their focus at the start. This way, when they come in, you will have a more open path for your direction. Additionally, if you do choose to acknowledge their desires, or lie, and your offerings do not line up, you will have created a very hostile first minute when they do arrive. This will present a situation in which your customer will be forced to lose their credibility before they can show a new interest. This may negate your offerings, even if they do like them. Don't ever ask, and always look to avoid this situation. Even if you are able to calm your customer initially, the factors that do not match up will likely present more of a challenge to overcome because you will have to overturn their interests rather than just help develop them.

WHY WE LIMIT

Since limiting our information has been such a large part of our appointment-setting process, let's take a little time to further our understanding of why. Please know that offering too much information is likely the leading reason most salespeople are not able to set the appointment.

I think it is safe to start by saying that all motivation to visit is either accomplished or not accomplished by the information that is communicated. If we are firm in our resolve to persuade our customers that they will have to come in for the most vital information, they in fact will be more likely to come in and thus open themselves up to more options and possibly a better decision. Please understand that curiosity in itself is enticing. People wonder about the unknown. People do not want to be left out. When a customer has a question, it is human nature to see that question through until it is answered. Their curiosity gives us the leverage to have them visit. Take this leverage and use it; do not throw it away by satisfying all of their requests. Increase their curiosity and build their desire. When your customers inquire about a specific offering, answer with a question like the one above. This is your best path to the appointment. If that question doesn't work, reword the question and try again. If their question is so specific that it requires a yes or no answer, find another variable with some additional inquiries: "Yes, ma'am, that offer is available until the end of the month; would you be interested in looking into our special finance offer as well? Yes? Okay, great. My name is J.B., and yours is? And in case you are running late or get lost on the way, let me give you my direct line. And your number is? Would it be convenient for you to visit now, or would this evening be better for you?" Always proceed as if it were simple and accepted.

If in this example she is not interested in financing, don't worry. We still have other questions. "Have you seen our latest color, the new shade of Autumn Red? Is anyone else involved in choosing the various options? Have they seen all of the available options? Would today be convenient to visit or would …?" Keep searching until you find a source for their curiosity, and every time you do, seek the appointment. As you can see, there is a never-ending supply of questions that can intrigue your customers' curiosities and develop their motivations to visit.

ESPECIALLY THE PRICE CALLER

Keeping the curiosity high is especially advised for the "What's your best price" caller. If you give this caller a discounted price on a specific offering, they will very likely never visit or call back. They will use your price as a basis for their next call.

When communicating with this customer, always look for a variable that is part of the price equation but hard to determine on the phone. This could be the trade value of their current solution or a non-specific option for one of your choices. Indicate that they might be missing out by not investigating all of the variables in the sale in addition to all of the other options, offerings, or programs. Let them know that many times in the past, when someone has come in with pre-set plans, they have altered their plans upon discovering one of your other offerings. Trust and believe in the power of curiosity. Ask them: "You wouldn't want to settle on a solution without investigating other choices and decisions, would you?" Have confidence in the solutions and purchasing options you represent. Be excited to convince them to "take a look." Know that with all of the offerings you have available, you probably have something that may interest them even more, so it would be better for both parties if they were to visit in person before opening a negotiation.

For the extra tough price customer, be persistent. Let them know that you have many similar offerings at similar prices, but your first concern is finding the one that is right for them. When customers tell you that they are not coming in unless they get a low sale price over the phone, you have to trust that they are bluffing. Do not let these customers mislead or pressure you.

Do not become unsettled and run to your manager for pricing every time someone wants to know your lowest price. Do not lose your sale here. Assure them that you will be extremely aggressive on price, but you will not discuss a final price on the phone. You want to make sure they are happy with your specific offering before they make a yes or no decision based strictly on price. It would be pointless to negotiate on a specific offering now if they choose another during the course of their visit. Let them know you feel compelled, as a conscientious salesperson, to make sure they will be happy both before and after they spend their money. You want to make sure the solution they choose is right for them before they get too caught up in price.

This should make sense to them because it does make sense. Make them feel as though they will be losing out if they do not come in to see what you have to offer before they make a decision based solely on price. Trust this. Do not give in. Although it might be difficult not to give your customers all the information all the time, you have to do what's best to make a sale, not what your customers say is best. You have to conserve your information to entice a visit. Too often, your caller's goal will be to get all the information that they can and then use it as leverage to get a better deal elsewhere. Do not let this happen to you. Search for a motive other than price and build upon it. It might be you, your company, your servicing ability, or even the city where your company is located. Whatever it is, find it. Conserve your information and create the curiosity and desire for them to want to visit. Please understand that setting an appointment is always best accomplished by offering select pieces of information and creating the promise of more when they visit.

SET THE APPOINTMENT

Set the appointment for a definite time. "Later in the week" is not an appointment that is likely to be kept. Narrow it down by giving your callers a choice of times. This will help you get the process started while still allowing them to choose the times. This way it is easy for them to choose and it kind of becomes their appointment. They will be less likely to break their own appointments, right?

For example, you may ask, "When would be a good time for you to visit?" Slight pause. "Would it be convenient for you to visit now, or would this evening be better for you? Great. Is it better for you around seven p.m., or would eight be easier? Great, I will see you then." Lead them to a specific time by narrowing in on the choices you give them. This is the best way to set an appointment, so it will be our only way.

When a caller does give you an appointment, simply confirm it. Do not go back to the information stage. That is like still selling after they say yes. We do not want to risk satisfying curiosity. Get the appointment and confirm the appointment.

CONFIRM THE APPOINTMENT

After you set the appointment, confirm the appointment. Reiterate the day and time the caller has chosen, so they will hear it again and further note it. Give them the impression that you take your appointments seriously. "Okay, Mary, it was nice talking to you, and again, we will see you at seven o'clock on Tuesday." Ask for the appointment, confirm the appointment, and reconfirm the appointment.

RECONFIRM THE APPOINTMENT

Sometimes the conversation may not always end exactly when you think it will. Some other small thing may come up.

Every time something does, always re-end the conversation with the confirmation of the day and time of the appointment: "Okay, Mary, great, and again, we will see you Tuesday at seven o'clock." Oh, and remember, do not allow this small instance to be specific-information-related. Keep it rapport-related. Know that some customers may make a final attempt to get a trip-saving piece of information.

OKAY, FAILED TO SHOW; NOW WHAT?

In our business, there will always be the occasion when our customers will not show up for an appointment. Because of this, we need to have a plan. When it is within a reasonable amount of time, call and ask if they will be running late. If so, ask if they are in need of additional directions. If they are unable to make it, say you understand and set another appointment.

Now, if you are unable to get a hold of them, here is our plan. At a later time, call and apologize for missing the appointment. Apologize almost to the point of embarrassment. Include an excuse or possible reason why you were unable to be there. When you've successfully convinced them of your regret, offer to make it up by meeting at their convenience. Then, offer to make the visit "extra worthwhile."

At this point, the customer will probably feel bad for you taking all the blame and look to make their next appointment. They will also want to avoid the feeling that you have displayed for missing the appointment. The customer will usually declare that they understand and will be eager to set another appointment to relieve their own guilt. This will allow your customers to save face and not feel as if they would be scolded by you if they did still want to come in. If they are still in the market, this almost always works; try it. The more you apologize, the worse they feel, and the more likely they will show.

CREATING OUR PHONE SUCCESS

When a salesperson finishes a phone conversation by asking, "And is there anything else I can do for you?" you can believe that it was the customer who had control of the conversation. You can also believe that there will be no visit. By finishing with this question, it is obvious that all of the customers' inquiries were in fact satisfied.

Earlier, in "Traits of a Top Salesperson," we talked about how our traits and habits influence what we are able to accomplish. We also talked about how we are sometimes limited by certain traits, and how difficult some habits are to alter. I think this is never more evident than when looking at our phone habits.

Taking the lead in our phone communications is something not readily accomplished. Very few people will become fluid on the phone overnight. It takes a lot of focus and conditioning to do what you are supposed to do, let alone do it well. Our callers will constantly challenge our phone process. Since it is the caller's purpose to seek information, it is often our impulsive reaction to answer. Our habits may likely be influenced by what we feel to be pleasing to the people with whom we are speaking. The easiest path to take is to respond in a manner that will satisfy their desired sense of wants. When interacting on the phone, we will always be susceptible to the slow conditioning that our callers' goals and our sense of help will generate. It is human nature to seek fulfillment, and the shortest path to receive fulfillment is always the easiest.

However, to be successful, we have to do what is best. We have to set our focus, take and keep control of our phone interactions, and only look to set the appointment. This conversation-ending question should be reserved for our customer service approach after they own their solution, not while seeking to set an appointment. You have to be aware of what to say and be skilled in saying it effectively. You have to condition yourself to follow your process, keep your sense of harmony, and keep your customers' desire intact. You also have to be extra careful on the telephone, because there is very little opportunity to correct a mistake.

FINAL NOTE

Making an appointment, like closing, is similar to solving a problem. It is having the creativity to decipher the best way to increase the chances that your customers will visit in person. The key to making an appointment is in influencing your customer to want to make an appointment, not in just asking for an appointment. It is being enthusiastic, friendly, inventive, and persistent to attain the appointment any way you can. Understand, and have your customers understand, that without visiting they will not have the opportunity to explore all of the opportunities available to them.

I understand that you may sometimes succeed in attaining an appointment by doing nothing more than being a source of information. Yes, it may happen that all of your information has lined up perfectly; no rapport, no curiosity, no name, no number, and no confirmation of the appointment time. This scenario is possible. However, the odds will not be in your favor. For consistently positive results, always position yourself for the best possibility for a sale to occur. Listen to your customer, understand their motivations and then build on their motivations to create their curiosity and desire to visit.

20

LISTENING

S ales is not just jumping in and telling your prospects why they should buy. Sales is first listening to your customers and understanding their goals before you start to speak. It is a two-way interaction that engages your customers with both listening and understanding.

Your ability to communicate effectively is one of the most important skills in sales, and listening is its foundation. It is both how we are able to understand our customers and how we show we are capable of helping them. When we are able to show that we are listening with concern, our customers will feel that we are qualified and interested in helping them. When our customers see our desire to understand before we go about our presentations, they will feel comfortable in providing us with the additional information we need to help influence a purchase. This is also the information that they will feel we need to have before they will allow us to influence a purchase.

AWARENESS

Were you ever unable to make a sale and couldn't understand why? Think back. Were you ever just left standing there all alone and confused? Well, ask yourself, was it possible that you missed what your customers were trying to say? Did you effectively enable them to speak by providing an open environment?

As I said in the introduction, there is a fine line between making a sale and not making a sale. In many cases, making a sale will be a challenge. To be consistently successful, you have to use every advantage you can. Often times, when you were unable to make a sale, these may have been the reasons. Proper listening skills are essential in sales. Although this will certainly be a short chapter, I do not believe that this is a skill that should be considered as something that is not crucial in making a sale. I really feel that you should stop and try to realize how much your ability to make a sale is so significantly affected by your ability to genuinely pay attention to what your customers have to offer before determining your next best move.

HOW TO LISTEN

To help us with our listening ability, let's take a look at the process of listening. Recognize and understand the relevance of each step. Allow yourself to become comfortable in listening by consistently following this pattern until it becomes second nature. Although listening is a process, it is not supposed to be seen as such within your interaction. Listening should always appear as just a natural flow of communication.

THE LISTENING PROCESS

- Clear your mind of your own thoughts when starting to listen.
- Face your customers to receive what they are saying.
- Encourage them to speak candidly through your own show of openness.
- Be interested in what they have to say.
- Adjust your stature to adapt to theirs.
- Do not let other salespeople, surroundings, or interruptions distract you or them.
- Ask questions that will further the flow of information.
- Acknowledge what they are saying.
- Don't argue or finish their sentences for them.
- Listen with all of your senses. Focus on their feelings as much as their words.

- Develop an understanding of their goals and parameters.
- Confirm what they are saying by repeating their main points.
- Save your response until they have finished with their points.
- Recognize and understand your next best action before you reply.

LISTEN FOR YOUR PATH

In some steps of the process, listening may actually be harder for many salespeople than talking. The reasoning behind this is that many salespeople will often be enthusiastic about the solutions they have to offer. They will know their offerings and will be desirous to present them. However, they will often present what they feel is important with their own wants or needs in mind, and will focus on their own specific routine. This routine will often sound canned and not intended for their specific customers. It is here that these customers will feel that their salesperson did not understand or care about what is best for them. They will feel that their salesperson did not even listen to them. Do not place yourself in this position. A successful salesperson will always present the features and benefits their customers deem important. They will listen to their customers' wants and needs and tailor a presentation just for them.

CREATE THE ENVIRONMENT

Please know that customers will not always walk up and volunteer everything needed to help find a solution. It is you who must often provide the environment for them to be forthcoming. Sometimes you will enable your customers to speak simply with your open manner; however, sometimes you will best encourage them with your inquiries.

The actual skill of listening is only part of the complete process of listening. Your ability to listen is often only possible if you are able to create an experience that will allow a communication with your customers, and listening is often the response that is only enabled by the questions you ask. In addition to increasing your ability to listen, be sure to increase your opportunity to listen. Understand the benefits of asking the proper questions. Understand that effectively inviting your customers to speak is always the best first step in understanding what they are trying to say.

INCREASE YOUR ABILITY

Earlier, when we talked about understanding people from our observations, our listening skills played an important part in our ability to understand. For your own future success, seek to further the efforts we talked about and focus on increasing your listening skills. Listening is more than just hearing what your customers are trying to say. It is taking in and absorbing their whole outward projection of what they are saying and how they are saying it. It is listening for your customers' true feelings and intentions. It is examining what was said, why it was said, and even what was not said.

The easiest way to understand the benefits of listening better is to simply spend more time listening than speaking. The next time you are involved in an interaction, pay attention to what your customers have to say. Become aware of how your communication is perceived and analyze your ability to act upon the information necessary to achieve the sale. Change your approach, if necessary. Temper your desire to just talk your way into a sale. Listening and understanding is always the best plan for every step in the sales process. You listen in order to greet, build rapport, select, present, negotiate, overcome objections, and close. Listening is how you start each step with the understanding of how you should proceed.

284

EMPATHETIC LISTENING

Empathetic listening is the deepest form of listening. It is feeling the way your customers are feeling by placing yourself within their emotions. It is putting yourself in their position and looking out from their point of view. Empathetic listening is important when your customers are confused, upset, angry, or concerned. Varying needs will often require varying intensities of listening. It will help resolve or lighten your customers' emotions in order to best allow them to move away from their current thoughts. It is also helpful whenever your customers are hesitant in moving forward. It will better allow you to understand what they are feeling.

Empathetic listening involves an open mind. It is not waiting for your customer to finish so that you can respond. It is not prescribing a remedy before they are through. It is not selective listening where you pretend to see their point of view. It is clearing your mind and focusing on truly understanding. Before you can begin to help your customers, you must first understand what they are thinking and feeling. Empathetic listening will allow you to receive the information needed to better defuse and resolve each situation. Yes, empathetic listening may involve slightly more time and patience, but it is an investment well spent. This form of listening is how you show the compassion needed to have your customers allow you to help solve their needs. It will save time in selecting their solution, in presenting their solution, and in persuading them to purchase their solution. It will also greatly lessen the possibility of losing the sale due to a misunderstanding.

ALWAYS LISTEN, YET KNOW WHEN TO FOLLOW

Due to the varying motives and shopping abilities of the customers you will likely face, I wanted to include a section that will further your understanding of why it's so important to listen and analyze before you act. When enacting your listening process, you should always listen to understand. And "listening to understand" means just that; it means to understand. It does not mean listening to follow or carry out whatever your customers may say or ask.

To listen effectively, you want to take your customers' information, combine it with the knowledge you already have, and then formulate the best path to help them realize their next best move. The information you receive while listening to understand is used to help lead them, not to lead you. We should always listen to what our customers are saying, however, there will always be varying situations in which we should first evaluate and then calculate our response. This is an important reality that you must become aware of and come to understand. Let's look at some examples.

- When a customer says he wants a networking solution that will accommodate four servers and support both internet and intranet use, you should listen and try to accomplish what he has asked.
- When a customer asks you to give her your best price on a particular policy so she can compare it to the next company's price, you should listen to her intentions and plan your approach.
- When a customer says he wants his monthly payment to be less than a certain amount, use it as a guide, but don't always assume that he will not be willing to pay more if the vehicle he really wants necessitates that he does.

Once you have successfully helped select their solution of preference, it is you who will want to set the direction of the sale. Understand and listen for your direction before you respond. For each situation, there will always be a best response. Always understand your objective and always understand your path.

LISTEN BETWEEN THE LINES

Most of the time, when communicating, our customers will be pretty straightforward in what they say, and we, as professional salespeople, should be pretty straightforward in how we should listen and answer. After all, we want to understand our customers' goals in their choice of a solution, and we also want to offer our best effort in making their future ownership experience a pleasant one. However, we must still always remain aware that in certain instances and at random stages in the process, our customers' words may not be best received at face value.

It is my guess that by now you have probably heard the advice to "read between the lines." Well, this is also how we should listen. What, where, when, and how someone tells us something is all information that we can use to better understand what it is our customer is actually saying. However, when responding or reacting, we still always want to take the best path, and this may or may not advise us to follow their lead.

In the day-to-day interactions that we will encounter, there will always be the occasion that will necessitate our own input on determining what action will be best for the sale. A common example of this can often be seen in the preparing-to-negotiate stage. It is here that certain customers may choose to enact certain methods that may be less than forthcoming to benefit their own negotiating position. Your degree of compliance should always depend on the individual customer's motives and agendas that you are working with. You must be prepared to interpret what their words are actually saying in order to understand each varying circumstance.

The best way to prepare yourself is always by effectively listening to your customers with the intent to uncover all that is said and expressed. It is to listen between the lines. It is to apply your listening process, through both verbal and physical understanding, to open yourself up to completely identify with all that is being communicated.

FINAL THOUGHT

In a perfect world, all of our customers would come in, say exactly what they are looking for, want to purchase right away, and be completely flexible in determining the purchasing terms and conditions. In reality, it is rarely that simple. In reality, you will have to learn the best path to take and then have the belief and trust to follow it. You will have to listen to your customers' wants, concerns, and intentions and then construct the best path to achieve them. You will have to understand when to follow and when to lead.

Trust that in some way, directly or indirectly, most customers will tell us exactly how to sell them their desired solution; however, we will have to be able to listen for the information that will help guide our way. Learn the process and trust the process. Listening to understand is the smart way to communicate and a sure step toward becoming a more successful salesperson. Our ability to listen is the foundation of our understanding. If you are able to listen with all of your senses for the true meaning of your customers' words and actions before you determine your next move, you will certainly increase your ability in providing their solution.

21

PROSPECTING

P rospecting is the act of developing your own customers. To be a top salesperson, you must not limit yourself to the people calling or walking in your door; you have to set yourself up to create your own business. The key to successful prospecting is to be proactive. You have to take the initiative to develop a way to build your customer base so that you will always have a steady supply of prospects.

CONSTRUCT A DATABASE

Before you actively go out and seek new customers, you should first set up a system to interact with them. Start today by developing a method in which to organize the lists of your potential future customers. From here, you can go about adding to and developing your lists to proactively pursue their business and the business of their friends, neighbors, coworkers, and associates.

One of the easiest ways to organize your prospective customers is with a mailing-list program. Basically, this is a modern-day Rolodex but easier to use and capable of so much more. This is simply the easiest way to create a list of your customers, and will enable you to contact them at will. All you need is an everyday computer and you will be set. This will give you the ability to create focused mailings for the unique events you choose, defined by the criteria you select. You will also have the ability to create different folders for each of the different lists you construct.

CREATE YOUR LISTS

Once you set up your database, you can start to develop the groups of people with whom you would like to keep in contact. Start with a list of your friends and relatives. Then add a list of your neighbors or the people in your community groups. As you start to sell, make a list of your customers. Just take a few minutes every other day or once a week to add your new sales. This is very easy to do. Once they are added, they will always be there for your use.

The most successful salespeople in your company will typically have some method they use to contact their customers. That is how they got to be successful. Every salesperson has prospects. The salesperson that stays in touch with their prospects is the one that will also have customers. If you spend all of your time waiting at the front door or sitting by the phone, your production will always mirror the current market conditions. During the slow periods, you will not have the traffic available to continue selling at a high level. It is smart business to take the time to develop future business.

If a paper company spent all of its time and resources harvesting trees without planting new ones, it would eventually run out of trees. For a short while, the company's production would be high, but it would be limiting its production ability in the future. Being successful in the present and the future necessitates a balance. Being a salesperson is much like running a business. Develop your business and your future now.

KEEP IN TOUCH

Once you have some prospects in your database, you can easily prepare them for delivery or have a mailing company do it for you. When you assemble your prospects using different criteria, you can create the selective mailings you choose. For example, you could mail your friends and neighbors an invite for an event, or mail your recent customers a thank you.

The more you are in contact with people, the more they will think of you when they or their friends are considering a new solution. Be creative with your letters or cards and include the small messages that will fit your selling style. I have always liked postcards because they are fast and relatively inexpensive. Also, most everyone will take a look at a postcard because there is little work involved and it will fit into their attention span. You could have your postcards preprinted on the front and handwrite a message on the back for a more personal touch.

COMPANY LIST

Another source of future customers is your company. Most businesses have been open for a while and will have many previous customers. As with most stores, salespeople will come and go, leaving many "orphan" customers. These people will likely be your store's future customers because they already have a history with your store. There is already a big head start here on the rapport. Be proactive and ask your owner or manager for a list of these customers. Enter them into one of your folders and treat them as your own. These are your inherited customers. This list is like gold. It still confuses me how few salespeople think to ask for orphan customers. If you can get a list of customers who bought three or four years ago, you will be in customer heaven. Many will ask for you right away upon receiving an inviting contact from you, and many more will come in after a few mailings.

In your first greeting, start out with a small introduction of yourself. Let your new customers know that you will be there for their company needs. Here it is probably best to start out as a customer service representative, then let your own personality and creativity take over. This is very effective with your neighbors and previous customers as well, as many will send you referrals. Not everyone will come in at once, but over time, people will come in asking for you. And when they do, they are almost a guaranteed sale. This will help you to keep your momentum and will create a good addition to the people coming through the door.

When mailing, include your name, phone number, and an incentive to visit. Be creative. Seek to develop your name as your brand, and come up with your own personal message as the theme of your trademark. With the messages you send and the proper amount of repetition, you can effectively create a positive perception of the service you seek to provide.

BUSINESS LISTS

There are also many different businesses that you can prospect. Introduce yourself to the owner or manager of a business that may be interested in your service and let them know what you do. Build rapport over time. Add each business to one of your mailing lists and keep in contact with them on a regular basis.

One of the best businesses to visit may be your own service or maintenance department. Get up early one morning and introduce yourself. In this surrounding, they will probably know what you are doing, so be upfront. You might say, "Hello, my name is J.B., and I was curious when you might have an interest in a new solution?" Always ask when, not if; you will get a more specific answer. They might just smile and take your card, but if their bill is more than expected, they might give you a call. Ask if it would be okay to get their information so you can keep them informed of any specials or upcoming promotions. Get their names and their addresses and add them to your list. Offer to be their contact for all of their company needs.

CARRY YOUR SIGN WITH YOU

Whenever you do business in the outside world, let people know what you do. Everybody knows somebody who is or might be in the market for a better solution. When you go out into the world, let people know that you like your offerings and that you like providing them. People enjoy doing business with people who like their business.

UNDERSTAND YOUR CUSTOMER BASE

Because having a steady supply of prospective customers is so vital to the success of any business, your company will usually provide you with a guide for contacting likely future customers. Usually it is the floor manager's charge to generate this flow. It will be rare for a company to set out a territory and say, "Okay, there you go." However, there will always be the variances in desire for some to gain a larger base.

As an extension of some of our earlier advice for finding new perspective customers, the first and last thing you must understand is: Who is your customer base? Who are your likely future customers, and where do they exist?

The key to prospecting, and the whole point of this topic, is for you to determine your most likely audience. Time is precious, and you must always look to conserve it by narrowing your focus. Search the Internet, ask your owners and managers, and learn from the other salespeople in your field. Because there are so many sources for each customer base, it is impossible to list them all, so you will have to use your own instinct and investigate a little on your own. Since the major limitations in any business venture are time and money, it makes sense to invest both as wisely as you can. Analyze your best source of potential prospects before you start to pursue them.

When you are able to find your path and start to build your base, simply follow the advice in this book to further your goal. Seek the decision maker, be nice to the people along the way, and follow the process to the sale.

QUALIFY YOUR CUSTOMER

Some companies or managers will not want newer salespeople to focus too much on qualifying. They will feel that they might miss a customer's potential, and for the most part, I agree. Most new salespeople will truly not understand all the avenues available for arranging a purchase. So I delayed bringing this up for a while. But time is important for the rising salesperson as well, so let's take a look at qualifying.

Is the person you are speaking with financially able to purchase, and are they the true decision maker? In order to best succeed, you will have to qualify the people you meet. You cannot afford to waste your time or energy if a sale cannot be made; you might as well have stayed in bed. Qualifying is deciding the ability to complete a transaction. There are an unlimited number of people available to talk to; the key is to determine those who are worth talking to.

Understand the importance of this topic and have the initiative to investigate your customer's potential. The reason that so much time is wasted here is not that qualifying is that difficult, it's just that no attempt is ever made. However, with just a few simple questions, your customer's worth should be obvious. Just ask. Don't be afraid or scared. As long as you are not rude, your questions will not offend. In fact, this will also often reveal your customer's level of interest. Save yourself time, money, and energy; know the person to whom you are talking.

FINAL NOTE

Prospecting is more than just a small advertisement. It is a continual form of branding yourself. It is choosing a message and strategically placing it for your audience to see. It is developing a way that your intended group of prospects will think of you merely by seeing the image or message you have chosen. All big companies have a logo or catchphrase; you should, too. It can be your name or just the fact that you keep in contact. Come up with some common factor for them to identify your mailings. Remember, what you are really offering is your service. What you are really selling is you. The more people "see you," the more familiar and comfortable they will become with you.

Prospecting is a continual process, one that only gets stronger with time. Do not get discouraged in the beginning and give up too soon. Think of prospecting as adding a little something extra now and building for your future. Once you get started, it will take very little energy to keep growing. Invest in your future. Understand that people will always prefer to do business with someone they know or have had contact with recently. So contact them. Market yourself. When you are able to attract and keep your own customers, you have truly reached self-employment. You will be responsible for your own destiny and well on your way to being a top salesperson.

22

THE INTERNET

T he Internet is much like the phone in that it is an opportunity to set an appointment. In relation to our business, it is a marketing tool, much like radio or print. It is a method for our companies to attract an interest and an avenue to obtain an inquiring prospect's contact information. It is a lead management system that will supply and organize our responding customers' information and provide us with an easy-to-use way to start our communication. For our purpose as salespeople, it is simply a resourceful means to encourage a visit.

UNDERSTAND THE LEAD SYSTEM

Most companies will have some form of a web-based system that will provide a platform to allow access to the internet-driven leads directed to your company. This is a website-hosted tool that will format your company's web-based communication into an easy-to-use management system. Meaning, all of the leads that come in from the various websites that your offerings may appear on will be directed to this one dedicated site. This is an easy way for your company to allow you access. Once they are received, you can then start the process of having your potential customers further their involvement by encouraging their visit.

UNDERSTAND YOUR MARKETING

Many of the websites that your company will use in its marketing effort will seek to engage the researching customer. This is accomplished by providing a way to make an offer, request additional information, or offer a response if they were to supply their contact information. The most likely reason your customers used the internet to contact your company is that they were searching for information, and the website they were on requested that they inquire.

The reason to understand your specific marketing is to understand how best to further encourage your customers' desires. Meaning, become aware of what your customers responded to, in order to better understand their motives and goals. Visit your sites to get a feel for what they offer, and how they offer it, so that you can better understand how your customers were driven to respond. It is up to your company or management team to decide how and where they will use the internet to market your offerings; however, a further understanding of these marketing ideas can be extremely helpful when interacting with your new customers.

SET THE APPOINTMENT

Our main objective in this stage, as with the phone inquiries we will receive, should be to set an appointment. We will not be able to sell our offerings over the Internet, just as we will not be able to sell over the phone. Our potential customers will still have to proceed through the steps of the sale. I am aware that in some circumstances, such as with businesses or buying services where customers are internally restricted to competitive bid prices only, an agreement may be able to take place; however, for the vast majority of the leads we receive, we should treat them no different than we would an incoming call. Besides, if all of your company's services or solutions were provided exclusively over the phone or Internet, it wouldn't have salespeople; it wouldn't need them. It would just have minimum waged order takers. If your future were to only include clicking a few buttons and placing a box in the mail, you really would not need this understanding. However, we are salespeople, or want to be, so please believe and understand that the average person uses the Internet simply as a point of contact, and this contact should be treated no differently than phone contact. The best way to work or interact with our provided leads is to keep the focus on one thing: setting an appointment.

RESPONDING TO THEIR INQUIRIES

Let's now look at how to engage our customers, and then some advice on getting our communication started.

ENCOURAGE THEIR INTEREST

The first step when responding to your customers' inquiry is to open a line of communication. It is to engage them. Seek to create a response that will encourage them to respond. Read and understand all of their goals or motives in contacting you and explore all of their information. Look for the motivating factor and create a question that will entice a response. Respond as fast as you can. If a phone number is offered, call them. If not, email them right away. Determine their goals and then develop preliminary strategies for your appointments.

I know that in some schools of thought, you should provide all the information requested, including price, as fast as possible; however, I disagree. Your objective here is to set an appointment, not to be a free source of information or a price provider. The best way to have your customers respond is to entice them with partial information and a question of your own.

Our goal in responding is to provide enough information to keep our customers' feeling of accomplishment high and yet limited enough to have them desirous to still learn more. Then, using their desire, create an interest and potential worth so they will want to visit. Encourage a response with your questions and further their interest by way of their curiosity. Use their inquiries as a way of determining their interests and then create a question based response that will encourage them to answer.

Determine their interest and then use it to open the lines of communication. Supply both comfort and a compelling desire all at the same time. Got it? I really hope this make sense, because completely understanding, believing, and trusting in this is absolutely essential in performing at your best.

ALWAYS KEEP YOUR FOCUS

Many average salespeople will simply issue a response to their customers with some included information, and then sit back and hope. They will hope that somehow their customers will appreciate their information so much that they will not seek any further advice or additional sources and come in and buy without being asked. They also hope that their customers will in no way want to compare or research the provided information anywhere else. In addition, these salespeople further must hope that all of their provided information will line up perfectly with all of their customers' parameters. These struggling salespeople have somehow convinced themselves that by being a great source of information, they will be rewarded. They believe that their job is simply to provide answers and then wait for their customers to offer a meeting.

A successful salesperson, however, knows that this is rarely the case. A successful salesperson knows that this "offer and hope" method will not usually fare well. As stated in our phone chapter, information alone will rarely manufacture a desire to visit. Conversely, it will quite often only manufacture a desire to seek comparative guidance from another company.

ENGAGE YOUR CUSTOMER

BY WAY OF PHONE

When your customer provides a phone number, use that as your first point of contact. Take the most direct approach; it is always easier and timelier to set an appointment over the phone. Your customer may have made another inquiry elsewhere, so time is important. When calling, you will either get your customer's voice mail or reach them in person. In either case, your first goal is to entice them to respond with interest. Let's take a more detailed look.

VOICE MAIL

When you reach your customer's voice mail, your initial goal is simply to have them want to respond. The best way to accomplish your goal is to leave a message to which they will want to respond. A good message would be one which lightly answers their initial request and follows up with a question of your own or a promise to provide additional information upon their return call. The easiest way to do this is with the promise of more or new information when they call back. Do not answer all of their inquiries on the machine.

An example may be, "Hi, this is J.B. from ABC Motors. Yes, I believe that offering is still available, when would be a good time to show you the new color chart?" or "Hi, this is J.B. from ABC Company. I have some information on the lease program you inquired about; how long were you thinking of leasing? Give me a call this afternoon if you could."

Vary your response depending on your customer's motivation. Remember your steps and keep your focus. When they call back, simply set your appointment so they can see their solution and you can explain the additional incentives available. Entice a response, entice a visit. Always keep in mind that you will only be able to sell something when they are in your presence.

IN PERSON

If you can reach your customer on the phone, simply set your appointment as we discussed in the phone chapter. Engage them, provide information, build rapport, and promise additional information when they visit. When you make contact, be sure to also follow up with an immediate email to reiterate your appointment time and personal information.

BY WAY OF EMAIL

If your customer does not leave their phone number or if you have received their voice mail, you will also want to send an email of encouragement, similar to the one you would leave on their answering machine. "Hi. Thank you for your interest in our solution, please know that we have that and many similar offerings available. Would it be convenient for you to come in this evening?" or, "Hi. Thank you for your inquiry. Would you be interested in the yearly or monthly contract?" Again, always tailor your message to their inquiry. In all cases, phone and email, always respond immediately.

ALWAYS FOLLOW YOUR BEST PATH

The key point to understand when responding is that your customers' future move will almost always be driven by their future wants. So make them want. I know certain Internet managers or even sales managers may disagree with this philosophy. Some will believe and even teach that the Web is sacred and should only be used for direct, fast information purposes. They will want you to send the invoice, the availability, and even the "bottom-line price." However, this should be questioned. In the very early stages of the Internet, when only information-oriented people used it, this may have been understandable. But now, the Web is such a regular part of everyday life that almost everyone uses it in some fashion. Meaning, normal everyday people are the majority of its users, so I believe that everyday rules should apply. Introduce yourself, build credibility and rapport with the sharing of certain information, and then further create their interest to visit by offering more for when they do.

THE CURIOUS WILL REMAIN

Have you ever noticed that when someone reads a top ten list, he or she will always start with number ten and then proceed toward number one? Is it fair to build on someone's curiosity like this? Wouldn't it be easier to know what number one is up front, so we could better decide when to tune in or out?

Have you ever noticed how a game-show host will always save announcing the winning answer until after the commercial? Is this fair? Is it fair that we have to sit through the commercial to learn the result? Is it fair that we must pay for the show's airtime by watching its commercials? Fair or not, do we hang around to see who won?

Have you ever started reading a book or thought of seeing a movie and then accidentally overheard the ending? Did your building desire and developing suspense continue with the same intensity? Did your curiosity compel you to stay interested? Did it? Well, if not, please know that it is the same for your customers. When you give your customers all of the information up front, they too will lose interest. Trust this. Do not squelch your potential customers' desire, instead learn to kindle and further build it.

Have you ever ventured further than you normally would just to uncover the whole truth? Have you ever been enticed into proceeding with the promise of additional information? Have you? Well, of course you have. In fact, this method of creating curiosity is effective and common. It has also become accepted.

The whole process of the sale both starts and finishes with the creating and building of additional motivation. Each step of the process is always best ended with an enticement to move to the next. This is the secret to sales. This is how the process of the sale starts and continues. In some sales transactions, this occurs accidentally, and in some transactions, this occurs by planned strategy. Please know that persons of success will always have this as their plan, not just as a chance happening. The purpose of our process is to take our customers through the steps and toward the sale smoothly and efficiently, without them knowing a process even exists. Build your customers' desire to visit and then build their desire to own, and always believe that it's all in the steps.

DEVELOP YOUR CREATIVITY

Creativity, to me, is the ability to achieve through an inventive means. The start of every contact should always be the same. It should be to examine your customers' inquiries, determine their key point of interest, and use that to develop a response that will further their interest and compel them to respond. It is to increase their desire. The idea of this seems pretty simple to me, except that I have learned where analysis and understanding come in to play, there will always be different levels of acceptance and resulting abilities.

To understand your customers' interests and put a creative response into words is going to take some thought. You will without question have to think before you respond. You will have to analyze your customers' inquiries to best determine their interests and best determine your path. Having the creativity that it will take to do this is not something you can learn from this or any other book. It is not random or simple knowledge. Being creative here will take some thought. This is something that is responsive to an action and must always reference that action. It is creating and catering a question or response to encourage a response to a specific instance; thus it is impossible to list somewhere every best response to every action or inquiry. Creating a further interest is the result of understanding your customers' eventual path. Sometimes it is best to respond directly, and sometimes it is best to respond in a manner that you have determined will better encourage your chosen direction.

To the experienced salesperson, the need for motivation is understood and instinctive. However, many beginning salespeople will not understand this. Many will start in this business and never understand the need to increase one's desire. They will operate without the ability to encourage an interest, and this will ultimately leave them without the positive experiences that they will need to learn from. Ultimately, they will set fewer appointments, sell fewer solutions, and become further discouraged. Well, if you are new, or if you feel you are headed down this path, stop. Change what you are doing. Quit trying to be simply a source of information and start contemplating how best to entice your customers creatively so they will want to move forward. I understand that it is easier and takes less thought to simply answer your customers' inquiries, but please understand that to be successful you will often have to prepare your path. Do not simply respond to your customers' questions with specific answers when that is not your best path. Understand their inquiries, understand their motivations, and then choose your path.

My advice for becoming better at creatively responding is to visually practice certain interactions ahead of time. Give yourself some quiet time with no distractions and just think. Visualize the reactions each of your responses may have and then try to visualize the most effective. Put yourself in your customer's position and analyze their motivation. Alternate from their position to yours and judge the effectiveness of each. Start with the small visualizations of various scenarios and then further refine your abilities as you gather additional information. Once you fully understand and set yourself to believe in this reasoning, and continue to learn from and grow from your future experiences, your positive abilities will only become easier. Soon, your creatively constructed initial responses and instinctive follow-up responses will become more and more natural and your success will become imminent.

FINAL NOTE

Your only goal when communicating on the Internet is to set an appointment. Take note of their motivations, look to increase them, and set the appointment. Set the appointment, set the appointment, set the appointment.

23

KEEPING YOUR FOCUS

The most successful salespeople are those who believe in themselves, believe in their offerings, and believe in the quality of the service they offer. These qualities, when combined with a set sales process, are the building blocks of success. With these principles, your career will be one of achievement and reward.

Keeping your positive qualities intact is essential to maintaining a constructive outlook and preserving your future success. Sometimes the most difficult challenge in sales is keeping your focus and not letting surrounding factors limit your abilities. Keeping this focus is looking at the big picture. It is creating and confirming your beliefs to help stabilize your focus through all of the fluctuations you will experience. It is not letting anything or anyone influence you in a negative way.

When you are up, it is easy to keep going. When you are down and can pick yourself up, you are on your way to becoming successful. To help establish and further create your success, take the time to discover your own set of beliefs and commit to them. Establish the philosophies that you have trust in, and use them for guidance and support. Whenever things are not going quite right or you feel stuck in a negative instance, concentrate on your beliefs. Think about what you have and where you want to go.

Many companies, in their efforts to be more successful in a competitive environment, have set themselves up with a "mission statement." A mission statement is an employee-sanctioned doctrine of the commitment and dedication that they will have to be the best they can. It is a writ of uncompromising allegiance to follow and believe in the philosophies and processes that will help them excel in their particular field. It provides the plan, the structure, and the goals for their companies to live by and forever improve themselves.

I like such a statement, and believe that both its creation and its following will help any size company achieve higher highs, even one-person companies such as ourselves. Your beliefs will help provide a source of determination that will give you the strength to remain successful through the challenges you will face.

THE PATH FOR SUCCESS

Here are some of the essentials that I believe are the foundation to a successful career in the sales profession.

BELIEVE IN THE PROCESS

An assembly line is a system in which each step of the process has to be followed, one in which each part of the process cannot be started until the previous step has been completed. The engine cannot be installed until the frame has been built. It is a process where there is no skipping of steps, and where each step builds off the previous.

All salespeople intent on success will have some type of system that they will follow. They will have a set means that will help guide them through the process of the sale. This system will be one of forward progression and consistency. In our business, our process is a set of steps that are ultimately designed to lead us on the proper path. It is a process that effectively helps us guide our customers from introduction to delivery. Each step relies on another, and each step is essential to the sale. You build the rapport to ask the questions to gain the knowledge and credibility to find a solution and influence a purchase. If you know you will have to handle certain objections down the road, you will be more likely to allow your process to

308

acquire your credibility in the early stages. If you know there will come a time when you will be presenting figures, you will more likely seek to build value throughout your preceding interaction. One of the attributes that makes our process so invaluable is its consistency. With your process, allow each step to be a new rung in your ladder. The way to eat an apple is one bite at a time; and this is the same to make a sale. Practice and rehearse the steps in your process until they become second nature. This will help you to better understand where you are with each step and how you will best get to the next. Having and following a set process will keep you focused on your results. The sales process has become habit to the top salesperson. Visualize your sale and you will better understand your path. Salespeople who are prepared with the proper skills, have set plans to follow and have become fluid in their delivery, are sure to be successful.

BELIEVE IN YOURSELF

Believing in yourself is how you radiate confidence, and confidence is a necessary trait for anyone who hopes to be persuasive. If you do not portray a belief in yourself, your customers will have a hard time believing in you or your advice.

Belief in one's self starts from the inside. The true projection of one's self is not what you do or say, but who you are; it is what you believe and have faith in. It is the result of your principles and your values. You cannot build trust without honesty and you cannot project trust without self-belief. These are the traits that will only shine through when they come from within. One who lacks the depth of these will be transparent to others. People are much more likely to see you for who you are than for who you pretend to be, so find strength in yourself. Take the time to measure your level of confidence and determine where you want it to be. Recognize and understand the importance of the beneficial traits of a salesperson, and become aware of where you may need improvement. Evaluate and realign yourself with the traits and habits that will give you strength, and then allow yourself to grow, improving your qualities as you proceed.

Once you build your foundation with good qualities and solidify them in your actions, your self-belief will likely better shine, and you will naturally be more successful. As you add to and adjust your traits, you will further gain your inner strength and ultimately have more belief in yourself.

Achieving a successful career in sales is much like building a relationship. We grow and obtain success by building successful relationships with our companies, our fellow employees, and our customers. In sales, in business, and in life, your relationships will always be more likely to excel if you can establish yourself as a person who has a true belief in himself or herself.

BELIEVE IN YOUR PRODUCT

Believe in the offerings that you and your company provide. Until you can convince your customers that you truly believe in the products or services you offer, you will not be completely effective in convincing them to purchase. First and most importantly, choose an offering that you like. This seems to makes sense to me, but it is surprising how many salespeople I meet who are selling a product they do not believe in. They feel their "technique" ability is enough to satisfy their income. Well, they are fooling themselves. You will never fulfill your potential unless you believe in what you are selling. There are thousands of companies in our world, and in each area there are a host to choose from.

Choose an offering and company that is right for you. Learn and study your offerings and the offerings of your competition. Discover and understand all of the possible benefits and shortcomings of each and become relentless in your pursuit of how each will line up with the customers you will meet. Dedicate yourself to knowing, understanding, and recognizing the features and benefits of all. When you are able to completely appreciate the benefits of your offerings, you will be better at helping others appreciate them as well.

STRIVE FOR EXCELLENCE

If this is the profession you have chosen, you owe it to yourself, your customers, and your company to perform at a high level. Commit yourself to perform to the best of your ability.

CONTINUE TO TRAIN AND SELF-EDUCATE

The best salespeople are constantly seeking to educate themselves. Great salespeople are not born; they study and learn their trade. One of the top traits that successful salespeople share is their ability and desire to learn. I think the expression "a natural-born salesperson" came about because some salespeople are so studied and practiced it appears they must have been born with it. They were not. Different actions provoke different responses from different people. Understanding this is not innate; it is a product of training and experience. Always believe in your ability to better yourself. A true achiever is never done learning.

Seek to expand your learning both within and outside your immediate profession. The more diverse your learning program is, the better you will become in your field. The differences in people are as multiple and complex as the differences in products. Studying a diverse background of products and intended clients is beneficial because it develops your ability to adapt to the people you meet. Just because you sell the same product over and over does not mean you are selling the same people. In addition to your company's training, visit and watch other salespeople in their places of business. Appliance stores, jewelry stores, clothing boutiques, and furniture stores are but a few with commissioned salespeople. Find out who the top salesperson is at each location and listen to what they say and do. Learn from others. Use every source you can. Watch the attorneys on TV, listen to the carnival stand operators, and hang out in the furniture showrooms. Pay attention.

Sometimes it is just as important to learn what not to do, as it is to learn what you should do. Study what works for other salespeople, and learn from their mistakes. Take note of their introductions and follow their interactions. Look for their process and analyze it. Learn from where they may have done better and from where they may have succeeded. Take note of their customers' language, actions, and responses. Learn to better read and understand people from their customers' reactions. Compare the similarities and differences in your sales process. Be excited the next time the phone rings and it is a sales call. Stay up one night for the late-night infomercial. Spend some quality time in local malls and shopping centers. Take advantage of all of the learning opportunities available and continue to increase your knowledge and understanding.

Learning is everything. It is how you obtain the knowledge that is essential to succeed. It is making an investment in yourself and your future. This investment is the essence of this book. Build a foundation in your career and then build upon it. Now that you have finished reading this book, keep and use it as a guide and reference for a successful career. Make a commitment to yourself to be successful.

Good luck.

If this is a book that you feel your salespeople or fellow coworkers could benefit from, please visit us at:

thesalesbook.net